Designing Usable Web Interfaces

Ameeta D. Jadav, Ph.D.

Prentice
Hall

Upper Saddle River, New Jersey 07458

Library of Congress Cataloging-in-Publication Data

Jadav, Ameeta Dhanesh.
    Designing usable web interfaces / Ameeta D. Jadav.
      p. cm.
    Includes bibliographical references and index.
    ISBN 0-13-088854-0 (pbk.)
    1. Web sites—Design. I. Title.
  TK5105.888 .J33 2003
  005.7'2—dc21
      2002070012

Editor-in-Chief: Stephen Helba
Director of Production and Manufacturing: Bruce Johnson
Executive Editor: Elizabeth Sugg
Managing Editorial—Editor: Judy Casillo
Editorial Assistant: Anita Rhodes
Managing Editor—Production: Mary Carnis
Manufacturing Buyer: Cathleen Petersen
Production Liaison: Denise Brown
Production Editor: Bridget Lulay
Production Management and Composition: Carlisle Communications, Ltd.
Design Director: Cheryl Asherman
Design Coordinator: Christopher Weigand
Cover Design: Joseph DePinho
Cover Printer: Phoenix Color
Printer/Binder: Von Hoffman Graphics, Inc.

Pearson Education LTD.
Pearson Education Australia PTY, Limited
Pearson Education Singapore, Pte. Ltd.
Pearson Education North Asia, Ltd.
Pearson Education Canada, Ltd.
Pearson Educación de Mexico, S. A. de C.V.
Pearson Education—Japan, Tokyo
Pearson Education Malaysia, Pte. Ltd.
Pearson Education, Upper Saddle River, New Jersey

10 9 8 7 6 5 4 3 2

ISBN 0-13-088854-0

This book is dedicated to

my parents
Sharada Jadav and Dhanesh Jadav

and

The Sisters of Lourdes Convent, my teachers

Walk-Through

This book is written for the beginning web designer. Throughout the book, the focus is on encouraging the reader to think about various considerations and arrive at sound design decisions. This is not a how-to book but more of a why-to book.

Chapters 1 through 4 present the larger view of the field of web design: outlining application areas, development processes, and roles.

Chapters 5 through 7 explore specific facets of design: information architecture, interface design, and writing.

Chapter 8 describes the approaches to establishing the success of a web site.

Chapter 9 presents a comprehensive case study of developing a web site and describes the experiences and challenges of each stage in the development process.

The Appendices present templates and sample documents generated at various stages in a web development project.

FEATURES OF THE TEXT

Examples of actual web sites accompany many of the points being discussed in the book.

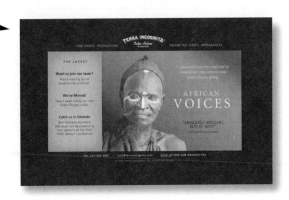

In addition, illustrations help communicate and enhance the message in all chapters.

Each chapter concludes with a list of Guiding Questions that will help the reader summarize and consolidate the content covered in the chapter.

GUIDING QUESTIONS

▶ What is the objective of web design?
▶ What are the three main components of web design?
▶ What aspects of a web site could we attribute to information architecture?
▶ What aspects of a web site could we attribute to interface design?
▶ What role does copy play in the effectiveness of a web site?
▶ What is the importance of project management in the development of a web site?
▶ What are the primary concerns of visitors, designers/developers, critics, and owners of a site?

Practical exercises at the end of each chapter encourage the readers to apply what they have learned in the context of real-life situations.

EXERCISES

▶ Select a web site that offers regularly updated news. Evaluate this site using the criteria discussed in this chapter.
▶ Select a web site that offers e-commerce transactions. Evaluate this site using the criteria discussed in this chapter. How does the e-commerce site differ from the news site?
▶ Make a list of heuristics that you would use to evaluate a web site. Evaluate the news and the e-commerce sites using these heuristics.

Contents

Foreword

The Internet is a fact of everyday life. Each day, more and more people interact with the World Wide Web for various reasons. Businesses utilize the Internet to communicate with consumers, to communicate among one another, and to streamline their in-house processes. The Internet has emerged, and it has changed the world's processing and delivery of information, data, and monies. Personally, I pay almost all my bills on-line and would prefer to pay all of them that way. I work with clients whom I have never met face to face because we can share work and communicate completely virtually. I read newspapers and conduct research and communicate with my colleagues over the Internet. As we continue on our historical path, the sharing of our data and information between ourselves via the Internet will become increasingly more important. More services will become available over the Internet as well as through web devices. As such, the increasing need for intelligent web development and design is a must, especially as communication through web pages becomes more ubiquitous to our culture.

Ameeta Jadav has put together a wonderful book giving anyone a true basis for designing successfully for the web. By reading this book, you will have a firm understanding of techniques, dialogue, and processes when approaching your web initiative. All chapters contain a wealth of knowledge. I have been increasingly impressed as I have watched the book develop.

In the past decade looking forward, we did not have a clue how much impact Internet technology would have on all of us. Whole industries have emerged because of the burgeoning presence of being totally connected all the time. Who could have imagined applying to institutions of higher education through the web, applying for jobs, purchasing a car and having it delivered to your door in a few days, or applying for a mortgage on-line? As the individual stakes of interaction rise on the screen, the stakes of the importance of interface design also rise. This important work demonstrates just how to achieve a successful interface by giving the reader a well-thought-out guide to designing successful interfaces and the processes involved.

In this book, Jadav has emphasized real-world practices when creating interfaces by using the right mixture of web site examples and industry references. She has worked hard to deliver a foundation for understanding the larger picture of web development. This book contributes to our understanding of the basics of the web development process. Each chapter builds on the previous one, allowing the user to fully comprehend all aspects of web development.

Jadav begins the book with an overview of web design. She quickly starts to dissect the process for the reader, and by Chapter 3 you are already learning about the makeup of the web development team. Chapters 4 through 7 detail how to approach a web design project and provide examples of best practices. Chapter 8 gives concrete advice on how to measure the success of your web site once you have developed it.

The web design and development industry grew fast simply because there was a need for Internet applications and web sites to be developed quickly. Consumers and businesses were fulfilling separate but equal needs to utilize the technology for their own convenience and growth. Industry processes and practices came about through a mix from the design industry, the software industry, and psychological and physiological research into human factors. I believe that Jadav is successful in creating a much-needed common vernacular for interface design processes. She truly leads us through and teaches us about all aspects of a web development project. It is appropriate that the book concludes with a case study where Jadav culminates all the practical knowledge of the preceding chapters into a demonstration of a web project from start to finish.

Thank you, Ameeta, for taking the time and effort to create this truly beneficial guide about and how to design usable interfaces for the World Wide Web.

Tina Miletich

March 2002

Preface

The contents of this book have twirled around in my head for several years, during which time I have been fortunate to experience the multimedia and the web industries in different contexts and in different parts of the world. I have had the opportunity to contribute to (and experiment with) the processes of the industry and observe the intricacies of the organizational and human interactions that impact these processes. My observations lead me to believe that a logical process, continuous evaluation, healthy team dynamics, and an ability to learn from our mistakes can make the industry much more efficient and effective. This book is an attempt to share some of these observations and thoughts.

I hope that this book will help web designers create comfortable, easy, pleasing, and meaningful experiences for their users. In addition, I hope that this book will not only provide answers to the questions of web design but will also help designers ask the right questions—to themselves, their team, their target audience, and their clients—the end result being the design of effective web-based communication.

Writing this book has been a challenging experience. However, I have had some of the most pleasant experiences as I interacted with artists, web designers, and organizations with a request to include their sites in this book. I have been amazed at how cordial, friendly, and receptive most of these people were. If the readers of this book find some value in it, a lot of that credit goes to the kind people who gave me permission to include their work in this book.

Raghu Reddy (whose illustrations you see in this book) has been a great friend and colleague to work with. We worked literally from halfway around the world (Singapore to the United States) to bring the text and the images together.

Christopher Altman, Sydney Aron, and Java Mehta worked on the Creations web site that is the basis for the case study in Chapter 9. Chris, with his ever-positive attitude, was a wonderful colleague to work with. Sydney carried out the critical stage of the usability study with extreme efficiency. Java was involved in the project for a short while but made significant contributions to the design of the site.

The Art Institute of Atlanta willingly agreed to be the "client" in the case study. Kim Resnik and Chef Paul patiently answered questions and provided the information that was essential for the completion of the project.

The contribution of Jeremy King, Brian King, Dr. Mildred Cody, and Wendy Riley as participants in the usability study was invaluable. Their candid comments and insightful observations were most helpful in identifying usability issues of the web site.

Tina Miletich has proven that usability, efficiency, aesthetics, and good design can actually work together. I am grateful to her for writing the foreword to this book.

My colleagues at The Art Institute of Atlanta are a great bunch of people to work with. Discussions with them have helped me ask the right questions and develop a deeper appreciation for the skills and perspectives that go into creating "effective" communication design.

Judy Casillo, the managing editor of this book, always had an encouraging word and was always prompt in responding to my many queries. Bridget Lulay, project editor at Carlisle Communications, has been amazingly patient in addressing my many "concerns." I have learned so much about the print production process from her. Denise Brown, Senior Production Editor, quietly worked in the background and was meticulous in her review of the manuscript. I am sure to use some of these lessons in my future web projects.

Dr. Vivian Beaty, Henry Ford Community College, and Deanne DelVecchio, Lake Tahoe Community College, provided excellent suggestions for improving the relevance of the book to students.

Jashoda Bothra provided valuable suggestions for improving the flow and consistency of this book. Thanks Jashoda for working against a tough deadline and for your support.

I would be naïve if I believed that this was *my* project. The truth is that this project has become a reality with the help of all those mentioned here and of family and friends (especially, Priya, Surangiben, Kathy, Ruma, Neepa, and Paddu) who have unceasingly provided direct and indirect personal support to me. I humbly thank you all.

What Is Web Design?

A friend, excited with the prospect of booking her flight to London through the web, went to a popular travel web site and found a great deal of information. After wading through the information, she completed the on-line ticket reservation form and then clicked on the Submit button. She waited for something to happen, and when nothing did, she figured that she had not actually clicked on the button and clicked on it again. In a few days, she received her tickets to London. The only problem was that she received two sets of tickets and, worse still, ended up with a double charge on her credit card. Needless to say, she has sworn to never book her tickets on-line again!

One just has to talk to some typical users of the web to appreciate the invariably exasperating experiences they go through. More often than not, novice users experience frustration, confusion, anger, and impatience when using the web (see Figure 1–1). It is possible that you, the designer of web sites, have also gone through some of these experiences. Is the web such a complex medium that we have to be highly experienced to make use of its tremendous wealth? I believe that it need not be so. This book focuses on how we can create positive and efficient experiences for the users of the web (see Figure 1–2).

Experienced users of the web are likely to overcome most design shortcomings to achieve the purpose for which they visited the site. However, the majority of web users are not "experienced" users. Most are inexperienced—a bit like someone who has walked into a building for the first time. These visitors do not "live" on the web. They visit a web site to get information, carry out a transaction, and maybe spend a little time interacting with and participating in the activities of a site. If they are not able to do this with ease, they could become apprehensive and skeptical about the utility of the web site and decide to leave and not revisit the site.

The main challenges faced by web designers are to ensure that the visitors are able to do the following:

▶ Figure out what information they could access and what transactions they could perform on the site
▶ Determine how they could interact with the site and navigate through it

FIGURE 1–1

Many users are
frustrated with their
experience of the web

FIGURE 1–2

A well-designed web
site can create a
positive experience for
the visitor

▶ Achieve what they came to a web site for
▶ Experience the site as a friendly, pleasant, and aesthetically pleasing
environment

Further, the designer needs to make sure that the site achieves the client's objective for commissioning its development.

Needless to say, the web designer's job is not an easy one. Even an ineffective site is difficult to design. Designing an effective site is many times more difficult. The purpose of this book is to help web designers optimize their efforts and get the best return for the time and energy they spend in designing web sites.

DEFINITION OF WEB DESIGN

Web site design refers to the process of conceptualizing and planning the experiences for visitors as they interact with the information and activities on the site.

Visitors to a web site experience its design in many different ways. Here are some examples:

- The first impression of the site on the welcome (home) page
- Selection of a navigation option
- Determining where they are on the site
- Locating specific information using the section labels or the search function
- Reading the copy on a web page
- Selecting and ordering an item on an e-commerce site

The designer of the web site attempts to make these experiences pleasant, easy, and intuitive. A web site has good design when the visitors can learn how to navigate and use the site with ease and also achieve the purpose for which they visit the site.

Web design is the process of creating experiences for users of the web. It involves decisions about the content structure, the look and feel of the web pages, the interactions, feedback to user input, the use of media, and the language style used for communication. Recognizing the importance of the totality of the experience rather than just the aesthetics ("look and feel") of the site, many experts have started to use the term "experience design" in place of "web design."

As mentioned in the preface to this book, there are many similarities between the processes of constructing a building and a web site. Here are some of these similarities:

- Both are conceived with a goal in mind
- Both go through (or should go through) intensive research and planning
- Both require the right tools for development
- Both are efficient when the development or construction closely matches design plans
- Both call for an amalgam of creative design, aesthetics, and functionality

And finally, in both, the success of the project is determined by how well the design meets the requirements of the people who use the building or the web site.

Web design (or experience design) calls for conceptualization and decisions about various aspects of a web site. These include the following:

- Information architecture
- Graphic (visual), media, and interaction (interface design)
- Copy (written communication)

Let us look at the components of web design with reference to my favorite web site: *http://www.terraincognita.com*. A simplified site structure is presented in Figure 1–3. Figures 1–4 to 1–6 present some pages from the site.

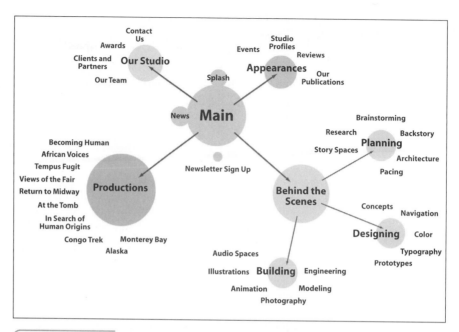

FIGURE 1–3 Site map for *http://www.terraincognita.com* © Terra Incognita

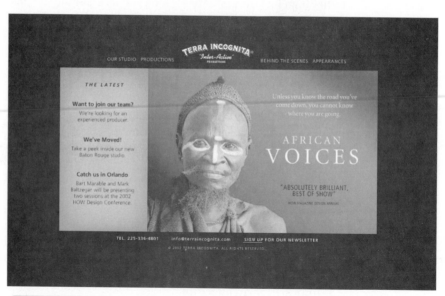

FIGURE 1–4 Main page from *http://www.terraincognita.com* © Terra Incognita

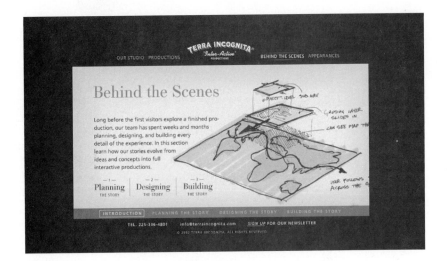

INFORMATION ARCHITECTURE

Information architecture refers to the structure and organization of the communication on a site. The information architect researches the target visitor, the content, the goals, and the requirements of the site. The architect attains a clear understanding of the anticipated visitor behavior and expectations on the site. The information architect also determines the scope of information to be communicated on the site, the specific message on each page, the labels for content on a page, and the navigation options on each page (see Figure 1–7). The message could be communicated using various media (sensory) options such as text, graphics, animation, photographs, audio, and video. Further, the information architect studies and identifies the specific process flows that need to be represented and supported on the web site.

FIGURE 1–7

Information architecture: content structure, navigation, labels, process

In the Terra Incognita site, some of the information architecture decisions are as follows:

▶ The hierarchy of navigation (e.g., the four global links)
▶ The sequence of listing (e.g., Our Studio, Productions, Behind the Scenes, Appearances)
▶ The labels (e.g., Introduction, Clients and Partners, Awards and Recognition, Contact Us)
▶ The process a visitor will go through when signing up for the newsletter
▶ The specific content on each page

Information architecture decisions are similar to those taken when creating the blueprint for a building: What is the building to be used for? Who will use the building? What will be the specific requirements of its occupants? How many rooms will be required? What activities will take place in each room? What facilities are essential in each room? How will the occupants move from one room to another?

INTERFACE DESIGN

Whereas information architecture is concerned with the organization of information on a site, interface design is concerned with how that information is presented to the visitor. Layout, colors, typography, icons, and illustration style are aspects of interface design (see Figure 1–8). So also are decisions about the type of media to be used on the site (audio, video, photographs, animation). Interface design decisions are taken both for the overall personality (the look and feel) of the site and for the specific pages within a site.

FIGURE 1–8

Interface design:
layout, colors,
typography, interaction

Going back to our analogy of designing a building, the interior design decisions about colors, layout, size and style of furniture, signage, and textures are similar to the interface design decisions taken for a web site.

Interactivity makes the web a unique medium. Interaction design, an important component of interface design, impacts the way in which users interact with a site. For example, when the visitors decide to go to the home page, what will they click on, and what response will they get from the page? Further, if they type in a word or a phrase in the Search field, how will the system process that input, and what response will it provide for the various input possibilities?

A similar situation in the design of the building would be decisions about how the lights will get switched on (voice commands, mechanical switch, up or down) or how doors will be opened and closed (position of handles, direction in which the door will open).

In the Terra Incognita site, the use of earth tones, the position of the first- and second-level links, the use of different colors for each section, the fonts used on the site, and the consistency in layout between pages are interface design decisions. So also are the method of navigation (text links, their position, indication of available and currently selected links) and the use of specific media.

COPY

While the web is very much a visual medium, most of the communication on it takes place through text. Writing for the web requires a slightly different approach as compared to writing for print. For example, delivery of a web site is largely through desktop computers and increasingly through handheld devices. The display area for the content is thus limited to the screen size of the device. The flow and continuity that are

FIGURE 1–9

Copy: saying more
with fewer words

possible in a print format are difficult to achieve on a web page (see Figure 1–9). Further, the interactive nature of the web enables chunking of information and nonlinear access. This too is significantly different from the message structure of conventional print media. Further, the fact that web visitors are likely to scan the copy rather than read it word for word makes it important to use representative labels for the content and pull quotes or highlights within the copy. Thus, the construction of the text-based message is an important design element on a web page. Again, the integration of the copy with the sensory (audio and visual) communication is important. The impact of the message will depend largely on how well these different communication media work together.

Information architecture, interface design, and the copy need to be supported by the technology that goes into building and supporting a web site. In this book, we do not go into any detail about the technologies that support web site development. However, we must maintain a healthy respect for it and keep in mind that however good the design is, it could quickly become irrelevant if it is technically not feasible or supportable.

Information architecture, interface design, copy, and technology are essential components of a web design process. These design components need to work harmoniously through a well-managed and efficient development process. In addition, the eventual output of the process needs to meet high-quality standards. This is a challenge of project management.

The illustration in Figure 1–10 represents aspects of web design that we have discussed so far. When taking web design decisions, it is important to consider all aspects and ensure that all elements work together in creating a successful experience for the visitor.

WEB DESIGN PERSPECTIVES

As we consider the challenges of designing a web site, we need to keep in mind that the priorities for the different "players" in web development are different. The four groups most concerned with a web site design are the following:

FIGURE 1–10

Considerations in web design

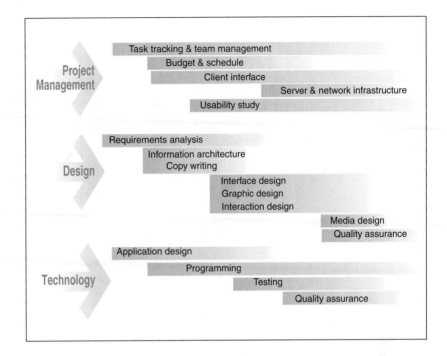

FIGURE 1–11

Perspectives of the web experience

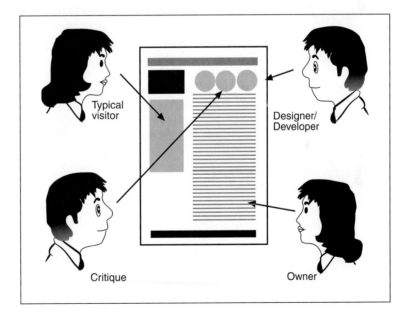

▶ The visitors to the site
▶ The designers/developers
▶ The experts critiquing or evaluating the site
▶ The site owner (the client who commissions and maintains the site)

Although the perspectives could differ among these groups, in the long run the success of a web site is determined by **site visitors and by the site owner (the person or organization who commissioned the development of the site)** (see Figure 1–11 and Table 1–1).

TABLE 1–1   Perspectives of the Web Experience

Perspective	Concerns
A typical visitor	• Concerned with achieving the objective for visiting the site. • Concerned with functionality and having a successful, pleasant experience when using the site. • Usually not concerned with the technology or software used to develop and deploy the web site. • Not likely to spend time "learning," "figuring out," and "thinking" about how and what the site has to offer. • Often not technology savvy. May get confused by messages such as "download plug-in." • Gets influenced by the first impression and experience.
Web designer/developer	• Interested in developing effective interfaces with the most efficient utilization of resources. • Often keen to use cutting-edge technology and pushing the creative envelope. • Can get influenced by the opinions of other designers/developers. • Is sometimes preoccupied with being unique and different. • Can get "possessive" of thoughts and ideas.
Critics	• Concerned with evaluating how the site fares on aesthetic, usability, and technical fronts. • Their opinion could be used to predict success of the web site over time (heuristic evaluation). • Have their personal preferred focus on aesthetic, usability, technical sophistication, uniqueness, etc.
The owner	• Has commissioned the development and is most concerned with getting the best return on investment. • May be keen on short-term as well as long-term strategic value of the web site. • Will usually want the best-looking, the best-performing, and the most economical web site, with the best returns. In other words, is concerned about the return on investment (ROI). • May sometimes be swayed by trends and focus more on the "bells and whistles."

WEB SITE EVALUATION

The real worth of a web site is established over the long term by examining how it impacts the visitor's and the client's communication objectives. Formal usability tests could be used to validate assumptions made during the process of design and to provide objective data on how the web site could be expected to perform. Further, actual data for site usage, such as number of visitors, time spent on the site, transactions completed on the site, revenue generated via the site, and feedback messages from visitors, could provide useful indication of the degree of success of the site.

Although these methods require time, planning, data collection and analysis, and of course money, there is a quick and effective method of evaluating a web site. This method (heuristic evaluation) calls for the opinion of an expert critic.

An effective critic first establishes the purpose of the site and the target audience and then evaluates the effectiveness of the web site on the basis of a set of criteria (heuristics). These heuristics could deal with aspects of aesthetics, usability, communication, technology, and overall impact. Table 1–2 gives an outline that an expert critic may use when evaluating a web site.

TABLE 1–2   Evaluating a Web Site

Understanding the Web Site

Purpose

Communication objective
- What change in information, knowledge, attitude, or skill should the site achieve?
- What is the anticipated action on part of the visitor during or after the visit?

Business Objective
- What is the target for direct revenue from this site?
- What is the target for business inquiries from this site?

Audience
- Who is the site targeting? What is the age, sex, education, interest level, reading ability, motivation, and so on?
- What are the objectives for the target audience?
- What level of technical sophistication are the visitors expected to have?

Technology
- What browsers and versions is this site designed for?
- What screen resolution is the site designed for?
- Does the site assume the availability of a plug-in or a special technology?

Evaluating the Web Site

Information Architecture
- Is the navigation organized in an intuitive manner, keeping in mind the needs of the visitor?
- Are links labeled adequately?
- Is the content in keeping with the communication and business objectives?
- Does the site provide adequate depth of content?
- Is the content on each page labeled (titles) adequately?
- Is there a need to update the information on the site? Does the content appear to be up to date?
- Are processes easy to execute?
- Do processes closely and accurately resemble real-life processes that the visitors are familiar with?
- Does the site inform the visitor about the browser version and plug-ins required on the site and where to get that technology?

Interface Design
- Is the visual treatment in keeping with the objectives and the audience?
- Are metaphors depicted with appropriate visual representations?
- Are principles of color, typography, illustration style, and layout used appropriately?
- Does the site adhere to design conventions and present the interface in a consistent manner throughout the site (visual identity, sequence, position, labels, colors, illustration style)?
- Is it easy for visitors to determine how to navigate through the site (where they are, where they can go, how they can go where they want to go, how they can get back to where they came from)?
- Do the media elements (animation, audio, video) add communication value to the site?
- Does the site have a personality that supports the overall message of the site?

Copy/Language
- Is the language on the site in keeping with the tone and content of the site?
- Does the language demonstrate consistency in use, grammar, and style?
- Is there too little or too much text?
- Are the salient points in the copy highlighted with appropriate labels and pull quotes?

continued

TABLE 1–2 *Continued*

Technology

- Does the site download in a reasonable time frame?
- Does it require technology (plug-ins, JavaScript, Java) that is easy to obtain, install and enable?
- Does the site provide an alternative to using plug-ins?
- Does the site work with all versions of browsers?
- Does the site work equally well on different computing platforms?

Quality Assurance

- Does the site have a consistent layout?
- Do all images load (no broken images)?
- Is the language free of grammatical and spelling errors?
- Is the content on the site readable across browsers and platforms?
- Do all links work (no broken links)?
- Are there any widowed pages (pages without a link back to the main site)?

Overall Impact

- Does the site invite you to explore it? Is the message engaging?
- Does the site appear to achieve its objectives?
- Would you recommend this site to a friend?

SUMMARY

In this chapter, we have seen that web design is about creating and facilitating experiences for the visitors to a web site. We have looked at the many faces of web design—information architecture, interface design, copy, technology, and project management. Different individuals (visitors, designers/developers, expert critics, and the site owner) are likely to hold different perspectives and expectations from web design. Finally, we have examined how a critic could evaluate a web site using a set of heuristics.

GUIDING QUESTIONS

▶ What is the objective of web design?
▶ What are the main components of web design?
▶ What aspects of a web site could we attribute to information architecture?
▶ What aspects of a web site could we attribute to interface design?
▶ What role does copy play in the effectiveness of a web site?
▶ What is the importance of project management in the development of a web site?
▶ What are the primary concerns of visitors, designers/developers, critics, and owners of a site?

EXERCISES

▶ Select a web site that offers regularly updated news. Evaluate this site using the criteria discussed in this chapter.
▶ Select a web site that offers e-commerce transactions. Evaluate this site using the criteria discussed in this chapter. How does the e-commerce site differ from the news site?
▶ Make a list of heuristics that you would use to evaluate a web site. Evaluate the news and the e-commerce sites using these heuristics.

Types of Web Applications

INTRODUCTION

The web is a young and dynamic medium of communication. Concepts, technology, uses, and trends are constantly changing in the world of the web. In conventional fields, change can be expected to be gradual. However, we can expect an almost new face of the web every few months. This makes it both exciting and difficult to develop generalized theories about the field.

In spite of this fast-moving scenario, some specific application or usage areas have emerged in the past few years. There is little standardization in the way applications are classified. However, even though the labels differ, by and large the application areas are similar across classifications. For example, in her book *Web Navigation: Designing the User Experience,* Jennifer Fleming classifies web applications as Shopping, Community, Entertainment, Identity, Learning, and Information. Though I have used slightly different labels, there is a significant similarity between her classification and mine.

It is common to find features of more than one application on any one site. This chapter will help us understand the basic objectives and features of broad classes of applications that could be combined on a site. Table 2–1 shows how a typical web site can be classified.

Going back to our analogy of a building, each category of web site is like a different type of building. Just as a structure could be built to serve as an office building, a school, a home, a secure laboratory, a warehouse, a restaurant, or a museum, you could build a web site to meet any one or more objectives outlined in Table 2–1. Let us look at these application types in some more detail.

BRAND SITES

Brand sites are often referred to as "brochureware sites." As the name suggests, these sites build a brand for a product or an organization. They are somewhat like the

TABLE 2–1   Types of Web Sites

Type of Site	Objective
Brand	Create an on-line identity and presence for an organization
Personal	Share information or opinions on a specific topic or person
Event	Share information and invite visitors to a particular event
B2C e-commerce	Business to consumer. Offer on-line shopping experiences and transactions between businesses and their consumers
B2B	Business to business. Support business to business communication and transactions
Training and education	Provide web-supported education and training
News	Provide up-to-date news or information
Intranet	Facilitate communication and interactions between and among management and employees in an organization
Entertainment	Provide engaging entertainment
Portal	Serve as a compendium of web resources on a specific topic
Community	Facilitate interactions between a group of people, leading to the formation of an on-line community

brochures and publicity videos that organizations use to inform the public about their products and services. These sites have the express objective of creating an identity and fostering an image for the organization. The sites are usually sleek and attractive and reflect the personality of the organization. For example, the Arden's Garden web site (Figure 2–1) helps create an on-line brand for the organization.

Most brand sites have a similar structure. They have sections on the organization and its people (about us), products and services, locations, job openings, and ways to contact the organization. Some brand sites provide a platform for community building where visitors could share and exchange views on topics related to the mission of the organization.

PERSONAL SITES

Personal sites are somewhat similar to brand sites, but they are not necessarily associated with a formal organization. The objective of these sites is to share "information" or "opinion." The subject could be anything—the flower rafflesia, the human genome, Tibetian Thangka painting, a personal art portfolio, or a fan page for a movie star. Personal sites vary greatly in the quality and depth of content. In a lot of ways, these sites are a manifestation of the "democratization" of the web. They could be expressive and experimental in nature and are not bound by guidelines of "effective web design." Renee Peter's portfolio site (Figure 2–2) is an example of a personal site. This site communicates her skills, values, and design approach and also allows visitors to contact her.

FIGURE 2–1 Example of a brand site: Arden's Garden (*www.ardensgarden.com*)

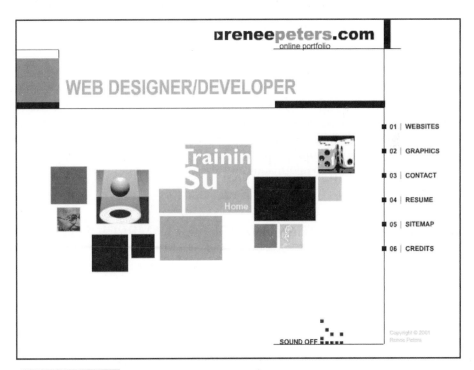

FIGURE 2–2 Example of a personal site: Renee Peters (*www.reneepeters.com*)

FIGURE 2–3   Example of an event invitation by Yuki Kawakita (*www.studioyk.com/a.htm*)

EVENT SITES

Event sites are built for a short "life span." They are tied to a particular event, such as the Olympic games, the Super Bowl, or a music concert. The primary objective is to disseminate information about the event and also support on-line sales of the tickets and merchandise associated with the event. Once the event is over, the site could continue to feature topics associated with the event or may be taken down.

Event sites are usually not extensive in content but often incorporate elements of a television commercial. A new breed of event sites for personal events, such as weddings, birth announcements, and birthdays, is also becoming popular. The invitation to an internship fair, shown in Figure 2–3, was a three-page site that provided just enough information and limited functionality that was required at the time of the event.

BUSINESS-TO-CUSTOMER (B2C) E-COMMERCE SITES

Business-to-Customer e-commerce sites have a primary objective of facilitating or supporting sales and on-line transactions between an organization and its customers. These sites emulate real stores and cater to the shopping behaviors of patrons. Though the original purpose of the Internet was not commerce, on-line sales and marketing have turned out to be some of the most popular (and perceivably lucrative) uses of the web. Many innovative commerce models have emerged to exploit the medium. Selling commodities (*www.amazon.com*), on-line auctions (*www.ebay.coms*), advertising (*banners on web sites*), on-line banking (*www.netbank.com*), on-line trading (*www.etrade.com*), and on-line subscription services (*www.nytimes.com*) have become popular in the recent past.

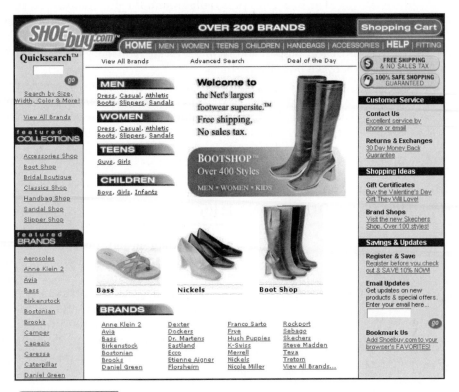

FIGURE 2–4 Example of a B2C e-commerce site: Shoebuy.com (*www.shoebuy.com*)

Business-to-Customer sites facilitate sales, but most of them also provide value-added customer support, such as tracking of an order and communication with the customer service departments.

Designing an effective B2C site requires a clear understanding of the anticipated user behavior and the back-end technology that supports secure on-line transactions. Such sites also need to stay current, and the information on the site needs to be regularly updated. Though in this book we do not discuss the intricacies of e-commerce, it is important to note that international commerce, taxation, credit card security, information privacy, on-line inventory management, and the behavior of an on-line shopper are topics that are at the core of B2C site design.

The e-commerce site in Figure 2–4 allows patrons to search, get information, and order shoes via an on-line interface. As you can imagine, the site display regularly changes in accordance with the seasons or events at different times of the year.

BUSINESS-TO-BUSINESS (B2B) EXTRANET SITES

Business-to-business sites allow business "partners" to carry out transactions on the web. Access to these sites is restricted to the business partners. Usage can include real-time inventory and supply chain management as well as access to exclusive pricing and product information.

The B2B concept is built around the possibility of creating an interactive, efficient, and economically viable transaction model for businesses to improve productivity and service. The objective is to create a relatively exclusive environment that will support and facilitate greater efficiency, ease, and economy in interactions between business partners.

For example, many web design organizations allow their clients to have on-line access to an exclusive web site. These clients are able to examine designs, provide comments, give approvals, submit media resources, and communicate with the project manager via this web site. Needless to say, the access to this web site is restricted to a specific client and members of the project team.

TRAINING AND EDUCATION SITES

The use of the web as a tool for training and education is one of the fastest-growing applications. The web can play three primary roles in supporting learning.

The first is as a **primary learning resource**. In this type of application, an individual works one to one with learning materials that are accessed on-line. It is important to note that one of the most popular uses of the web has been as an information resource. Although information sites certainly can support learning, Web-based Learning (WBL) sites are designed with the explicit purpose of supporting specific learning objectives. The term "web-based training" is derived from an older and well-recognized term, "Computer-Based Learning" (CBL).

The Activities section of the site (On Becoming Human), shown in Figure 2–5, allows visitors to construct a human and a chimpanzee skeleton. As the skeleton is being put together, relevant comparative information is presented. This not only

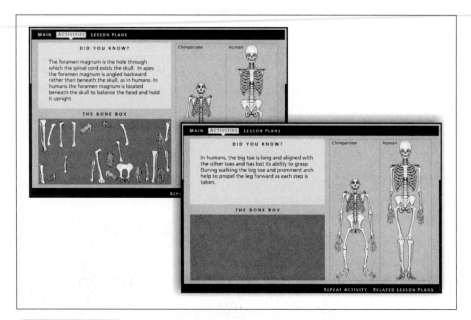

FIGURE 2–5   Example of a web-based learning site: On Becoming Human (*www.becominghuman.org*)

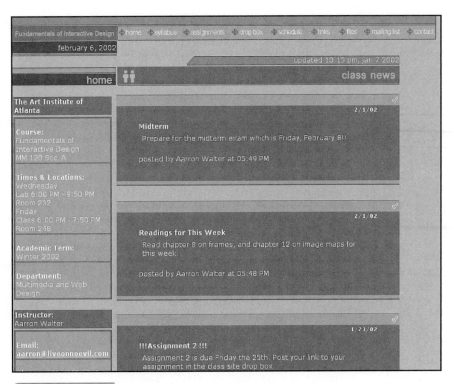

FIGURE 2–6   Example of web-supported learning: course site designed by Aarron Walter (*www.thecreativityengine.com*)

enables the "learner" to identify the skeletal structures of humans and chimpanzees but also gives him or her an understanding of the comparative features of these structures.

The second training and education application on the web **supports learning** by providing educators and learners with a platform for sharing information, initiating and participating in discussions, tracking performance, managing access, and generating various reports. Several platforms for this type of learning management system exist on the web. These web sites allow students and instructors to interact with each other in an asynchronous manner (all need not be present at the same time). Courses can be offered entirely through such web sites, without requiring any face-to-face interaction. With the growing need for providing access to learning over distance and time, on-line courses have gained popularity and will continue to do so over the next several years. Aarron Walter has developed a web-based tool that instructors can use to post course-related information and activities on a web site. Instructors and students can interact with each other via this site and also share comments, course documents, and announcements through the site (see Figure 2–6).

Although some people would be inclined to compare on-line instructional delivery models with in-class instruction, we need to keep in mind that these two modes of instruction address two very different needs of education and training. As such, the effectiveness of instruction needs to be measured in terms of achievement of learning objectives, economic savings, convenience to instructors and learners, affective outcomes, and the potential of reaching the "unreached."

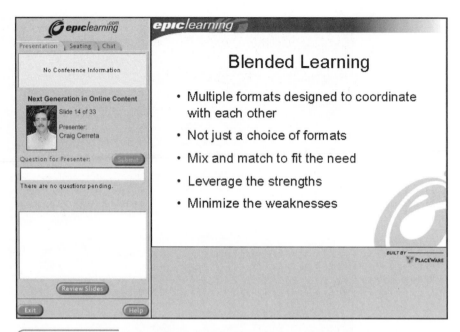

FIGURE 2–7 Example of an on-line synchronous virtual classroom: EpicLearning (*www.epiclearning.com*) and Placeware, showing one of the delivery vehicles in EpicLearning's patented "Blended Learning" technology

The third web-based training and education application emulates a real classroom in which all learners and instructors participate in an on-line **real-time virtual classroom.** These virtual classrooms allow audio- and chat-based group interactions, document exchange, interactive presentation, and individual queries (similar to raising a hand to ask a question in a classroom). Video-based interaction is also possible wherever a higher bandwidth is available to all the participants. EpicLearning and Placeware's web application allows "learners" and instructors to gather in a "virtual classroom" and interact with each other via voice while sharing a "white board" (see Figure 2–7).

Although the previous discussion could lead to an impression of exclusive application areas, in reality an e-learning environment could consist of a combination of all three. A typical e-course could consist of WBL lessons, scheduled participation in a virtual classroom, and involvement in activities such as chat and threaded discussions through an on-line learning management system.

NEWS SITES

News sites present frequently updated information. These sites emulate the traditional radio and newspaper media. While some news sites tend to be general purpose (such as a daily newspaper), others specialize in topical news (such as technology, sports, finance, arts, and weather). Just as individuals have their favorite newspaper and radio stations, we can expect that over time they will also identify a favorite news site. This means that we can expect that once the loyalty has been established, the visitor will regularly revisit the same site. This consideration has led

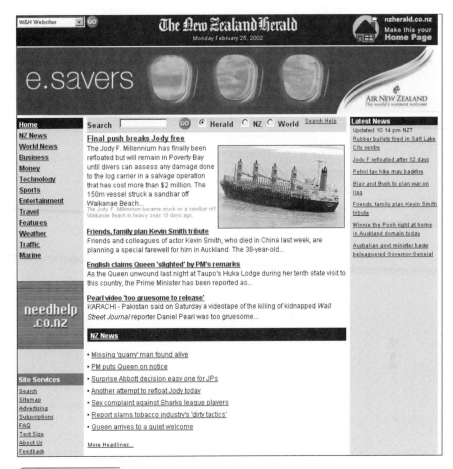

FIGURE 2–8   Example of a news site: *The New Zealand Herald* (*www.nzherald.co.nz*)

to the availability of personalization on many sites (e.g., www.yahoo.com). A visitor is able to access customized news pertaining to specific topics (finance, sports, medicine, region, and so on) and also have the "news" delivered to an e-mail address or computer desktop (through screen savers) at specified times.

The web site of *The New Zealand Herald* presents news and information that could potentially be updated every minute of the day (see Figure 2–8).

INTRANET SITES

Intranet sites facilitate transactions and communication *within* an organization. They are built to enhance productivity and communication among employees and different departments within an organization. Typical uses of intranets include access to up-to-date organizational news and policies, leave applications and approvals, filing of expense reports, sharing of documents, on-line audio and video conferencing, e-mail, and chat.

Transactions over intranets are often sensitive in nature. Therefore, information and access security is an important consideration when designing the site. In a way,

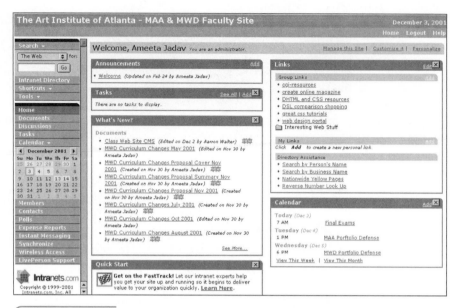

FIGURE 2-9   Example of an intranet site: Intranets.com (*www.intranets.com*)

this is similar to designing buildings with limited and secure access. Only authorized persons have access to the building, and only certain individuals have access to special rooms (e.g., payroll and employee information).

Intranets provide a valuable tool for supporting the organizational culture and building a strong sense of community for employees who may otherwise be in geographically diverse locations. Easier information access can also facilitate a participatory work culture and increase a sense of "ownership" for employees.

Designing intranets requires a clear understanding of the work flow (e.g., how tasks get done, how information is generated and shared) and processes (e.g., how a leave application gets approved) within the organization. In addition, it needs to reflect organizational culture and values. Further, the transition from manual to on-line interactions needs to be carefully considered when designing an intranet system. If the intranet looks and feels very different from what the employees are used to, its integration in their daily work ethos is likely to be difficult and could even lead to a "failure" of the intranet.

Organization-based intranets are exclusive and highly customized, but it is common to find relatively simpler intranets being used by small groups to communicate and share information. For example, an intranet of the department of Multimedia and Web Design at The Art Institute of Atlanta facilitates document and information sharing and communication between faculty (see Figure 2–9). This simple intranet was set up using a template provided by www.intranets.com.

ENTERTAINMENT SITES

Entertainment sites offer activities that engage and entertain the visitor. These are not sites about entertainment (such as movie sites) but rather sites that provide entertainment. Several gaming sites can be found on the web (e.g., *www.shockwave.com*).

FIGURE 2–10   Example of an on-line game: © Estate of Keith Haring (*www.haringkids.com*)

Some of them allow interactions among a group of individuals, creating a virtual gaming environment that allows individuals to interact with each other in real time.

Design of a gaming site requires not only a creative game concept but also the use of sophisticated technology to support the processing and speed required for such games.

The Haring Kids web site allows visitors to solve a puzzle by picking the animal shapes and placing them in the right place (see Figure 2–10). The site uses sound and animation as feedback to these actions. As you can imagine, the target audience (children) could be effectively engaged and entertained through this activity.

PORTAL SITES

As the name suggests, portal sites provide an "entry" to a compendium of links to sites on a specific topic. General-purpose portals, such as Yahoo.com, provide an entry to the world of the web. On the other hand, specific-purpose portals, such as CNet.com, present topic-specific information and links (in this case, computing technology). The advantage of a portal is that comprehensive information pertaining to a topic can be accessed from the same spot. Naturally, identifying the information and organizing it in an intuitive navigation interface is one of the bigger challenges for designers of a portal site. A portal also needs to ensure that the information it features is current. Since visitors access information with a certain degree of trust, it is

FIGURE 2–11

Example of a portal
site: Poetry Portal
(*www.poetry-
portal.com*)

important that the information on portal sites be valid and authentic. A portal is a good place for the "gathering of like-minded people." Many portals facilitate on-line community building activities (discussed next).

For example, the Poetry Portal at www.poetry-portal.com provides access to information on genres, events, courses, poets, and so on (see Figure 2–11). The site also supports community building by providing a forum for exchange of ideas, opinions, and information—all pertaining to poetry.

ON-LINE COMMUNITIES

As we have seen, on-line communities are powerful and unique features of the Internet. Bulletin boards, newsgroups, discussion lists, and chat rooms facilitate the creation and support for virtual on-line communities. A relatively standard interface for these applications has evolved over the past few years.

A whole new "social" culture has emerged through these community features. Anonymity provides individuals the safety and confidence for expressing opinions and observations with relative ease. The environment facilitates building relationships with other "regulars" who frequent the same chat room, list, or bulletin board.

Typically, a site that supports community building also provides content support for its members. As such, news, portal, B2C, B2B, and brand sites could all incorporate one or more community-building feature.

SUMMARY

In this chapter, we have discussed a range of web applications: brand, personal, event, B2C e-commerce, B2B extranet, training and education, news, intranet, entertainment, and portal sites as well as on-line communities. More often than not, one site could incorporate features of many different applications. Understanding the fundamental features of each application can help designers select the most appropriate feature that can meet the objectives of a site.

REFERENCE

Fleming, Jennifer. (1998). *Web navigation: Designing the user experience.* Sebastopol, CA: O'Reilly & Associates.

GUIDING QUESTIONS

▶ Describe the main features and give one example of the following type of web site:
  ▶ Brand
  ▶ Personal
  ▶ Event
  ▶ B2C e-commerce
  ▶ Training and education
  ▶ Entertainment
  ▶ Portal
  ▶ On-line communities
▶ How do B2B and intranet sites differ from the previously listed ones?
▶ Looking into the future, which new areas of applications do you see evolving on the web?

EXERCISE

Assume that you are a web developer and that you have been asked by a magazine to design a web presence for them. (For the purpose of this exercise, pick your favorite magazine and pretend that you are developing the site for the magazine.) Review various magazine sites on the web and draw up a list of features that must be present on your site.

The Project Team

I n this chapter and the next, we examine factors and processes that could enhance the efficiency of a web development project and in turn lead to development of an effective web site.

In my opinion, the composition and climate within a project team is one of the most critical (if not *the* critical) factors that impacts the success of a project. Web organizations vary greatly in how they set up project teams. Typically, smaller projects have teams of two or three persons (sometimes even one), while larger projects could have teams of more than 20 individuals.

As we discuss the designations of team members and the definition of their roles, we must keep in mind that individuals in a team often play more than one role. As a matter of fact, the web industry encourages expertise in more than one area and an ability to tackle multiple tasks. For example, a web designer is invariably expected to know Hypertext Markup Language (HTML) and basic JavaScript coding. The designers will not only carry out visual and interface design but also do basic coding. Similarly, the creative director may be required to not only establish standards, provide guidelines, and monitor the quality of visual and interface design but also design the layout and graphics for web pages and maybe even code the HTML for these pages. Multiplicity of roles and skills has become a norm in the web industry. This is not to say that all people play all the roles in web development. There certainly are specialized skills and roles in the industry. However, multiskilled professionals are common, and at the least, web professionals are expected to have a clear appreciation and understanding of the skill, process, and technology requirements for each role in the team.

This is similar to what happens in the construction industry (to which we have compared the web industry). The roles in the construction industry (architect, interior designer, civil engineer, electrical engineer, and construction workers) are probably more clearly delineated than those in the web industry. However, both industries require a range of disparate yet highly dependent skills. The more each expert understands the skills and requirements of the other experts, the more efficient and effective the overall process will be.

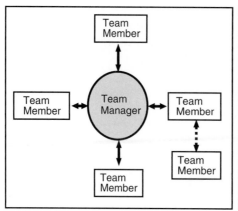 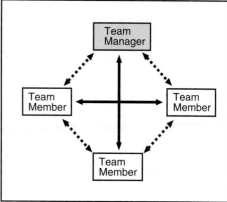

Each web organization functions with a formally or informally identifiable set of values that form the foundation for the way the organization interacts with its employees, clients, and business partners and the way it does business. The same set of values guides an organization's approach to project management and team culture. For example, an organization may be built on values that encourage participatory decision making. We can expect this organization to have a relatively nonhierarchical management structure.

Other organizations may have a hierarchy-based management structure in which the manager determines the tasks to be completed by each team member and sets expectations. The manager monitors the completion and quality of the tasks and serves as a "control center" for input and output of information to the project. In large projects, more than one control center may be established. In either case, the line of control, accountability, and the decision-making authority are clearly delineated.

It is difficult to say that any one these cultures is better than the other. Each team's culture is defined by the organizational culture, the manager's personal leadership style, and the personalities of the team members. The success of a team is determined by the synergy that exists between these cultures, styles, and personalities within the team (see Figure 3–1).

Whatever the management structure and culture a team works with, its members will invariably perform one or more specific roles. These roles are discussed in the next section.

ROLES IN A WEB PROJECT

A typical project team consists of individuals who perform one or more of the roles shown in Figure 3–2. It is important to remember that titles, role definition, and requirements vary significantly across the industry. For example, many organizations expect the web master to perform the role of the web designer (as defined in this chapter). In other organizations, the project manager is expected to also play a marketing

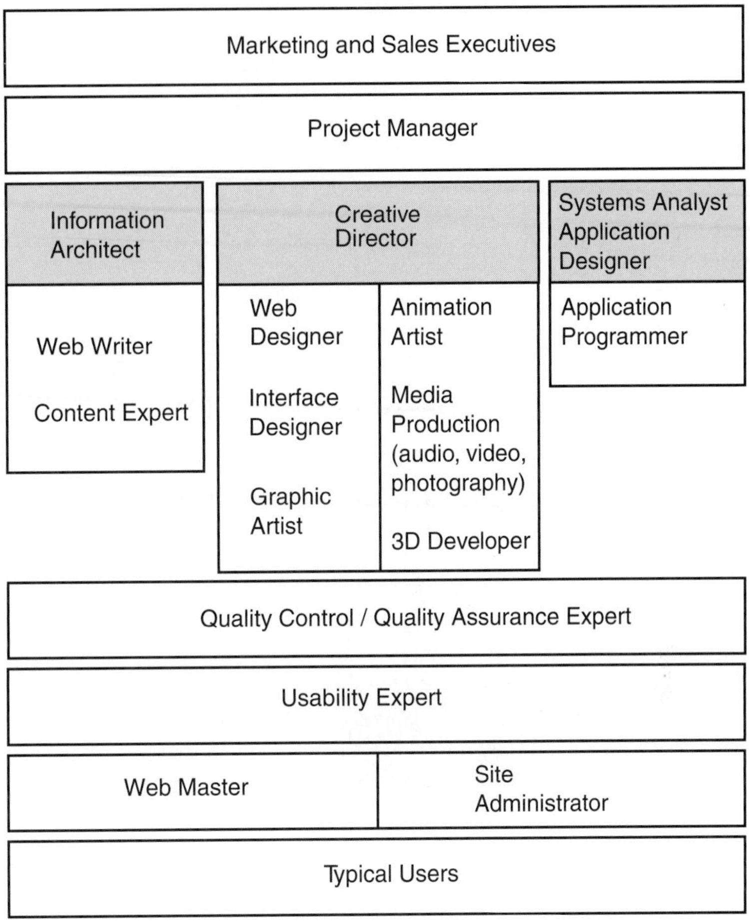

FIGURE 3–2

Roles in a project team

Marketing and Sales Executives			
Project Manager			
Information Architect	Creative Director		Systems Analyst Application Designer
Web Writer

Content Expert | Web Designer

Interface Designer

Graphic Artist | Animation Artist

Media Production (audio, video, photography)

3D Developer | Application Programmer |
Quality Control / Quality Assurance Expert			
Usability Expert			
Web Master		Site Administrator	
Typical Users			

role. The important thing to recognize is that regardless of the title of a role, certain skills and activities are critical to the successful execution of a web project.

Let us now look at each title and define the activities and expectations of that role.

Marketing and Sales Executive

The marketing and sales executive is the client's first contact (see Figure 3–3). He or she establishes the credentials for the web development organization and gains the confidence of the client. Once the contract is signed and the project is under way, the marketing and sales executive may continue to liaison with the client and build a relationship for an ongoing business partnership.

The marketing and sales executive is responsible for the following:

- Conducting the initial requirements analysis
- Developing and presenting the concept proposal to the client
- Developing and presenting the business proposal to the client
- Formalizing the contract with the client

Project Manager

The project manager orchestrates and manages the show (see Figure 3–4). At any point in time, the project manager is aware of the status of the project in terms of the schedule, budget, deliverables, client relations, team climate, and so on.

FIGURE 3–3

Marketing and sales executive

FIGURE 3–4

Project manager

Most project managers in the web industry have either migrated from other industries such as software and media production or have gained experience as a team member in some other capacity.

The project manager is responsible for the following:

- Drawing up a list of project tasks
- Determining roles and responsibilities of team members
- Establishing reporting and communication protocols within the team
- Assigning tasks to the team members
- Tracking the completion of tasks
- Monitoring and managing the budget
- Monitoring and managing project resources and infrastructure
- Interfacing with the client
- Maintaining a healthy climate in the team
- Establishing norms and methods of quality assurance
- Monitoring quality
- Communicating with relevant groups outside the team (client, marketing, finance, other project teams, technology support, and so on)
- Managing change control (scheduling, cost, effort modifications on account of changes initiated by the client or the team)

Information Architect

The information architect has a clear understanding of the target audience, the content to be presented on the site, and the business and communication principles that will form the basis for the site design. In a way, the information architect holds the larger "vision" for the web site and is able to translate that vision into a concrete content structure, process flow, and navigation system for the site (see Figure 3–5).

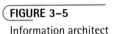

FIGURE 3–5

Information architect

The information architect is responsible for the following:

- Researching content and target audience
- Conducting the requirements analysis
- Researching and creating different use case scenarios and process flow diagrams for the site
- Determining the most appropriate scope and hierarchy for content on the site
- Designing the navigation and interaction structure
- Determining the content to be presented on each page
- Identifying the appropriate labels for content and links on the site
- Designing and conducting usability tests

Web Writer

The web writer works closely with the information architect, the content expert, and the creative director. The writer researches and composes all written (verbal) communication for a web site (see Figure 3–6). Many web writers have a background in journalism, copy writing, script writing, or technical writing. The web writer attempts to create cohesive, clear, and concise communication while capitalizing on the nonlinear and interactive features of the web.

The web writer is responsible for the following:

- Researching content and target audience
- Writing the copy
- Determining the labels for different sections (with the information architect)
- Specifying the pull quotes (brief excerpts or phrases that capture the message in a section of the copy)
- Ensuring that the verbal communication on the site is well integrated with other communication modes, such as images, audio, video, animation, and photographs

FIGURE 3–6

Web writer

Content Expert

Depending on the complexity of the content, a web team may work with one or more content experts. These experts may not belong to the core project team, but they play the critical role of validating the content information on the web site. They are usually from the client organization. In the initial phases, they help the team understand the content. In the later phases, they help the team by evaluating the communication and verifying the validity of the content on the site. Content experts serve as consultants throughout the project and direct the project team toward the relevant content resources whenever it is required (see Figure 3–7).

Creative Director

The creative director (also called the art director) establishes the overall design parameters and directs the conceptualization of the aesthetic and experiential design for the site (see Figure 3–8). As with the information architect, the creative director needs to have a holistic perspective of the target audience and the objectives of the site. The creative director is concerned mostly with the visual interface and aesthetics of the site, while the information architect is concerned mostly with the organization of content and navigation. They need to work with each other and share a concern for usability.

Most creative directors have played the role of a designer at some point in their careers. Their vast design experience is now brought to play in helping other designers develop their concepts and creativity.

The creative director is responsible for the following:

▶ Establishing and maintaining a high design standard
▶ Providing guidance to the web designers and artists
▶ Researching design approaches and style
▶ Conducting quality assurance for all aspects of interface design

FIGURE 3–7

Content expert

Web Designer (Graphic Designer; Visual Designer)

The web designer is largely responsible for conceptualizing and developing the visual personality of the site (see Figure 3–9). The creative director guides the web designer in creating the most effective experience on the site. Typically, a web designer would work on one project at a time, while the creative director could be working with designers on several projects at the same time.

FIGURE 3–8

Creative director

FIGURE 3–9

Web designer

The web designer is responsible for the following:

- Researching content and target audience
- Experimenting, exploring, and determining the visual design (layout, colors, typography, illustration style)
- Documenting the design approach
- Developing the storyboards (also known as "comps")
- Documenting the design standards (size and position of elements, color values, interaction design)
- Ensuring that the design is technically feasible
- Providing guidance to the artists as they work on the development of visual elements
- Integrating the different visual elements on a web page
- Coding and editing HTML, Cascading Style Guide (CSS), and basic JavaScript

The roles of the web designer and interface designer are close, and in many organizations the same individual performs both roles. However, theoretically, the web designer is concerned with the "visual" experience on the site, whereas the interface designer is concerned with the way visitors interact with the content on the site. Naturally, there is significant interdependence between these two roles, and it is most critical that there be clear communication and interaction between individuals performing these two roles.

Interface Designer

The interface designer is often called the GUI (graphical user interface) designer. This person is responsible for designing the way in which a visitor will interact with the site (see Figure 3–10).

FIGURE 3–10 Interface designer

FIGURE 3–11 Graphic artist

The interface designer is responsible for the following:

▶ Determining the requirements for specific interactions on the web site
▶ Researching user behavior with respect to different types of interactions
▶ Flowcharting various processes (user response, system feedback, and action for each interaction)
▶ Designing and deploying the interaction using appropriate visual interface and technology
▶ Carrying out usability evaluations

Graphic Artist

The graphic artist works with the web designer and the interface designer. He or she develops and optimizes the visual elements (scanning, icons, illustrations, photo touch-ups, buttons) to be incorporated on the site (see Figure 3–11).

Animation Artist

The animation artist specializes in creating and implementing web sites involving two-dimensional animations and interactivity (see Figure 3–12). Flash software from the Macromedia corporation has become a defacto standard development tool for web animations, and so some organizations may refer to this position as "Flash artist or developer." The animation artist works with the creative director.

Media Producers

Media producers work with audio, video, and/or photo production teams to shoot/develop, edit, digitize, and optimize the audio, video, and photographs to be integrated on a web site (see Figure 3–13). Beside the core media production skills, media producers need to have expertise in preparing and deploying rich media content over the Internet.

FIGURE 3–12
Animation artist

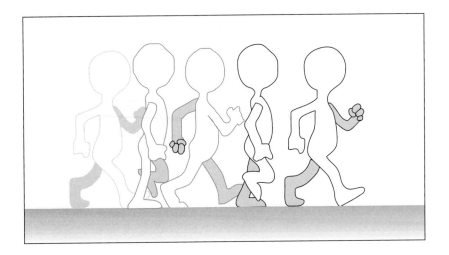

FIGURE 3–12
Animation artist

FIGURE 3–13
Media producers

3D Developer

If a web site design calls for three-dimensional (3D) images and animation, a 3D developer is called on to develop these elements (see Figure 3–14). The 3D developer creates animation storyboards and uses 3D modeling and animation software to design and develop the 3D media assets. The 3D developer is also responsible for optimizing the 3D media for integration on the web.

FIGURE 3–14
3D developer

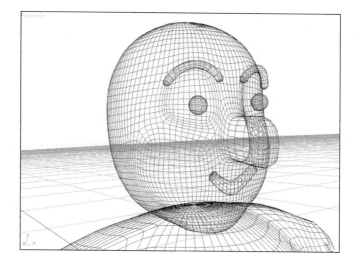

FIGURE 3–14
3D developer

FIGURE 3–15
Systems analyst

FIGURE 3–15
Systems analyst

Systems Analyst/Application Designer

The systems analyst (also known as the application designer) conducts technical research and designs the software application and databases for the web site (see Figure 3–15). This person also provides technical guidance to the application programmers. The software applications designed by this person are usually server-side applications and are also known as back-end applications. The systems analyst has an intricate knowledge of how different technical elements of a web site interact with each other. This person is able to visualize and define a technical solution that best meets the requirements of the web site.

FIGURE 3–16

Application
programmer

Application Programmer

The application programmer develops the web site using programming environments such as Java, Perl, PHP, C++, VisualBasic, ASP, ActiveX, JavaScript, and databases (see Figure 3–16). The application programmer may also specialize in using development environments such as Cold Fusion.

Quality Control (QC)/Quality Assurance (QA) Experts

The QC/QA experts have an eye for detail and a lot of patience (see Figure 3–17). The industry often uses "quality control" and "quality assurance" as interchangeable terms. Theoretically, quality control refers to the process of certifying a product as being ready for the next stage (usually site release). On the other hand, quality assurance refers to the processes that are incorporated throughout development to achieve a high degree of quality in the product.

The QC/QA experts develop test plans and then implement these plans to evaluate a site. They test the web site for technical bugs, media (image) quality, language, consistency, and adherence to the design standards that have been established for the site.

Usability Expert

The usability expert evaluates a site and provides direction for enhancing its usability (see Figure 3–18).

The usability expert is responsible for the following:

- Gaining a clear understanding of the objectives of the site and the target audience
- Anticipating and predicting the behavior of the visitors to the site

FIGURE 3–17
QC/QA expert

FIGURE 3–18
Usability expert

▶ Conceptualizing, designing, conducting, and analyzing a usability study to establish empirical parameters for the usability of a site
▶ Providing suggestions for enhancing and improving the usability of a site

Web Master

The web master's role is often confused with that of the web designer. In this book, we define the web master as the individual who tracks the traffic to a web site and manages the site once it is released (see Figure 3–19). The web master's responsibilities require a good appreciation for the workings of the search engines, marketing principles, and user behavior. The web master is responsible for ensuring that the content on the site is current and also for employing strategies for maximizing the traffic to the site.

FIGURE 3–19

Web master

FIGURE 3–19

Web master

FIGURE 3–20

Site administrator

Site Administrator

Once the site has gone live, the site administrator uploads new content, monitors the site for possible breaches in security, and ensures maximum uptime for the site (see Figure 3–20).

FIGURE 3–21

Typical users

Typical Users

While users do not really belong to the team, they play an important role in the success of the project. Typical users are involved in focus groups, usability studies, and informal evaluation of the web site throughout the development cycle (see Figure 3–21).

As the web industry becomes more specialized, we could come across different roles that perform overlapping and similar functions. Three roles in particular (information architect, instructional designer, and systems analyst) are similar and yet require specialized skills in niche areas. Let us briefly examine these roles.

INFORMATION ARCHITECT, INSTRUCTIONAL DESIGNER, AND SYSTEMS ANALYST

The information architect, instructional designer, and systems analyst must understand the requirements, the content, the target audience, and the business and communication objectives of the site. In addition, each role requires a specialized perspective.

The information architect's focus is on organizing the information and interactions on the site such that they are intuitive and easy to use and help achieve the goals of the site.

On the other hand, the instructional designer plays the role of the information architect for web-based learning applications. The instructional designer has a mastery of training strategies for different learning objectives and is able to design a solution that addresses the training objectives on a site.

The systems analyst's focus is on technical feasibility and the design of the software application such that it best meets the objectives of the site. In order to do this effectively, the systems analyst starts with a clear understanding of the information architecture for the site. The complex technical solutions (including database design, security, transaction processing, and so on) are then conceptualized and designed.

As the industry develops, newer terms, such as "cognitive engineer," "communication strategist," and "content strategist," may evolve and become popular. However, at the core of these roles will be skills for analysis of the requirements, understanding the audience, determining the resources and constraints, identifying communication and business objectives, organizing content in the most intuitive structure, and defining process flows such that they facilitate business and process transactions.

SUMMARY

In this chapter, we have seen the various roles that web team members could play.

Most projects do not have as many individuals as the roles described in this chapter. Typically, an individual may play more than one role in a project.

The success of a project team is defined largely by the leadership style of the managers, the communication between team members and with the client, and the culture of the team.

The roles of the information architect, instructional designer, and systems analyst call for common core skills though each role focuses on differing perspectives—each calling for highly specialized skills.

GUIDING QUESTION

Small web development projects are often executed by teams of one or two persons. On the other hand, large projects may require teams as large as 20 individuals. What are the likely differences in dynamics within these teams? What size team would you like to work in? Why?

EXERCISE

Determine the role you would like to play in a web project. Describe your role and its interactions with others in the team. Go on-line and find at least three position descriptions for this role. A good place to begin is *www.monster.com*.

The Project Development Process

Carrying out effective web site design requires understanding the stages in the life cycle of a project, their interrelationships, and their dependencies. The efficacy of the development process determines the eventual effectiveness of the web site, the profitability for the web developer, and the long-term sustenance of the industry as a whole.

In this chapter, we discuss one of the many possible project process models that could be used for web site development. We briefly examine the process model and then discuss each stage.

The chapter ends with a discussion of idea generation methods, which are important in generating creative, usable, and practical design concepts.

As we will see in this chapter, every stage in the project calls for creative and collaborative problem-solving and ideation strategies. Some of the best designs have emerged out of a discussion of diverse viewpoints through a constructive idea generation process.

THE MODEL OF A PROJECT LIFE CYCLE

Each web organization uses its own model of the project life cycle. The infancy of the field has resulted in erratic standardization in nomenclature and project processes. Though in content and concept most of these processes are similar, they may appear very diverse in format, terminology, and representation. Figures 4–1 and 4–2 show examples of the project model from two web development organizations.

In the "real world," the project process tends to vary according to the size of the project. Smaller, low-cost projects are often carried out through informal stages, whereas larger, high-cost projects are based on formal and structured project development methodologies.

Ideally, all projects, whatever their size, should follow the basic stages of project development. Doing this could help reduce wastage of time and effort and increase

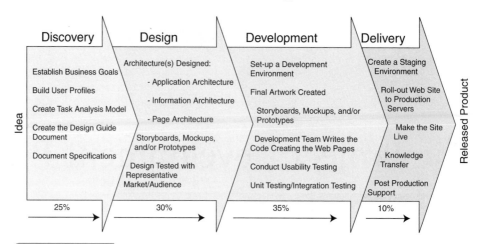

FIGURE 4–1 Project methodology used by Girlzilla, Inc. (*www.girlzilla.com*)

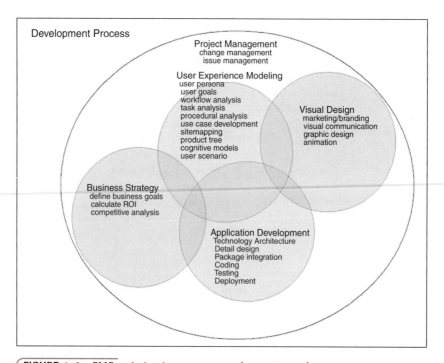

FIGURE 4–2 PMG.net's development process (*www.pmg.net*)

the return on investment. Well-informed clients often look for a formalized project process before they sign the contract with a development company.

Returning to our analogy of the construction industry, a systematic and structured process for constructing a building is very critical. The individual stages in construction are highly dependent and interwoven. Failure or imperfection at any one stage can result in escalation in cost and time and the eventual dissatisfaction of the client. For example, the interior design work cannot begin until construction is complete, yet inputs from the interior designer are important when enacting the plans for construction. Timely inputs, appropriate planning, logical sequencing of tasks, and quality checks at each stage are essential for constructing a building within the stipulated budget, in the available time, and with the required quality.

Even though a model for the project life cycle makes the process appear very formal, structured, and systematic, in reality creative problem solving is required at almost every step of the way. The efficacy of a web development process depends largely on the project team's ability to creatively and cooperatively meet the challenges of the project.

The project model presented in this chapter has evolved through my experience of the industry and an academic examination of the various project processes being used in the industry. As mentioned earlier, most project models are based on similar stages as listed below:

- Requirements analysis and research
- Conceptualization, design, and prototype production
- Media asset production, programming, and integration
- Testing and evaluation
- Hosting
- Maintenance

The project model presented in this book follows the same basic stages. This model differs from some other models in that it includes a navigation prototype at the end of the information architecture phase. This recommendation is based on the conviction that an experience of navigation and process flow (e.g., what will happen when the visitor inputs certain information) will give the client an opportunity to validate the information structuring and process flow without getting caught up in the visual presentation of the site. This in turn could save rework after the expensive visual and media design stages have been completed.

The model assumes strategic involvement from the client at all stages of development. In fact, a formal client orientation meeting at the beginning of the project is crucial. At this meeting, the client is apprised of the stages in the project life cycle, the activities that will take place at each stage, the essential inputs from the client at each stage, and the communication and approval protocols. A signed formal approval from the client at various stages is critical in the development process. The approvals provide an opportunity for review and validation of the activities of each stage.

The main stages of the project are classified as proposal, planning, design, production, evaluation, and maintenance (see Figure 4–3).

The progress from one stage to another can be linear, but only if the client and developers implement the review and approval process. At the same time, the processes within each stage could be iterative. Expert developers have learned the trick of retaining the iteration to improve quality and at the same time completing the activity within the time set aside for the stage.

Any experienced developer will respond to the previous paragraph with an emphatic "impossible." No changes after an approval and completion of work within deadline are often pipe dreams. However, as the industry matures, professionals will find ways of achieving high quality as well as timely completion. These factors may determine the eventual survival and profitability of the industry. In the meantime, it is best to approach web development as a systematic process and to define the project activities and milestones on the basis of its specific requirements.

FIGURE 4–3

Overview of a project
life cycle

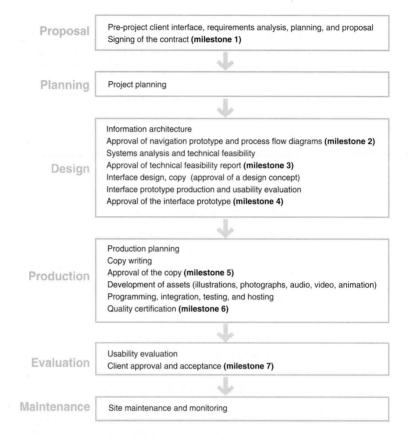

FIGURE 4–3

Overview of a project
life cycle

One of the success factors of a project is the effectiveness of communication among members of the team and also between the team and the client. The project manager also needs to continuously monitor the progress and climate of the team. The success of the project often depends on the project manager's ability to communicate effectively, creatively manage conflicts, predict disasters, do contingency planning, and take tough, proactive decisions in the face of uncertainties.

The project stages we have seen here can be represented in a process-chart as shown in Figure 4–4. Let us examine the specific activities that take place at each stage.

PROPOSAL

Significant involvement: **marketing and sales executives,** *project manager, information architect, systems analyst, creative director*

In a typical situation, the marketing and sales team makes the first contact with the client. The sales team establishes the credibility of the organization and gains confidence in the organization's ability to meet the client's needs in terms of value for money, quality, production time, postproduction support, technical sophistication, and creative communication design. Different clients may have different critical considerations. For example, some may prefer to look at cost, some may focus on support for maintenance of the site, and others may be interested in the use of

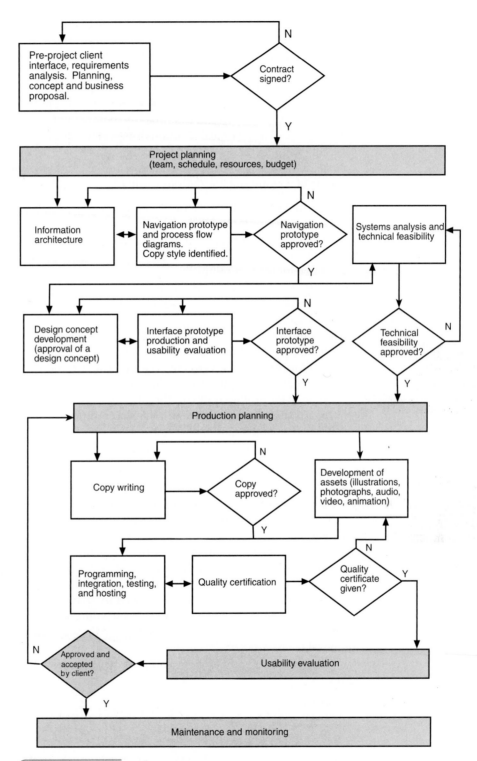

FIGURE 4–4 Project process chart

cutting-edge technologies. It is the responsibility of the sales team to understand the client's requirements, evaluate their own organization's readiness to meet the client's requirements, and carry out a productive dialogue that eventually converts into a business contract.

In order to understand the client's requirements, the sales team may call on the information architect, project manager, and systems analyst to conduct a preliminary study. This study would examine the requirements, consider possible communication as well as technical solutions, and carry out preliminary project planning. Although the specific questions and issues addressed through this study may vary, here is a list of some of the issues that could be examined (see Appendix A for an example of a requirements analysis outline):

- Information about the client organization
- Goals of the proposed web site
- Business and communication objectives of the site
- Competition analysis
- Target audience profiling
- Objectives to be achieved for each group of target audience
- Desired design treatment (visual interface, copy, use of media, site personality)
- Benchmark sites to be emulated and not emulated
- Updation requirements, resources, and available infrastructure
- Plan for providing advertising space on the site and the revenue to be generated through the sale of this space
- Strategy for driving traffic to the site
- Desired technical infrastructure for development and deployment of the site
- Available content and media sources
- Detailed content inventory and process documentation

The proposal is developed on the basis of the data gathered through this exercise. The proposal consists of three main components: the requirements analysis, the concept proposal, and the business proposal.

The requirements analysis documents the needs for the web site. These needs are identified through the information gathering exercise outlined previously.

The concept proposal specifies the problem, the proposed solution, and an analysis of how this solution best meets the needs of the clients.

The concept proposal is used to determine the schedule of deliverables and project costs. In turn, this information is used to arrive at details of pricing, payment schedules, penalty clauses, copyright, arbitration, and other legal issues (see Appendix B for a template for project costing). All these items constitute the business proposal.

The table of contents for a comprehensive proposal submitted to a client is given here:

Introduction
Requirements Analysis
    Site objectives
    Target audience
    Overall communication strategy for the site
    Resources and constraints
    Hosting and delivery specifications

The Solution
  Site personality
  Information architecture
  Interface design
  Advertisement strategy
  Traffic strategy
  Technical solution
  Updation strategy
  Content and media sources
Contractual Terms
  Schedule of deliverables
  Project pricing
  Payment schedule
  Penalty clauses
  Arbitration
  Copyright

The client evaluates the proposal and, more often than not, enters into negotiation of terms with the developers. Once the terms are agreed on, a formal and legal contract is drawn up and signed by all parties.

Contract

The contract is a legal document that specifies responsibilities, schedule of deliverables, payment schedules, penalty for delays, arbitration in case of dispute, and termination of contract. Attorneys are usually involved in drawing up the contract because of its legal nature and implications.

Once the contract is signed, the project is planned in terms of specific activities, roles, responsibilities, budget, resources, and so on.

PLANNING

*Significant involvement: **project manager**, information architect, systems analyst, creative director*

Project planning is the primary responsibility of the project manager. However, the information, technical, and creative leaders usually contribute to the planning process.

This is a critical stage in the project life cycle because a well-conceived project can contribute to efficiencies in project execution and save all parties from escalation of project costs. The project manager usually builds in buffers at each stage to address the possibility of iterations and contingencies. Planning is usually considered a matter of documenting a list of tasks, responsibilities, budget, resource allocation, milestones, and making informed assumptions. As we have seen earlier, it is important to remember that a successful project is as much a function of good planning as it is of synergistic work ethos within the team and between a team and the client.

Once the project manager has identified the skills required for the project and determined who is going to fill those roles, he or she then generates a task list and determines the schedule of deliverables.

Task Scheduling

Task scheduling is probably one of the most frequently visited activities of project management. The task list starts off being broad but gets specific and detailed as the project gets under way.

The project manager generates various versions of the task list. One is the comprehensive list (from the beginning to the end of the project). The second is the list of tasks for specific team members. The third could be the list of critical deliverables (milestones). The task list also includes dependencies. Task dependencies are based on assumptions that certain activities cannot be started unless other activities are completed. Figure 4–5 is an example of one such task list. It identifies the activities, their "owners," the duration for the task, the start and end date, and the dependencies.

Once the project is under way, the project manager revisits the task list several times. Tracking the progress of each task allows the project manager to make decisions about cost overruns, corrective actions, reallocation of resources, communication with the client, and so on.

The task list also serves as a valuable resource when conducting performance evaluation for individual team members.

Budgeting

The project planning process includes budgeting. The typical cost heads for a project are given here:

- Salaries of full-time team members
- Salaries of part-time team members
- Fees for consultants
- Fees for external evaluators
- Payments to subcontractors (including media producers)
- Purchase of reference materials (books, videos, CDs)
- Cost of capital equipment (usually amortized over several projects)
- Cost of software tools (usually amortized over several projects)
- Cost of office supplies, digital media, and communication
- Cost of web servers
- Miscellaneous costs

As with the initial task list, the project manager revisits the budget on a regular basis to monitor it and, if the budget is slipping, to realign it. Delay in task completion and the time spent in reworking deliverables are among the chief causes of cost overrun in projects. At the same time, they are the most difficult to control. One of the biggest challenges for the project manager is to ensure optimum quality in the minimum time.

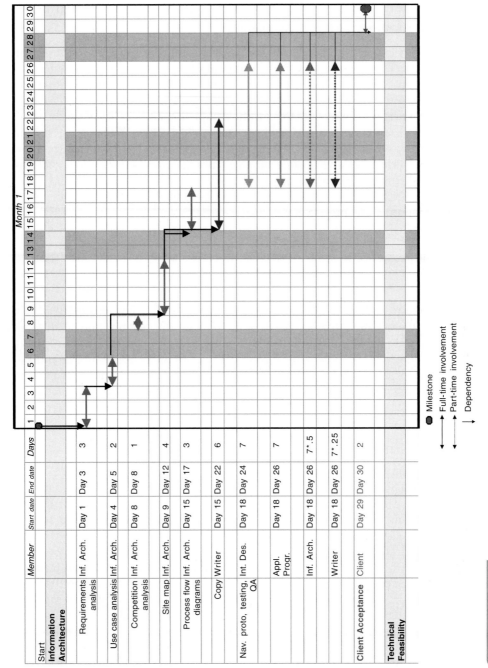

	Member	Start date	End date	Days
Start				
Information Architecture				
Requirements analysis	Inf. Arch.	Day 1	Day 3	3
Use case analysis	Inf. Arch.	Day 4	Day 5	2
Competition analysis	Inf. Arch.	Day 8	Day 8	1
Site map	Inf. Arch.	Day 9	Day 12	4
Process flow diagrams	Inf. Arch.	Day 15	Day 17	3
	Copy Writer	Day 15	Day 22	6
Nav. proto, testing, QA	Int. Des.	Day 18	Day 24	7
	Appl. Progr.	Day 18	Day 26	7
	Inf. Arch.	Day 18	Day 26	7*.5
	Writer	Day 18	Day 26	7*.25
Client Acceptance	Client	Day 29	Day 30	2
Technical Feasibility				

● Milestone
↑ Full-time involvement
↑ Part-time involvement
↓ Dependency

FIGURE 4–5 Example of a project task list

53

Project Processes (Communication, Reference, Tracking, Reporting, Quality Assurance

Every project team is effectively an organization in its own right. Accordingly, it needs to establish methods of communication and reporting, systems of quality assurance, and conventions that the team will follow in storing, backing up, transferring, and archiving documents and files. Each process in the project should have an "owner" who is accountable for the completion and quality of the tasks. As we have seen earlier, the best-planned projects could go awry if the team dynamics are destructive. Thus, one of the biggest challenges for a project manager is establishing and cultivating synergistic team dynamics that are conducive to higher productivity and efficiency of the output of the project.

Once the project planning has been completed and a start date for the project identified, the project moves into the design stage.

DESIGN

We discuss design in much greater detail in the next few chapters. The design stage addresses four distinct facets of a web site: the organization of information and process flows (information architecture); verbal communication (copy); the design of the visitors' experience through visual interface, use of media, and interactions (interface design); and the design of the technical solution (systems analysis). Let us get a quick overview of these activities. Because each of these activities calls for special expertise, we will also examine the roles in the context of each activity.

Information Architecture

Significant involvement: **information architect,** *web writer*

The information architect gains a keen understanding of the business and communication objectives of the web site along with the profile of the target audience. Further, the information architect researches and documents the processes and systems that are to be supported on the web site (e.g., the process of leave application and approval).

Once this understanding has been arrived at, the navigation plan of the basic web site is developed. This process (information architecture) specifies the paths the visitors will take to access the information, the specific content in each section, and the step-by-step documentation of the interactions and processes that will be supported on the web site.

In order to arrive at these specifications, the information architect may conduct use case analysis (how a typical visitor to the web site is likely to behave) and enact use case scenarios (simulation of a visitor's behavior and expectations from the site). The outputs of this stage are the site map, process flowcharts (for specific processes to be incorporated on the site), and the navigation prototype (representing the content, navigation, and process flow on all pages of the site). In some projects, the actual copy that will go on each page is integrated in the navigation prototype. Although this requires a lot of up-front work for the copywriter, it may provide the client a better feel for the navigation and content flow on the site. The navigation prototype is sometimes referred to as a "click-through."

Approval of the Navigation Prototype and Process Flowcharts

When evaluating the navigation prototype and process flowcharts, the client is able to validate the organization of the information and the processes that will be supported by the web site. The navigation prototype simulates the information experience on the final web site. Authentication of this flow by the client allows the systems analyst and the interface designers to further design the web site with the confidence that the basic flow and structure of the site will not change. Inclusion of the copy in the navigation prototype also gives the designers a clear idea of the length of text and the number of subsections on each page.

Systems Analysis and Technical Feasibility

Significant involvement: **systems analyst,** *information architect*

Once the scope of the web site and the processes that it will support have been decided, the systems analyst (also known as software application designer) designs the technical approach and plans the organization and development of the software elements of the site. For example, the systems analyst determines how the database is to be designed and how the software program will retrieve and process the data in this database. The file naming and storage conventions and the software testing methodology are also identified in this process. This work defines the software systems design and establishes the technical feasibility for the project. In this book, we will not go into the details of this process.

Typically, highly qualified computer scientists or information technology experts perform these tasks. The outcome of this exercise is encapsulated in a comprehensive systems design and technical feasibility document. Invariably, the systems design document is technical in nature, and a typical client is not likely to understand or have much use for its contents. On the other hand, the client would normally be interested in the summary of the technical feasibility report.

Approval of the Technical Feasibility Report

It is important for the client to be aware of and approve the technical aspects that are critical to the deployment and maintenance of the web site. The technical feasibility summary could include specifications for the hosting server, server space, special server software (e.g., streaming media server), plug-ins, compatibility with browser versions, directory structure (important for maintenance of the site), and so on. The technical feasibility report is relevant to planning and budgeting for the hosting and maintenance infrastructure for the site. In many instances, the technical requirements will call for addition or modification to the client's existing infrastructure. It is thus critical that the report be approved by the client before proceeding with the project.

If this approval is not given, the earlier assumptions may need to be revisited and the overall solution reconceptualized.

Interface Design and Copy

Significant involvement: **creative director,** **web designer,** **interface designer,** **web writer,** **animation artist,** *media producers, information architect*

In this phase of the project, the site is given a personality. Approaches for interaction, layout, colors, typography, media use, and copy style (if the copy was not integrated in the navigation prototype) are explored and documented in a design concept document.

The design process could include rough layout explorations (on paper or white board), wire frames (identification of the position and size of elements on a page), and design explorations using software application tools such as Adobe Photoshop and Adobe Illustrator. The web and interface designers work on developing the visual storyboards (comps) and obtaining feedback on their effectiveness. The feedback could be obtained through brainstorming sessions, discussions, and heuristic evaluation.

The designers determine how audio, video, and animation will be integrated as a part of the overall communication on the web site. While the interface design is being explored, the web writer determines the copy style and develops the copy that will be integrated in the prototype. The objective of this phase is to explore interface design alternatives. Most often, the client is presented with alternate designs through storyboards (comps). Depending on the clauses in the agreement, the client may select one of the comps or could request redesign and submission of more comps. Approval of one design comp is the outcome of this stage. This design forms the basis for all further development of the site.

The specifications of the design for the approved comps are documented in a production document that specifies the attributes of the different elements on the page, for example, color values for the background, width of HTML tables, font size and color, size of images, alignment of objects, and so on. An interface prototype is developed using the production storyboard as the guiding document.

Interface Prototype Production and Usability Evaluation

Significant involvement: **creative director, web designer, interface designer, web writer, graphic artist, animation artist, application programmer, usability expert, media producers,** *systems analyst, information architect*

The culmination of the design stage is the interface prototype. The interface prototype (also called a mock-up) is a representation of the personality and experience of the site. The interface prototype also affords validation of technical feasibility. A prototype is a miniaturized version of the final web site. In developing the prototype, the designers select the most representative and typical sections of the site and create a fully functional interface for these sections.

At this stage, it is important to establish a "proof of concept test." Usability evaluation of the interface prototype is one way of determining the potential success of the fully developed web site. The usability evaluation provides an indication of how easy and intuitive the site is to use. The evaluation indicates the effectiveness in terms of achieving the site's and the visitor's objectives. It also helps identify specific trouble areas with the interface. Depending on the findings of the evaluation, the interface design may be reworked or tweaked. See Appendix K for an example of the usability evaluation.

Approval of the Interface Prototype

It is wise to pause at this point and make a comprehensive presentation to the client on the design approach, interface prototype, and results of the usability test. Depending on how the contract is drawn up, if the client disapproves of the prototype, they could ask for redesign or modifications. Of course, if the client has been kept informed through the design process and has approved the design comps, it is likely that the changes requested by them will not be significant. It is important that the client and the designers understand that changes to design after approval of the interface prototype could prove to be expensive in terms of time, effort, and budget. It is thus important that designers present a well-thought-out prototype and that clients spend adequate time evaluating the prototype before signing the approval document.

PRODUCTION

Once the interface prototype has been approved, the team is given the go-ahead to produce the assets (audio, video, graphics, animation, copy), code the web pages, develop the back-end applications, and integrate these elements into the final web site. As the assets get integrated into the site, the site is tested to ensure that there are no bugs, broken links, broken images, or invalid system responses to user inputs and that the performance of the site is optimum when it is hosted on the server. In order to achieve this, the project manager carries out detailed production planning with the help of the creative director, media producers, lead copywriter, systems analyst, and lead programmers.

Production Planning

*Significant involvement: **project manager**, creative director, web writer, media producers, systems analyst, usability expert*

Production planning involves a systematic approach to carrying out the production of individual media assets, finalization of the copy, integration of media assets on web pages, and development of the application program that will drive the back end (database, interaction processing, report generation). Further, it calls for a plan for testing and quality certification before the final release of the site.

The production plan for a web site is more than just the schedule for completion. It further establishes the specifications of the elements that will constitute the site and also the method for ensuring the required production values (quality) for these elements. For example, the production document for a web site contains specifications for the size and position of images, such as the logo, the color value for backgrounds, the width of columns in tables, the size of banners, the directory structure for storing the files, the process of taking backups, and so on.

Once the production planning activity is over, the team carries out concurrent activities of copy writing, development, and integration of assets (graphics, photographs, audio, video, animation); programming, integration, testing and hosting; and quality certification.

Copy Writing

*Significant involvement: **web writer**, information architect*

The copy (text) that will appear on every page of the site is specified. The copy also identifies the titles for each section and subsection and the media elements (graphics, photographs, audio, video, animation) that will be integrated on each page. The web writer works on the pull quotes that will appear along with specific sections of the copy. A thorough quality assurance of the copy is essential. Failure to do this can result in spelling and grammatical errors on the site. As we saw earlier, the copy can be presented to the client by integrating it in the navigation prototype. If that is done, the task at this stage is limited to finalization and evaluation of the copy.

Approval of the Copy

The copy constitutes a blueprint for a significant component of communication that will take place through the web site. It is thus important to get an approval for the copy from the client. This approval provides a page-by-page validation of the content and media elements.

Development and Integration of Assets

Significant involvement: **creative director, web designer, interface designer, graphic artists, media producers, animation artist**

In this book, we will not go into the details of production planning for individual media assets such as photographs, 3D animation, audio, and video. These industries are relatively mature and have well-established production processes of their own.

The animation artist, the graphic artist, the web designer, and the interface designer work with the creative director in developing the individual 2D animation and graphic assets for the web pages. The creative director typically provides guidance and carries out quality assurance for the output of this group. Depending on how the web site is to be deployed and the way the roles for team members are defined, the animation artist and the web designer may also integrate the media assets on a web page using technologies such as HTML, JavaScript, Macromedia Flash, Macromedia Dreamweaver, Adobe LiveMotion and Adobe GoLive.

Programming, Integration, Testing, and Hosting

Significant involvement: **systems analyst, application programmers**

The application program is usually developed using established systems design methods. As we saw earlier, software application development is a rather complex and skilled field. The professionals who develop the technical aspects are well versed not only in programming environments such as Java, Active Server Pages (ASP), Perl, PHP, XML, WML and SGML but also in database technologies and Internet security. These professionals use sophisticated application design approaches and development environments.

The application programmers integrate the programs they write with the front-end web pages developed by web designers and animation artists. As the web site is integrated, it is tested not only on the local servers but also on the servers that will host the site (staging servers).

Testing for quality assurance of each component of the web page is carried out as it is developed and integrated. For maximum efficiency, it is best to trap an error as close to its origin as possible. Thus, spelling errors are best corrected before the copy is integrated on a web page, and it is best to validate the size of icons as they are developed by the graphic artist. The quality assurance process requires that errors be detected, documented, and corrected. It is an ongoing process and usually carried out by all the project team members.

On the other hand, an external evaluator conducts quality certification. A web site needs to receive the quality certificate before it goes "live."

Quality Certification

Significant involvement: **quality control expert**

There are many sites on the web with the most blatant errors. Some of these are errors of spelling and grammar. Other errors are caused by broken links (clicking on a link results in an error message), broken images (images do not load), inconsistent display of elements (elements displayed in different sequences), dead links (nowhere to go from the page), and program errors or bugs (JavaScript error). More often than not, these errors go undetected because the publishers have not put the site through a quality certification process before publishing the site.

Quality certification is carried out after the site has been hosted on the target server. If the site meets the quality requirements, it is given the quality certificate and "released." Several quality experts may be involved in the process. Each may test a specific aspect of quality, such as program bugs, download times, process validation, spelling and grammar, layout, and so on. The testing is also done for compatibility with different browser versions, plug-ins, and computing platforms.

USABILITY EVALUATION

Significant involvement: **usability expert**

We saw that the interface prototype is taken through usability evaluation. Once the site is completed and hosted, it is taken through another comprehensive usability evaluation. This evaluation gives the client and developers confidence in the effectiveness of their site. Naturally, if problems are identified at this stage, they could still be fixed. The usability evaluation examines the totality of the user experience in terms of how easy it was to learn to navigate the site (learnability), how easy it was to find information on the site (ease of use), and how well the users liked the site.

Both the clients and the developers usually acknowledge the value of usability evaluation. Unfortunately, when budgets are running short, the first thing to go from a project is the usability evaluation. This can result in the clients accepting a site that appears effective from their own perspective even though it may not be the most effective site from the target visitor's perspective. Failure to carry out even an informal usability test can leave such problems undetected and result in a substantial long-term wastage of resources.

So, at best, a web development project will end with a usability evaluation; if not, it will end with a quality certification process.

CLIENT APPROVAL AND ACCEPTANCE OF THE SITE

After either or both the quality certification and usability evaluation have been completed, the client may carry out an acceptance test, and the project gets wrapped up.

If the client has been involved in the project process throughout the life cycle, it is very likely that the acceptance at this point will be a matter of formality. However, projects that do not involve the client at regular and frequent intervals can give the client a rude surprise if the site is not up to their expectations. In such cases, the site may need to go through substantial redesign and reprogramming at a rather late stage. As we have seen earlier, this could in turn result in substantial escalation in project costs and time.

Once the acceptance process is over, the final payments are made, and the project can be deemed complete.

Although many developer organizations offer maintenance and monitoring as a service, the next stage is an entirely separate process that could very well be carried out by a different organization.

SITE MAINTENANCE AND MONITORING

*Significant involvement: **web master, site administrator***

Once the site has been accepted by the client and published, it invariably requires maintenance and monitoring. Maintenance refers to the process of updating the content and fixing bugs. Monitoring, on the other hand, refers to examination and analysis of the traffic to the various sections of the site and also ensuring that the server is not accessed by unauthorized individuals.

EVALUATION AND IDEA GENERATION METHODS

As we saw earlier, just about every stage in the project requires a creative and collaborative approach to idea generation. We now examine some methods that could help project teams not only to generate ideas but also to develop, enhance, and support innovative yet feasible solutions.

The methods described in this section encourage sharing and building of ideas for the purpose of generating a solution or arriving at a clearer understanding of a situation. Effective project execution calls for such sharing on a regular basis. Although the value of such an exercise cannot be questioned, the invitation to express opinions does need to be managed constructively.

Brainstorming

Brainstorming is a process by which a group of individuals generates ideas about a specific topic. The size of the group may vary, but a typical group would be composed of five to seven individuals. A leader is identified to steer the group and ensure that anarchy does not occur.

The objective is to obtain a large number of perspectives and suspend the judgment on the details, coherence, or worth of the ideas. The individuals are not under the gun to produce the "right" solution or the most practical suggestions. They are encouraged to go "wild" and come up with uninhibited thoughts. Here is what the Imagineering team at Walt Disney says about brainstorming: "While conceptualizing, our thoughts are unrestrained. Limitations only weigh on the wings of an idea

FIGURE 4–6

Brainstorming

as it soars wild and free on the updrafts of possibility. Creative freedom allows us to do anything imaginable, anything at all."

A brainstorming session is usually conducted in a relaxed atmosphere. The group is presented with the "problem" and asked to generate ideas. These ideas may be written down on paper or on a board by one individual as others call out the idea. The group may also decide to have all individuals claim a part of the board and jot down the idea on the board.

During the process of brainstorming (see Figure 4–6), the group follows these basic guidelines:

▶ Spellings are not critical.
▶ No idea is to be criticized as it is written.
▶ At the same time, no idea is to be defended.
▶ It is not important to use the most appropriate words.
▶ The ideas do not need to follow a particular organization, system, or hierarchy.
▶ It is okay to build on someone else's ideas.

As the group generates ideas and documents them, the leader may initiate a discussion to clarify and reflect on a particular idea. The group may also attempt to classify ideas into groups to further analyze them.

A web design team may explore some of the following using brainstorming: content scope, information structuring, layout, illustration style, visual metaphors, and navigation.

Focus Groups

A relatively close-knit group such as a production team generates ideas using brainstorming. On the other hand, focus groups are typically comprised of a representative group of individuals brought together to reflect on and share their opinion about a particular issue. The objective of a focus group is not to generate a solution but rather to gather views and insights.

Focus groups are often used to generate ideas for product specifications and/or obtain opinions about effectiveness of a product concept. The members of focus groups are members of a typical target audience or experts who are in a position to reliably predict the behavior of the target audience.

A focus group consists of 5 to 10 individuals who are presented with a specific concept or problem and asked to express their opinions about its viability and impact. The group responds to specific predetermined questions. At the same time, the group leader often encourages the free and open exchange of ideas that help clarify responses.

Web development can benefit from focus groups at various points. First, during the requirements analysis stage, the target audience could be invited to reflect on what they would expect from the site. The focus group may also be called on to reflect on a specific marketing strategy and how the web site fits within that strategy.

The interface prototype for the web site could be presented to a focus group to determine whether it is likely to meet its communication and business objectives. It is important to validate the findings of a focus group by conducting a formal usability test of the prototype. Opinions may turn out to be inaccurate when compared to actual experiences of using a web site.

One-on-One Discussion/Feedback

Focus groups are relatively formal events that require special planning and organizing. However, web designers often use a less formal and less expensive method of gathering ideas and validating decisions: one-on-one discussion or feedback. Designers often seek opinions about specific designs from members of the target audience. This may mean obtaining verbal opinion or an observation about a specific feature. The designer may also call on an expert designer, content expert, or application developer to validate a concept. Although this method is not scientific, if the representatives are selected carefully, valuable design inputs could be obtained.

Heuristic Evaluation

Heuristic evaluation calls for establishment of a set of heuristics (or guidelines) by an expert. The expert then evaluates the web site with the heuristics in mind. The outcome is a set of informed opinions arrived at by the expert. This type of evaluation is ideal for evaluating web sites at the stage of prototyping or a web site that has already been deployed. The evaluation may provide valuable insights in a relatively short period.

SUMMARY

In this chapter, we have examined the systematic process for developing a web site. The main stages in development are the following:

- Pre-project client interface, requirements analysis, planning, and proposal
- *Signing of the contract (milestone 1)*
- Project planning

- Information architecture (and copy)
- *Approval of navigation prototype and process flow diagrams (milestone 2)*
- Systems analysis and technical feasibility
- *Approval of the technical feasibility report (milestone 3)*
- Interface design and copy *(approval of storyboard)*
- Interface prototype production and usability evaluation
- *Approval of the interface prototype (milestone 4)*
- Production planning
- Copy writing
- *Approval of the copy (milestone 5)*
- Development of assets (illustrations, photographs, audio, video, animation)
- Programming, integration, testing, and hosting
- *Quality certification (milestone 6)*
- Usability evaluation
- *Client approval and acceptance (milestone 7)*
- Site maintenance and monitoring

A systematic development process results not only in an effective web site but also in efficiency of effort and resource utilization. However, it is important to remember that synergy and cooperation within the team can help not only in creating an effective web site but also in making the process of development stress free and enjoyable.

Besides project processes, we have also examined methods of generating and building on creative concepts: brainstorming, focus groups, one-on-one feedback, and heuristic evaluation.

REFERENCES

The Imagineers (Rafferty, Kevin, & Gordon, Bruce). (1996). *Walt Disney Imagineering: A behind the dreams look at making the magic real.* New York: Hyperion.

England, Elaine, & Finney, Andy. (1999). *Managing multimedia: Project management for interactive media.* Reading, MA: Addison-Wesley.

Strauss, Roy, & Hogan, Patrick. (2001). *Developing effective websites: A project manager's guide.* Stoneham, MA: Focal Press.

GUIDING QUESTIONS

- What is the value of a model for a project life cycle?
- Besides a systematic approach to developing a web site, what factors are important in the success of a project?
- List the main stages of a web project life cycle.
- Typically, who interacts with the client before a project team is identified? What activities take place at this stage?
- What is the output of information architecture?
- At what stage would storyboards (comps) be presented to the client?
- What is the importance of an interface prototype?

- How does the interface prototype differ from the navigation prototype?
- Between completing the interface prototype and presenting it to the client, what activities could you undertake to enhance your confidence in your design decisions?
- Assuming that the client has approved the interface prototype, what other output should they approve before it is integrated on the web site?
- What is the difference between quality assurance and quality certification?
- What are some approaches for generating creative concepts and solutions?

EXERCISE

Assume that you are a part of a team that has been asked to develop a web site for a popular magazine. If you were appointed the project manager for this project, what stages would the project go through? What will be the milestones for the project. In your opinion, what are some possible hindrances to a successful completion of the project?

5

Information Architecture

I n Chapter 4, we discussed the stages in the development of a web site. We now come to the process of making decisions about specific design aspects of a web site. In this chapter, we focus on designing the architecture of the site. It is fortuitous that this process is called information "architecture." Earlier in this book, we compared web development with designing and constructing a building. The information architect's role is similar to the role of a building architect. Both work with the specified requirements and determine the layout, organization, activities, movement, dimensions, and so on in relation to the building/web site.

Both the building and web architects combine scientific principles and design guidelines with creativity and aesthetics. They are considered to be successful when their design meets the requirements for which the building/web site was developed.

While working in the field of web development, we often come across arguments such as "If only we had more time and more money and more people and more resources. . . we could come up with the most impressive design." Unfortunately, the real world rarely provides such "ideal" work circumstances. The challenge to designers is to make the most of the available resources and work within the existing constraints to develop the most optimum solution. Thus, among the first things information architects do is understand the objectives, target audience, resources, and constraints of the project (see Figure 5–1).

INFORMATION ARCHITECTURE ACTIVITIES

The information architect's initial task is to thoroughly understand the requirements for the web site. The process of documenting and specifying the requirements starts even before the contract is signed with the client. The information architect analyzes and elaborates the specific content and processes that the web site is expected to address. This requires an in-depth study of the hierarchy and grouping of the information to be presented on the site. Furthermore, this relationship needs to be examined from the perspective of the visitors to the site.

FIGURE 5–1

Considerations in
information
architecture

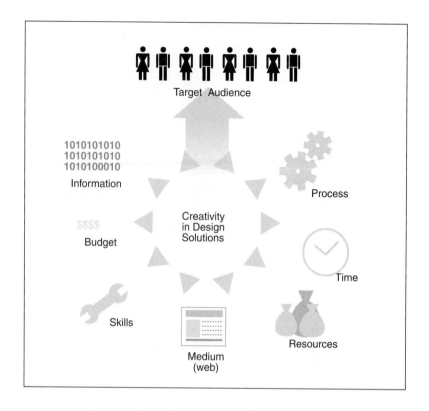

FIGURE 5–1

Considerations in
information
architecture

As more and more web sites incorporate business, employee, and customer processes, the information architect also studies the existing processes that the web site will emulate. Some examples of this are the process of selecting and ordering an item in a store, the process of registering a learner at a web-based learning site, and the application and approval for leave within an organization. Very often, this involves visualizing specific instances of use (user scenarios) and documentation of business processes and rules that would guide these interactions.

Once the information architect has a good understanding of the requirements of the site, he or she lists the content and processes that are to be incorporated on the web site. This information is then organized into a hierarchy of sections and subsections. A navigation structure is then designed to allow visitors to move between these sections. The navigation structure is based on the understanding of the content hierarchy, the assumptions of the visitor's navigation requirements, and the business rules that drive the processes on the site. After the navigation structure is designed, the processes and interactions that take place at specific points are documented. Further, the information architect does the information design (presentation approach for the information) for each section of the site. The creative director and interface designer usually work with the information architect on this activity (information design) (see Figure 5–2).

INFORMATION LISTING

The information listing activity starts with making an exhaustive list of all the content that need to be represented on the web site. These are not broad classification of in-

FIGURE 5–2

Information architecture activities

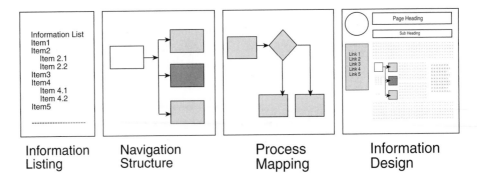

Information Listing

Navigation Structure

Process Mapping

Information Design

FIGURE 5–3

Card sorting

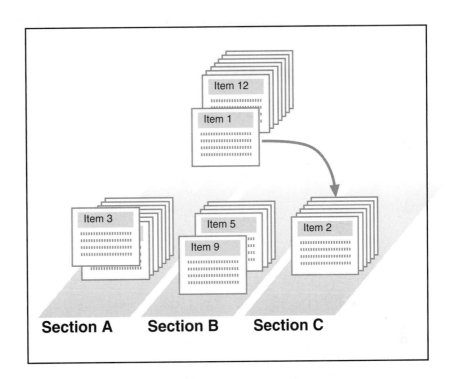

formation items (such as company) but specific items (such as the firm, the team, awards, and publications). Once the content list is created, many information architects list each content item on an index card and carry out a card-sorting exercise with a few members of the target audience. The card-sorting exercise invites the individuals to organize the cards into piles that seem to belong together and then determine a label that best describes the contents of each pile. The card-sorting exercise serves as an indication of how the target audience perceives the content and helps determine the content organization on the web site (see Figure 5–3).

As information architects carry out this exercise, they attempt to provide meaning to raw data. This is achieved by providing labels that identify clusters of data. Although this may appear to be a simple exercise, finding labels that appropriately describe the contents of a section is one of the toughest challenges to an information architect. As you may have imagined, the writer can play an important role in identifying these labels.

Once the labels for the information have been determined, the information architect organizes the information in a hierarchy of sections and pages on the site. The navigation structure is designed such that the visitor is able to intuitively find information and move through the site.

NAVIGATION STRUCTURE

The navigation structure identifies the paths available to a visitor to the web site. In the next few paragraphs, we examine different types of navigation structures. Keep in mind that a web site will rarely be based entirely on one type of structure. It is, however, easier to understand the basic classification of the structure and then select the most relevant structure for specific sections of a web site.

Linear Navigation Structure

The simplest navigation structure is linear. However, a linear structure does not offer real navigation options to the site visitor. The most common use of this type of navigation structure is for slide shows where the visitor is required to move through information in a predetermined sequence (see Figure 5–4).

In Pilar Plata's web site, the slide show allows a visitor to sequentially view a list of projects by clicking on the forward and back arrows (see Figure 5–5).

FIGURE 5–4

Linear navigation structure

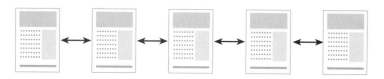

FIGURE 5–5

Example of linear navigation: slide show (www.pilarplata.com)

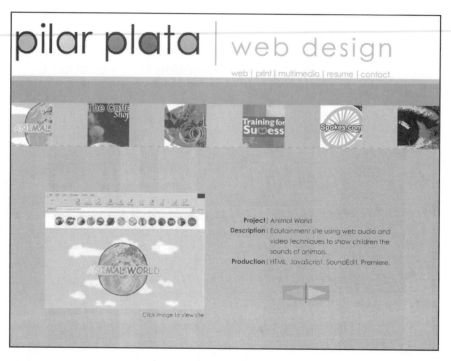

Hierarchical Navigation Structure

The hierarchical navigation structure provides access to information modules via specific entry points. Many corporate sites provide this type of navigation (see Figure 5–6).

In Andy Lim's web site, the content is organized in a hierarchy (see Figure 5–7). The home page allows access to the sections on Andy, Work, and Play. Each of these sections in turn allows access to subsections (e.g., in the section on Play—Millennium Greetings, Intro + Navigation, Particles, Dreamscape, 1999 Screensaver, Motion Study, Splash Study, Sanctuary Under the Sea, and Aikido Virtual Dojo).

The Grid Structure for Navigation

When information can be classified in more than one way and when we can assume that the visitors may want to access the information via multiple access points, the navigation is organized in a grid structure (see Figure 5–8). For example, a web page about an individual in an organization can be accessed through either the department or the designation within the organization.

In the Shoebuy site, it is possible to navigate to a specific item through the type of user (Men, Women, Teens, or Children), brand (Bass, Birkenstock, or Caparros), or type (All, Comfort, Heels, or Mules) (see Figure 5–9).

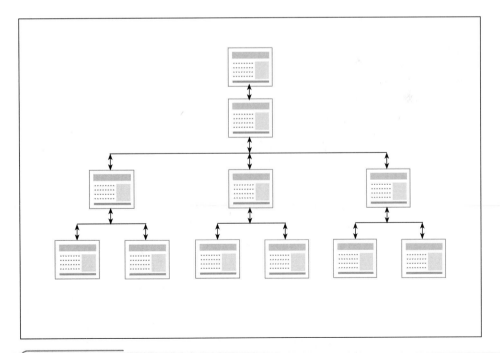

FIGURE 5–6   Hierarchical navigation structure

FIGURE 5–7

Example of hierarchical
navigation: Andy Lim
(*www.andylim.com*)

FIGURE 5–8

Grid navigation
structure

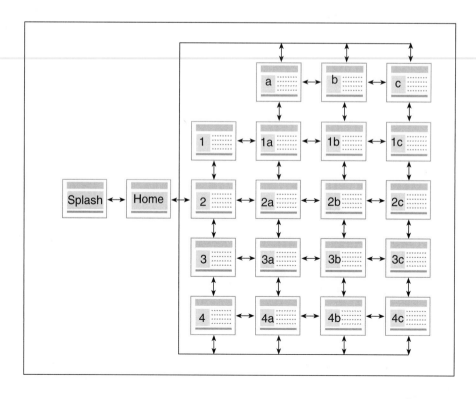

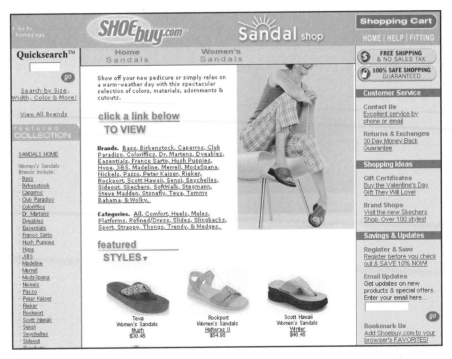

FIGURE 5–9   Example of grid-based navigation: Shoebuy.com (*www.shoebuy.com*)

Hypertext/Media

Hypertext/media refers to text or image links embedded within a web page (see Figure 5–10). This type of navigation can be "unstructured" in that the links are provided as per the requirement on each page. Typically, these links provide additional information about a specific word or an image.

The web page for the Jane Goodall Institute illustrates the use of hypertext links embedded within the text on the page (villagers are planting trees. . .) (see Figure 5–11).

Hybrid Navigation Structure

A typical web site is most likely to adopt a combination of navigation structures. For example, an e-commerce site is likely to have a linear slide show of products a hierarchical navigation for specific categories of products, a grid-based navigation for locating products by price and features, and hyperlinks for details of product features.

Global and Local Navigation

The navigation structure of a web site is based on the path that visitors are likely to take. However, it is nearly impossible to anticipate all the possible paths that visitors to a site will want to take. The information architect attempts to create a navigation structure that will allow maximum flexibility in navigation and at the same time not confuse the visitor. This is typically achieved through global links (links that are available on all pages of a web site) and local links (links that are specific to a particular page of a web site).

FIGURE 5–10

Hyperlinked navigation
structure

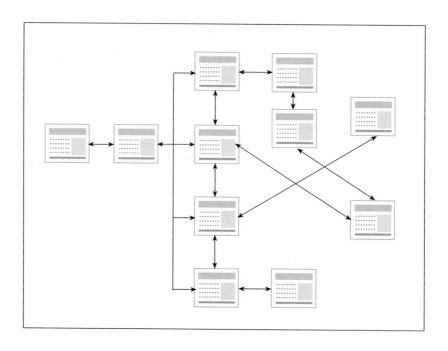

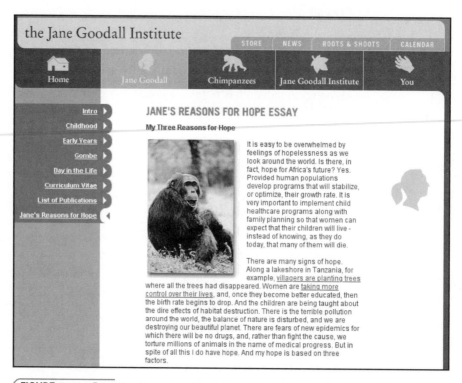

FIGURE 5–11   Example of hyperlinked navigation: Jane Goodall Institute (*www.janegoodall.org*)

Information architects grapple with the issue of which links should be made global. They do not want to overwhelm the visitor with too many navigation options, yet they need to anticipate and provide the links that visitors would expect at various points in the site. Typically, links to the home page, the main sections, the contact page, the site map, and the search function are available as global links.

Another consideration in this decision is that of links, which are critical to achieving the business and communication objectives of the site. For example, though one can assume that the Contact link may not be absolutely essential from the visitor's perspective, it may be important to keep the Contact option in front of them, just in case they may need to use it.

Local links can be made available through clearly defined links on a web page and also through embedded text and image links.

Local links can be categorized into two types: those that take a visitor to another page and those that take the visitor to another location within the same page. Page-to-page links are relevant when related topics need to be accessed from a page. For example, the biography of an artist whose work is featured on a web page could be accessed from the Artwork page.

On the other hand, within-page links are useful when a single page contains a number of subtopics and it is important to provide direct access to these subtopics. An example of this type of link can be found frequently on news sites where the headlines are listed at the top of the page and clicking on them takes you to the full story in the lower part of the page.

Navigation structure defines the options available to a visitor for moving around the web site. The information architect also needs to determine the structure of interactions that will take place on the site. This is achieved through process mapping.

PROCESS MAPPING

Process mapping is different from the navigation structures we have seen previously. In the structures we examined earlier, the visitor navigates to a different section of the site through links. On the other hand, the process structure is driven by business rules. This structure incorporates conditional navigation. For example, unless the visitor has items in the shopping cart, the option for "check out" is not presented to him or her. As another example, if the employee is entitled to 3 days of leave, he or she is not offered the option for selecting more than 3 days of leave. Each of these interactions is determined by a set of rules that drive the process.

One of the challenges to an information architect is to understand existing rules and determine how these rules will be implemented on a web site. In doing so, it is important to take into consideration the varied situations that will arise for different visitors. One way of ensuring that the site caters to these variations is to construct "user scenarios."

User scenarios describe the series of events and actions that "users" will engage in to achieve a desired outcome. A typical user scenario is a narrative (story) of a

TABLE 5–1   User Scenario

User: Jacqueline Shroff. Female. 21 years of age. Well versed with using computers and web site. Does not want to stand in a line for registration. So decides to go to the school web site to register for the summer quarter. Jacqueline has been in school for three quarters and is somewhat familiar with the sequence of courses in her program and the fact that some courses have prerequisites. This is the registration week. Jacqueline is in the seventh week of the spring quarter.

Event: Jacqueline logs on to the school web site using her user name and password. On her personal home page, she is offered the option to view grades, transcript, course sequence, schedule, web sites for courses she is currently registered in, register for the quarter, and so on.

Since she wants to make sure she is doing well in her current courses, Jacqueline first goes to the section on grades and checks on her midterm grades. Now, she is curious to see what her overall performance in the program looks like. She next checks the transcript and is happy to see her GPA. She is now ready to register. She clicks on the registration link.

On the registration page, she notices that she can register for up to five courses. She sees an option for help and clicks on it. A pop-up window displays the recommended course sequence, prerequisites, the courses she has successfully completed, the courses she is currently registered in, and the courses she could take in the next quarter. Jacqueline selects the courses for summer by looking at the recommendations on screen and the printed schedule in her hand. She closes the pop-up window and enters the course numbers and section for three courses. She then clicks on the Register button. The system informs her that she has successfully registered for summer and displays her summer schedule. She uses the print option on the screen to print her schedule and logs out.

particular user. The story describes the user and pictures a scenario in which he or she is attempting to achieve a goal on a site. The story narrates the thoughts and actions of the user as he or she attempts to navigate and interact with the site. Since the user scenario is constructed before the web site is developed, it cannot specifically identify the label or the link that a user would click on. Rather, the scenario explores an imaginary process and attempts to capture possible actions and system responses.

Table 5–1 presents a simplified example of a student attempting to use a school web site to determine the courses to take in the next quarter. You may notice that the flow in this story is very simple. When creating user scenarios, we would also want to consider errors and difficulties that a user would face in interacting with a system. As such, we may construct several user scenarios, each dealing with a different experience for the user.

Whereas the user scenario helps us visualize possible situations when users interact with the site, flowcharts allow us to capture the specific rules and processes that will drive the interactions. The flowchart shown in Figure 5–12 represents the partial process for learner interaction with a web-based training system.

INFORMATION DESIGN

The information architect takes decisions about the components that will be displayed on each web page. At the same time, the layout and presentation of these elements (information design) is the joint responsibility of the information architect, the creative director, and the interface designers. It is important to reiterate that though the design process can appear very compartmentalized and regimented, in

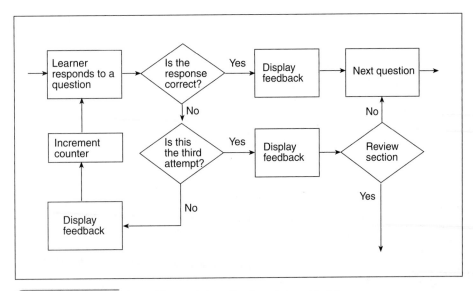

FIGURE 5–12   Flowchart of learner interaction in web-based training

reality there is continuous interaction between all team members. It is the synergy and collaboration between the team members that typically results in an effective web site interface.

Information design refers to the process of determining the presentation of information in the most meaningful and easy to understand format. For example, let us assume that we need to present the grade distribution for a class on a web page. There are many different ways of doing this. We can present a table with the grades and percentage of students, or we can present a pie chart that visually indicates the distribution of grades. The decision about the best way to present this information is an information design decision. At a broader level, the information architect needs to determine the specific components of a web page and then work with the creative director and interface designer in creating the most effective presentation of these components.

Typical web pages may have some, all, or more of the following components (see Figures 5–13 and 5–14):

▶ Banners
▶ Branding and identity
▶ Page title
▶ Page heading
▶ Breadcrumb links
▶ Global links
▶ Local links
▶ Embedded links
▶ Text links
▶ Information presentation
▶ Pull quotes
▶ Images and other media
▶ Search
▶ Footer
▶ Forms

FIGURE 5–13

Components of a web page

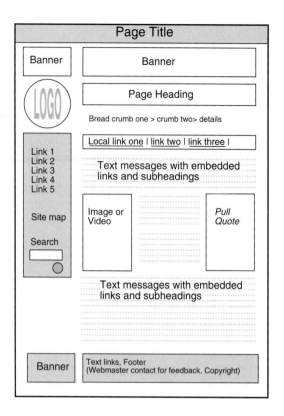

Banners

Banners are typically used for advertising. They could also be used to draw attention to specific items within a web site. Although banners have grown in popularity, their impact and success are still being researched. The Internet Advertising Bureau (IAB) and the Coalition for Advertising Supported Information and Entertainment (CASIE) have published a list of standardized sizes for banners for web pages (see p. 107 in Chapter 6). Banners are the billboards of the web. As such, they are usually animated, display terms that will compel the visitor to click on them and provide just enough information such that the interest of the visitor is piqued. The success of banners is determined by the click-through rate (the number of times it is clicked on) and the impression rate (the number of times it is "seen" by a visitor).

Branding and Identity

We can safely assume that each web site has an "owner." The owner could be a corporation or an individual—the entity who invested in getting the site designed. It would naturally be important to identify the owner of the site on every page of the site (most often through the display of the logo). It is equally important for a web site to communicate its main "offering." The offering could be a product, a service, information, entertainment, and so on. A random survey of web sites will show that many web sites do not tell you who the owner is or what the site is attempting to communicate. Experience with sites like this can cause confusion about the purpose of the site, and the visitor could leave the site with an unpleasant feeling. The experience is somewhat like walking into a store that does not display its name anywhere

FIGURE 5–14

Components of a web
page: Jane Goodall
Institute
(*www.janegoodall.org*)

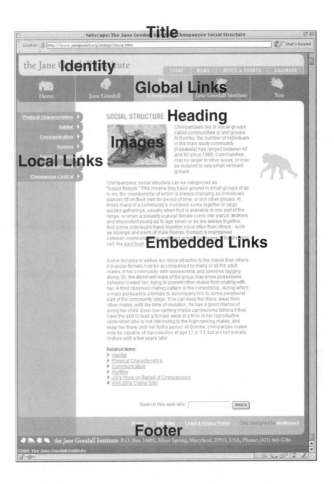

FIGURE 5–14

Components of a web page: Jane Goodall Institute (*www.janegoodall.org*)

and also does not indicate what it sells. It is important that all pages of the site carry an indication of the site's owner and a clear message about what it communicates. The information architect determines how this branding and identity will be achieved. Considering that the solution involves a significant visual element, the decision typically is taken in consultation with the creative director.

Page Title

Every web page can display the title at the top of the browser window (see Figure 5–15). If the title is not specified (in the HTML code), the word "untitled" appears at the top of the window. The title should ideally represent the contents of the page. More often than not, the title is identical to the page heading. Many search engines use the web page title when indexing the page. Thus, the page title is important not only for the visitors but also for ensuring appropriate indexing by search engines. Furthermore, when a web page is bookmarked, the page is identified in the bookmark listing by its title. It is thus important to make sure that every page has a clear and descriptive title.

Page Heading

Obvious as it sounds, each web page needs to have a heading. The heading should reflect the contents of the page. In order to aid navigation and cognitive mapping of

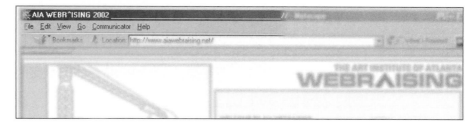

FIGURE 5–15   Title of a web page: The Art Institute of Atlanta (*www.aiawebraising.net*)

<u>HOME</u> : <u>Section one</u> : <u>Sub section</u>: **Example one**

FIGURE 5–16   Example of breadcrumb links

the site, the page heading should closely match the name of the link that the visitor clicked on. The information architect specifies the label that will be displayed as the heading for each page (often in consultation with the web writer). The most effective page headings identify the site, the section, and the subsection of the site. As we will discuss in the next chapter, consistency in the position and visual design of the heading is important for creating an effective and easy-to-use interface.

Breadcrumb Links

Breadcrumb links, as the name suggests, is a trail of links that allow the visitor to trace the path and access any node along that path. "Breadcrumbing" is especially helpful when the site is complex and easy to get lost in. Invariably, breadcrumb links are text links placed near the top of the page (see Figure 5–16).

Global Links

Global links allow the visitor to "jump" between the main sections of the web site. As we discussed earlier, the information architect identifies the links that will be displayed as global links. The information architect then decides the order in which these links will be displayed. Although many web sites tend to list the links in terms of the perceived importance to the owner organization, it is important to compare this sequence with the intuitive navigation approaches of the visitors to the web site.

Local Links

Local links differ from page to page. The information architect determines the links that will be provided on each page. Once again, the sequence of presentation is important. It is important to visually distinguish between the global and local links. It is equally important to establish the association between the currently selected global link and local links. If this is not done, it is possible that the visitors will get confused about where they are on the site and where they could go from there.

Embedded Links

Embedded links allow visitors to navigate to a different section by clicking on words or images embedded within the page. Sometimes these links provide a redundant navigation option for the local links on a page. When determining the position and label for the embedded links, it is important to ensure that the visitors have an adequate clue about where these links will take them.

Text Links

A web page that uses images or icons as links needs to provide text links for browsers that are incapable of displaying images. Such redundancy is important to make the site accessible by visually impaired individuals. The information architect determines the wording of these links and also the sequence of presentation. Typically, these links are displayed at the top or bottom of the page.

Information Presentation

Effective communication is one of the biggest challenges to the information architect. Once the decision on the information to be presented on each page has been taken, the most intuitive and meaningful organization of this information needs to be worked out. Organizing information involves identification of the label for topics and subtopics and determination of the sequence of presentation. It is also important to determine whether the information is to be presented in the form of a narrative or visually represented in the form of a chart, graph, or metaphorical imagery.

Determining the appropriate labels for the topics is critical because most visitors tend to first scan the contents of the web page. If the label is not accurate and does not appeal to their interests, it is possible that they will completely ignore the critical information that has been so carefully verbalized in the body of the text. For example, if a magazine has a section on expert reviews, the label "Gray Matter" may not be meaningful as a representation of the contents of the section. At the same time, "Gray Matter" could be an effective label if it is accompanied by an elaboration of the section contents either through text or through mouse rollovers. The same argument is relevant for the use of icons. We will examine this in some detail in the next chapter.

Another area where labels are critical is for actions that are to be taken in a form. The labels need to clearly identify the action that will be performed after clicking on a button. For example, "Get" may be a better label than "Go" for requesting stock quotations (see Figure 5–17).

The sequence of presenting the information is also a significant challenge. Information architects could choose to present the information using organizational approaches such as the following:

- Alphabetical order
- The order in which events occur (temporal sequence)
- Order of assumed importance or familiarity
- As per the metaphor that is used to communicate the information

Information architects also need to determine (often with help from the creative director) whether specific information will be better presented via a visual representation. For example, in Figure 5–18, the number is displayed in a relative

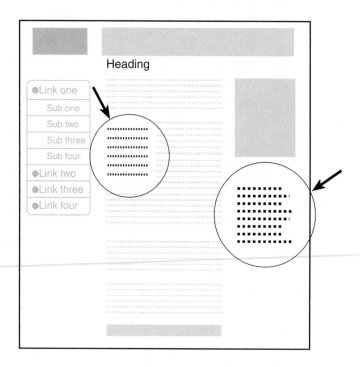

position, providing both the value and the positional context for interpreting the rating information.

Pull Quotes

The pull quotes encapsulate the critical messages of a page (see Figure 5–19). They are extracted from the body of the text. As we saw earlier, most visitors are likely to scan the message on a page. If something does not grab their interest, they are likely to move on out of the page (maybe even the site). Pull quotes help grab and focus attention on the critical message. The information architect works with the web writer to determine what messages should be displayed via pull quotes.

Images and Other Media

The information architect identifies the images and media that will be displayed on each web page. As the Internet moves toward better capabilities for serving multimedia content, web design can be expected to offer better integration of media in the composition of the message. The information architect determines how audio, video, animation, photographs, illustrations, and virtual reality could be used to enhance and support the message. As we have seen with many other decisions, the decisions about media in message design are taken in consultation with other team members, such as creative director, animation artist, media producers, web writer, application programmers, and so on.

Search

Considering the increasing complexity of web sites, it is common to find the search feature on most sites. The information architect decides on the way in which search will be conducted. Text search is the most common search method. In this type of search, the user types in a word or a phrase, and the search results return web pages or items that match the search "string."

Some sites implement powerful search engines and incorporate complex search involving boolean (either/or, and) and conditional operators (if. . .then. . .).

Although search is certainly an important component of a web page, it is generally not effective as the primary navigation tool. Thus, it is important to effectively design the navigation through links and provide search as a backup method for reaching specific locations within the web site.

Footer

The footer on a web page is usually a text copyright statement, the date of updation and an e-mail link to the web master. The global links for the site are also usually repeated via text links in the footer.

Forms

Just about every component we have discussed so far is concerned with how information is organized and presented on a web page. Forms on a web page take the user experience one step further. They allow interaction between the visitor and the web site. The simplest example of this is when a visitor types a word in the search field and clicks on Search. On the other hand, banking and on-line trading require complex inputs from the visitor. This input needs to be processed by the system (usually referred to as back-end application), and an appropriate feedback needs to be presented. Form design poses the challenges of making instructions unambiguous, providing essential options, anticipating visitor expectations, and providing appropriate feedback for valid and invalid inputs. As we have seen with other components, effective forms are designed through synchronization of the skills of the information architect and the creative director (see Figure 5–20).

Forms on a web site could be used for inquiring about a product or an organization, surveying the background of the visitor, inquiring about the status of a brokerage account, and placing an order for items in a shopping cart. Form filling could

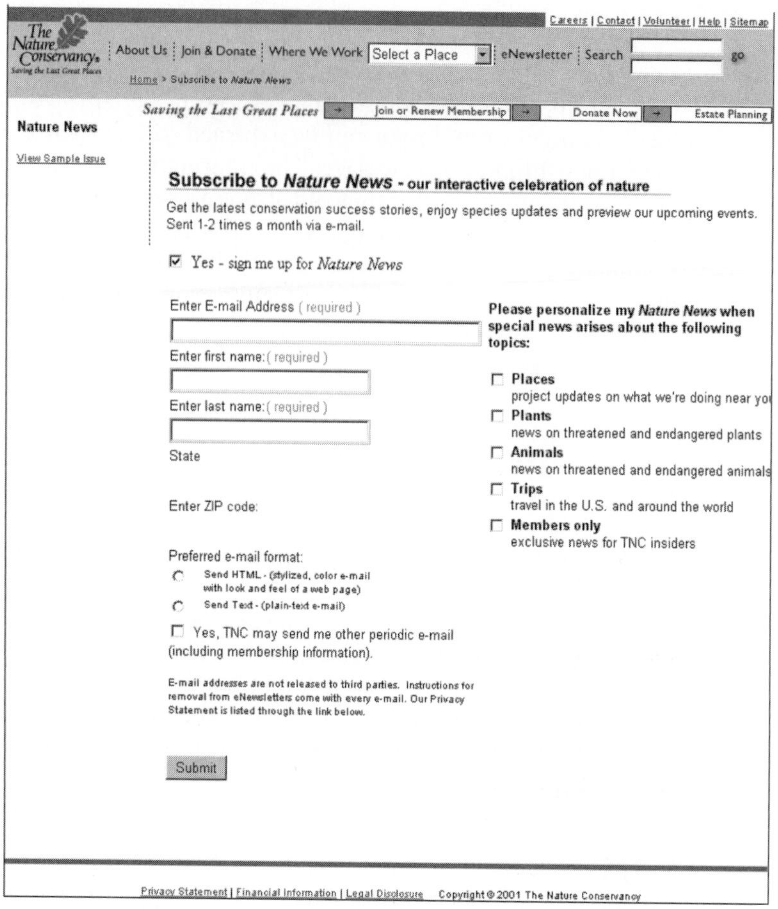

FIGURE 5–20 Example of a subscription form: The Nature Conservancy (*www.tnc.org*)

cause apprehension among the visitors. First, people usually do not like giving out personal information. Second, they are concerned about security of the information they type in. Finally, there is the fear of the unknown, as the visitors do not see where the data is going and what is going to be done with it. This apprehension gets compounded and results in frustration when the interaction is not supported by intuitive interface. In addition, visitors are likely to be completely confused if the form validation results in messages that are difficult to interpret.

Here are a few suggestions for designing easy-to-use forms (see also Figure 5–21):

▶ Ask for information that is absolutely essential. Avoid redundant information, such as date of birth and age.

▶ Provide clear text-based instructions and labels for fields (areas that are to be filled in by the visitor).

▶ Provide the visitors with a list of options to select from rather than asking them to type open-ended responses. The information architect would need to ensure that the list provided to the visitors includes most of the options that they are likely to enter. One way of collecting this information is to ask typical visitors what they would enter and then match their inputs with the categories in the list.

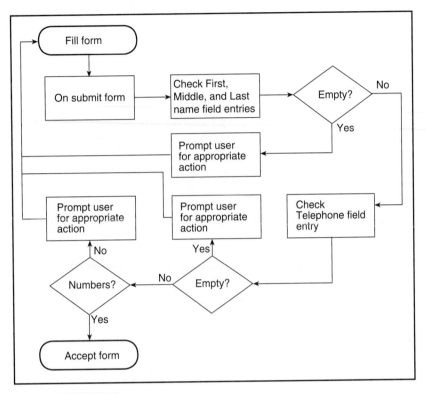

FIGURE 5-21 Form validation flowchart

- A form requesting personal information, such as credit card number, account number, and password, should provide reassurance about security of the data and inform the visitors about what will be done with the data.
- Make sure that form validation (a method of checking that the data entered in the fields meets specific criteria) results in clear feedback and instructions on what is incorrect.
- It is a good idea to provide immediate "feedback" to user action such as "your request is being processed." A confirmation about the receipt of the information and what to anticipate further will help allay the visitor's apprehensions.
- Finally, it is important to examine all the possible inputs and actions that will be required to process a form. A very simple transaction such as "username" and "password" validation, can have multiple possibilities, and it is important that all these eventualities are predicted and planned for.

SITE MAP AND FLOWCHART

So far, we have discussed the considerations and approaches that an information architect will use when planning a web site. The output of this design process is the site map with specification of page content and process diagrams (flowchart).

Whereas the site map represents content and navigation on a site, the flowchart represents the rules that will guide the processing of visitor inputs and interactions.

Flowcharting tools, such as Microsoft Visio, are often used for creating the site map and flowchart.

Some essential features of a site map are the following:

- Each page on the web site should be represented on the site map.
- The site map should indicate grouping of pages (e.g., several pages for one section).
- Each page should be represented by its heading.
- The content details of each page should be listed via brief descriptions.
- Global links should be identified.
- Links specific to a page or a section should be identified.
- The presence of a process on a page should be identified, and a separate flowchart should represent this process.
- The site map is a communication tool used by the project team to indicate the content, process, and navigation options available on a site.

Figure 5–22 presents an example of a site map. It is important to distinguish between the site map that the information architect generates during the process of design and the site map that is often displayed on the site itself. The first one guides design and production of the site, whereas the second one helps site visitors understand the organization of content on the site and access specific sections listed in the site map.

Formal flowcharts are built using standardized icons and shapes that represent different technical features and processes. The symbols that are most commonly used for representing the process flow for web sites are the rectangle (for a page), the diamond (for a decision point), and the circle (to identify the start and exit points). Here are some essential features of a flowchart:

- It needs to indicate every possible condition that is likely to arise when a visitor interacts with the system.
- It should be possible to trace various user scenarios using a flowchart.

The flowchart in Figure 5–23 has been developed by Jennifer English, Kim Garrett, and Sacha Pearson for a site that allows visitors to create personalized travel guides. The flowchart illustrates the process flow that a visitor would experience as he or she interacts with the site.

NAVIGATION PROTOTYPE

The navigation prototype (also called the functional prototype or click-through) provides a method for evaluating and presenting the information architecture for a site. The navigation prototype is a fully linked web site with all representative pages. The visitor is able to move between pages and read a description of the contents for each web page. Processes are also realistically represented in this prototype, though they may be emulated and not actually programmed. Emulation refers to creating specific instances of the usage and demonstrating the interaction. In some projects, the copy can be completely developed and integrated in the navigation prototype. This provides the client with an opportunity to examine the overall message on the

Site Map for The Art Institute Student Web Site

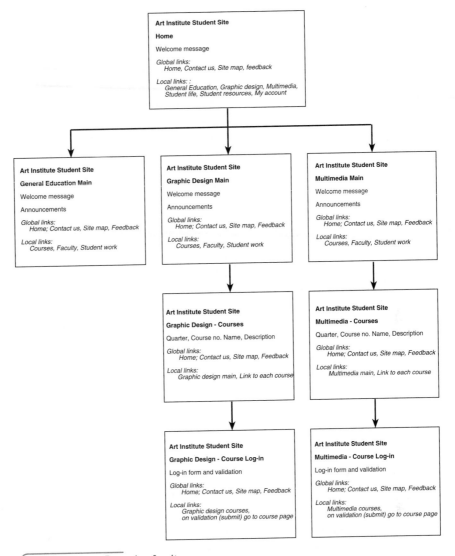

Art Institute Student Site

Home

Welcome message

Global links:
Home, Contact us, Site map, feedback

Local links: :
General Education, Graphic design, Multimedia,
Student life, Student resources, My account

Art Institute Student Site

General Education Main

Welcome message

Announcements

Global links:
Home; Contact us, Site map, Feedback

Local links:
Courses, Faculty, Student work

Art Institute Student Site

Graphic Design Main

Welcome message

Announcements

Global links:
Home; Contact us, Site map, Feedback

Local links:
Courses, Faculty, Student work

Art Institute Student Site

Multimedia Main

Welcome message

Announcements

Global links:
Home; Contact us, Site map, Feedback

Local links:
Courses, Faculty, Student work

Art Institute Student Site

Graphic Design - Courses

Quarter, Course no. Name, Description

Global links:
Home; Contact us, Site map, Feedback

Local links:
Graphic design main, Link to each course

Art Institute Student Site

Multimedia - Courses

Quarter, Course no. Name, Description

Global links:
Home; Contact us, Site map, Feedback

Local links:
Multimedia main, Link to each course

Art Institute Student Site

Graphic Design - Course Log-in

Log-in form and validation

Global links:
Home; Contact us, Site map, Feedback

Local links:
Graphic design courses,
on validation (submit) go to course page

Art Institute Student Site

Multimedia - Course Log-in

Log-in form and validation

Global links:
Home; Contact us, Site map, Feedback

Local links:
Multimedia courses,
on validation (submit) go to course page

FIGURE 5–22 Example of a site map

site. Industry experts may agree that a significant amount of time is "wasted" on re-working the copy after the site has been fully integrated in many web development projects. Evaluating the copy in the early stages of the project can help avoid these costly revisions.

The navigation prototype is not a visual representation of the site. Rather, the purpose is to focus on content, navigation, and interaction on the web site before fully developing the interface design. The client, typical members of the target audience, content experts, and information architecture experts could be called on to evaluate the navigation prototype. This evaluation certainly increases the time taken to complete the project. However, the evaluation helps improve the overall efficiency of the project. This is because it can save the time, energy, and cost of

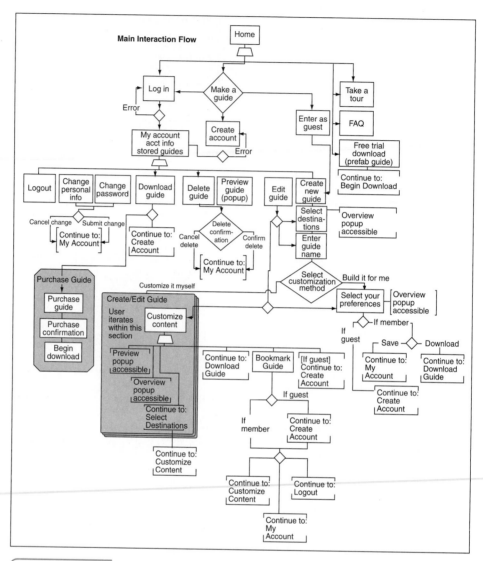

FIGURE 5–23 Example of a process flowchart: Jennifer English, Kim Garrett, and Sacha Pearson (*www.sims.berkeley.edu/courses/final-projects/travelite/*)

reworking navigation after the interface has been developed, the programming has been completed, and media elements have been integrated.

Typical pages for a navigation prototype are shown in Figures 5–24 and 5–25.

CONSIDERATIONS FOR INFORMATION ARCHITECTURE

In the next few paragraphs, we discuss some considerations that may help increase the effectiveness of information architecture. Keep in mind, however, that the best way of ensuring effectiveness is to work cooperatively within the team and to frequently invite comments and feedback.

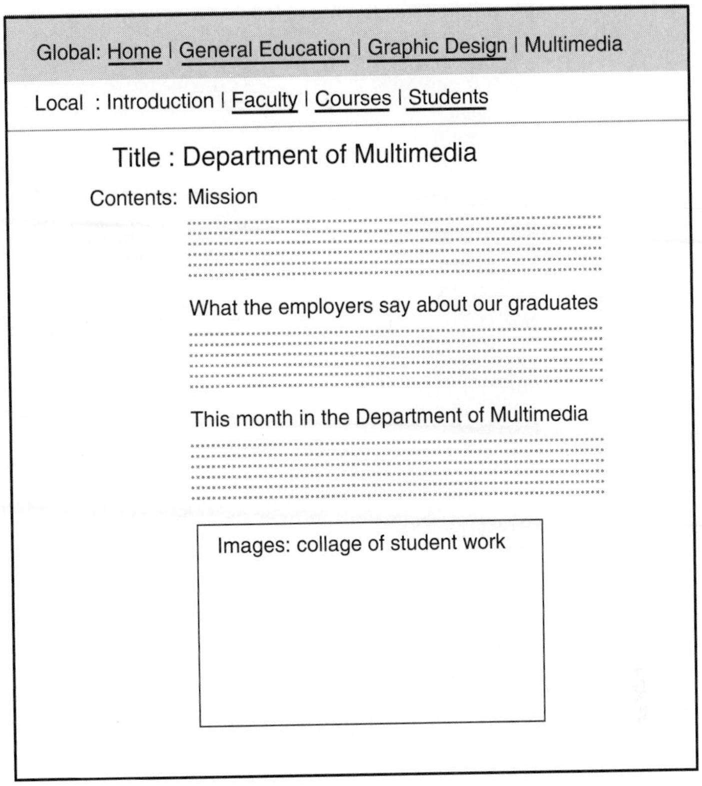

FIGURE 5-24

Navigation prototype
screen 1

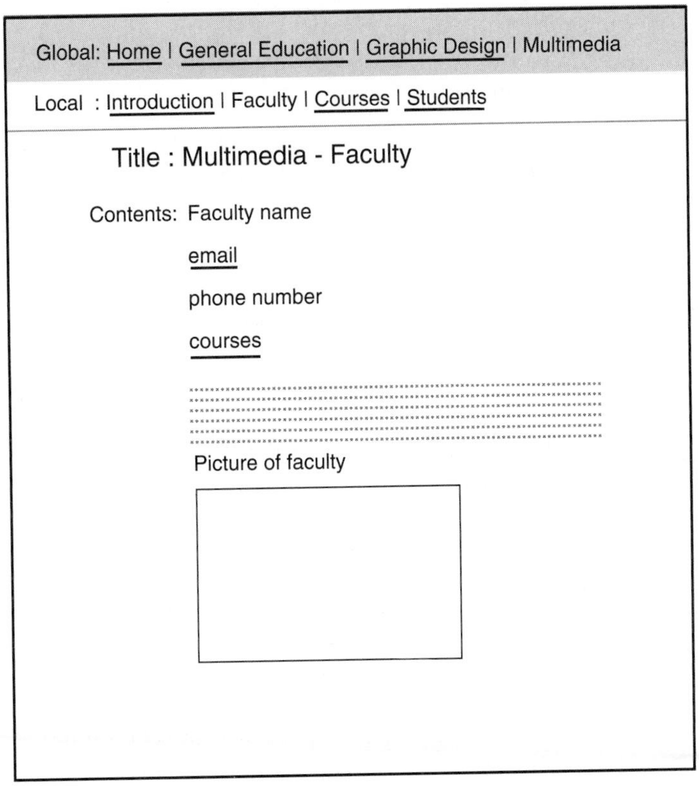

Global: <u>Home</u> | <u>General Education</u> | <u>Graphic Design</u> | Multimedia

Local : Introduction | <u>Faculty</u> | <u>Courses</u> | <u>Students</u>

Title : Department of Multimedia

Contents: Mission

What the employers say about our graduates

This month in the Department of Multimedia

Images: collage of student work

FIGURE 5-25

Navigation prototype
screen 2

Global: <u>Home</u> | <u>General Education</u> | <u>Graphic Design</u> | Multimedia

Local : <u>Introduction</u> | Faculty | <u>Courses</u> | <u>Students</u>

Title : Multimedia - Faculty

Contents: Faculty name

<u>email</u>

phone number

<u>courses</u>

Picture of faculty

Splash/Home Page

The initial pages of the site need to attract, invite, and encourage "revisits." Thus, you may want to put content that will appeal the most on the home/splash pages. The objective of the splash page is not so much to inform as to attract. The information content on the splash page is minimal. The home page, on the other hand, needs to provide substantial information and clarity on what a visitor will be able to do on the site. The splash page is a bit like the foyer in the building. It creates a comfortable space that is inviting and not overwhelming (see Figure 5–26).

Currency of Information

The information on a web site needs to be updated regularly. Stale content discourages revisits and can also get irrelevant. For some sites, content needs to be current, that is, up to the minute or second. While planning a site, it is important to identify sections that will require updating. Naturally, these sections need to be designed and implemented such that updating will be easy. The simplest way of achieving this is by ensuring that content that needs to be updated is presented as text rather than images.

Web sites should also display the date on which the content on the site was updated.

Quantity of Information

The site needs to cater to the visitors who seek a quick summary as well as to those who wish to get an in-depth analysis. The use of headings, subheadings, summaries, and pull quotes can be effective strategies for drawing visitors into the site.

Consistency and Familiarity

The information on the site needs to be up to date, and the organization of information needs to be predictable. We can expect regular visitors to select sections of the site without ever looking at the interface they are clicking on (a bit like someone going straight to the sports page of a newspaper without thinking about it).

The sites need to use icons and labels (or section titles) that visitors are familiar with. Whenever metaphorical titles are used, they need to be supported by descriptive titles so that if a visitor is unable to decipher the metaphor, the descriptive title will provide the required information. For example, we had seen that "gray matter" was not an obvious representation of "expert comments." However, it could be a clever title if it is supported by an explanation of the contents of the section.

Overall Marketing Strategy (Media Plan)

Many web sites are a part of a larger marketing strategy or media plan. Print, billboards, television, and web communication need to leverage off the reach of each medium. When designing a web site, it is important to understand how the site fits into and interacts with other components of the marketing strategy.

Search and Site Map

Most visitors to the site are likely to use the navigation system (links) to find the information they are interested in. It is thus important to build intuitive and easy-to-use navigation systems on a web site.

The search option on a site allows visitors to quickly find specific information they are looking for. A keyword (preclassified) and an open-ended search are important features of a comprehensive web site. Search should also be prominently displayed so that visitors do not have to search for "search."

The site map on a web site provides a different way of navigating through the site. It presents the content structure for the site and allows the visitor to go directly to a specific point of interest. As with the search feature, the site map should be a secondary and supportive navigation aid. Site maps are especially useful in providing orientation and quick access to information on web sites with a complex content hierarchy. Site maps could indicate "you are here" in different sections of the site and thereby serve as an effective orientation tool.

Personalization

Personalization is an important feature of many web sites. Personalization allows a web site to prioritize and select the content that is presented to the visitor on the basis of previously defined preferences and surfing habits.

Along with personalization, we need to consider the issue of privacy of information. If a web site gathers information about a visitor with the purpose of personalizing the content (or for the purpose of marketing other products), the visitors need to be informed about how and where this data will be used. Naturally, the visitors also need to have the option of not entering their personal information.

Security

Whenever a site requires confidential information (e.g., social security or credit card number), the visitors must be assured that the transaction is secure. Although implementation of security features is a technical function, the information architect needs to determine what information is critical and also how that information will be managed.

Planning for Search Engines

When developing sites, it is not enough to do great planning and design for the site. It is just as important to plan the strategy of bringing visitors to the site. Search engines play a critical role in this strategy. Although in this book we do not go into the specific steps one could take in preparing the site for search engines, the information architect needs to keep in mind the features that would increase the chances of a site being indexed and displayed prominently in search results.

It is possible that a visitor may enter the site on any page. This may happen if he or she uses a search engine that directly references a page of the site. Each page should thus stand on its own and provide adequate navigation and contextual aids. The title, heading, branding, identification of current location, and global links become critical in such situations.

Community

Community building is an important feature of the Internet. Topical web sites could enhance their value by including community features, such as chat, bulletin boards, or listservs, and by incorporating features that encourage community interactions, such as contests.

Web Accessibility Guidelines

The World Wide Web Consortium (W3C) has published guidelines for making web sites accessible for all persons. Increasingly, there is a movement toward making web pages accessible to individuals who may not be able to hear, see, move, or easily process some types of information. The W3C's recommendations are in keeping with the universal nature and original intention of the web. As such, when one designs web sites, it is important to keep some simple guidelines in mind. For example, the use of text descriptions for images using the "alt" attribute will enable visually impaired individuals to "read" the description of the images using special devices. Information on the guidelines can be found at www.w3.org/TR/WCAG10/.

SUMMARY

In this chapter, we have discussed the activities and considerations for an information architect's role. The information architect's primary role is that of analyzing the requirements, generating a navigation and process structure, and doing page-by-page information design for the web site. The site structure is best represented through a site map, process flowcharts, and navigation prototype. The navigation prototype is the completely linked site with specification of content on each page—without the visual and aesthetic representation. In many projects, the full copy can be integrated in the navigation prototype. A thorough evaluation of the navigation prototype can help increase the efficiency of the project and also lead to greater effectiveness in achieving the business and communication objectives of the site. Increasingly, web sites need to adhere to the standards of accessibility as defined by the W3C.

GUIDING QUESTIONS

▶ What is information architecture?

▶ What aspects does an information architect examine as he or she starts the process of information architecture?

▶ Describe the following types of navigation structures and find an example of each on the web:
  ▶ Linear
  ▶ Hierarchical
  ▶ Grid
  ▶ Hypertext/hypermedia

▶ Visit an e-commerce site and trace the process for selecting and purchasing items on the site.

▶ Differentiate between global and local links on a web site. What is the advantage of using each type of link?

▶ What is information design?

▶ What is the purpose of a form? What are some considerations for designing forms?

▶ Differentiate between a site map, a flowchart, and a navigation prototype.

▶ List the important considerations in information architecture. Analyze a web site in terms of these considerations.

EXERCISES

▶ Develop a process map for starting a car. Assume that you start with unlocking the door to the car.

▶ Visit the web site for a well-known corporation. Identify the components of the page on its home page.

▶ Prepare an exhaustive list of all the components that you could find on a web page.

▶ Write down the contents of a magazine site on a set of index cards. Ask a friend to sort these cards into piles of similar topics. Compare your friend's sorting with the way in which content is organized on the site.

▶ Assume that you are designing a web site for a popular weekly magazine. How would you structure the content on the web site? How similar is this structure to the one in the printed magazine? Prepare a site map for the site.

Interface Design

As we have seen, web sites provide a plethora of experiences on the Internet. As designers, we make an effort to ensure that these experiences are pleasant, engaging, and productive. Naturally, we do not want to design experiences that are initially pleasant but eventually unproductive. We also want to ensure that the experiences are engaging and encourage the visitor to return to the site. The quality of experiences on a site is determined by factors such as ease of navigation, readability, aesthetics, content organization, effective integration of media, and the overall approach to communication design. Some of these are issues of usability and functionality, whereas others are challenges of creative design.

In Chapter 5, we examined information architecture as the first "design" activity. Once the functionality of the site has been designed, the creative director, web designer, and interface designer step in to design the sensory experiences. These designers are concerned with giving a concrete form to the functional interface that has been designed by the information architect. Thus, while the information architect works on the process flow, business rules, information structure, labels, and navigation, the web and interface designers create a means of experiencing them. This process is often referred to as experience design, site personality design, front-end design, and graphic or visual design. In this chapter, we examine the considerations and processes for interface design that could contribute to a usable site.

As we saw in Chapter 3, the roles of the web designer and the interface designer are very similar. Although some organizations do have distinct positions for these roles, more often than not the web and interface designers perform almost the same function. For the purpose of this chapter, we will refer to them as "interface designer." Keep in mind that the creative director provides the design leadership and guidance on all design approaches for the web site.

The interface designer is responsible for the following:

▶ Selecting the graphic style
▶ Selecting the typography
▶ Selecting the colors
▶ Designing the layout

- Designing the illustrations
- Designing the branding and identity
- Designing the interaction elements, such as buttons and icons
- Designing the forms requiring visitor input and the processing and feedback for that input
- Designing the experiences that a visitor will go through as he or she interacts with the web site

According to Alison Head (1999), "An interface is the visible piece of a system that a user sees or hears or touches."

Patrick Lynch and Sarah Horton (1999) state that "the graphic user interface (GUI) of a computer system comprises the interaction metaphors, images, and concepts used to convey function and meaning on the computer screen."

Lisa Graham (1999) describes interactive design as "the meaningful arrangement of graphics, text, video, photos, illustrations, sound, animation, three-dimensional (3D) imagery, virtual reality and other media in an interactive document."

The interface design for a web site requires creativity and an understanding of the concepts of visual design, the target audience, the communication objective, and information architecture. An awareness of technical feasibility and time and budgetary constraints are also important.

So where does the interface designer begin? As we saw earlier, involvement of all team members throughout the project is important. However, the interface designer gets actively involved once the information architect has conducted the requirements analysis and defined the site structure, section and subsection labels, process flow, and navigation. The interface designer uses this information and creates the "face" and "personality" of the web site. To do this, he or she considers a number of design issues. The collaboration between the information architect, creative director, and interface designer continues throughout the project life cycle.

Before we get into the specifics of these issues, let us address a broader issue. Is interface design a science or an art? Is it driven by a series of rules and procedures, or is it essentially a creative process? Unfortunately, there is no simple or clear answer to these questions. The concepts, rules, guidelines, and thinking inside or outside the box can be only the launching pad. Eventually, a designer is successful if the site achieves what it was designed to achieve. A good designer builds on experience and guidelines and takes considered decisions—sometimes breaking rules and at other times working within their boundaries. Whatever the designers' personal leanings (art or science), it is important that they are able to support their design decisions with sound rationales.

Another dichotomy in the field is that of usability versus creative design. Unfortunately, these two camps seem to be driven by rhetoric rather than by a serious consideration of the purpose of the web as a medium of communication. A successful web site is one that has achieved high aesthetic value (and thereby created a pleasant experience for the visitor) and at the same time is easy and intuitive to use. Finding this balance is the challenge to web designers.

A similar challenge is faced in fields such as industrial design, product design, and architecture. These disciplines attempt to strike a balance between form and function. Successful professionals in these disciplines design products that not only look beautiful but also work successfully in achieving the objective for which they were developed. Going back to the analogy of a building, designers of a building strive to make it look good (and unique), make its occupants comfortable, facilitate the activities that will take place in the building, and make the building structurally sound.

In creating the interface for a web site, the designer considers many options and zeros in on what appears to be the most appropriate decision. In the next few paragraphs, we look at some possible decision areas.

METAPHORS

In this book, I have used designing and constructing a building as a conceptual metaphor to represent web sites and web development.

The best way to understand a metaphor is to look at some examples. One of the best-known metaphors in the computing industry is that of the Apple Macintosh desktop. Users are able to successfully interact with the "desktop" because it is similar to a desktop they use in their noncomputing life.

When the new Beetle was introduced by Volkswagen, the site used the metaphor of the periodic table (chemistry) to create an interesting and intriguing interface (see Figure 6–1).

From the previous examples, you can see that a metaphor is usually an object, a concept, or a situation that the target audience can be expected to be familiar with. The metaphor also bears similarity with the concept that is being introduced. The metaphor thus creates an easy bridge between the familiar and the unfamiliar content.

The new Beetle site uses the metaphor of the periodic table to represent the content for the whole site, but we often find metaphors being used to represent navigation links (icons).

For example, the image of a home is often used to represent the link to the home page (see Figure 6–2).

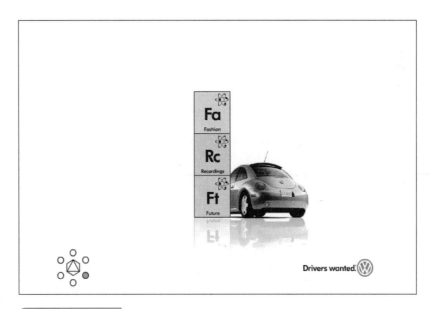

FIGURE 6–1　Example of a metaphor: the Volkswagen Beetle

FIGURE 6–2

The home: a metaphor for the home page

FIGURE 6–3

"On" in the United States, "Off" in Singapore: cultural implications of metaphors

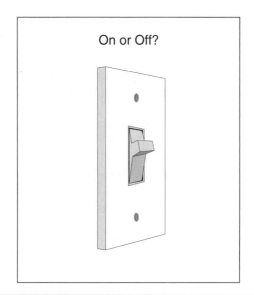

As designers, you may need to decide whether a metaphor is essential to enhance the communication. You will often find that although on the face of it a metaphor seems to fit, it falls apart when you try to relate it to the content of the whole web site. A metaphor needs to fit both in terms of the conceptual interface and in terms of the visual interface. You also need to keep in mind the cultural relevance of a metaphor. For example, consider the metaphor of an electric switch for representing the on and off state of an interface. In the United States, the "on" state would be represented by the switch being at the top, whereas in Singapore, the switch would be at the bottom for the "on" state (see Figure 6–3).

Though a metaphor can be a very powerful tool of communication, we must keep in mind the dangers of interpretation, familiarity, and culture when using them. Figure 6–4 represents icons that could possibly be used on a web site. Would you be able to figure out their functions without the text labels?

Take a look at the metaphors in Figure 6–5. The icons are in keeping with the personality of the site and, also, it is easy to figure out the function or section they represent.

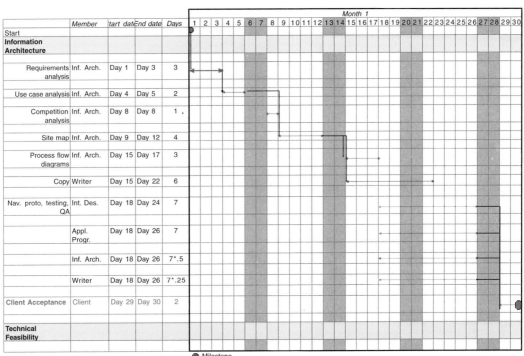

	Member	Start date	End date	Days
Start				
Information Architecture				
Requirements analysis	Inf. Arch.	Day 1	Day 3	3
Use case analysis	Inf. Arch.	Day 4	Day 5	2
Competition analysis	Inf. Arch.	Day 8	Day 8	1
Site map	Inf. Arch.	Day 9	Day 12	4
Process flow diagrams	Inf. Arch.	Day 15	Day 17	3
Copy	Writer	Day 15	Day 22	6
Nav. proto, testing, QA	Int. Des.	Day 18	Day 24	7
	Appl. Progr.	Day 18	Day 26	7
	Inf. Arch.	Day 18	Day 26	7*.5
	Writer	Day 18	Day 26	7*.25
Client Acceptance	Client	Day 29	Day 30	2
Technical Feasibility				

● Milestone
⟷ Full-time involvement
⟷ Part-time involvement
↓ Dependency

FIGURE 4–5 Example of a project task list

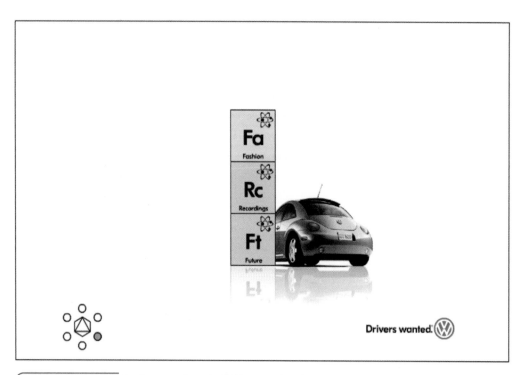

FIGURE 6–1 Example of a metaphor: the Volkswagen Beetle

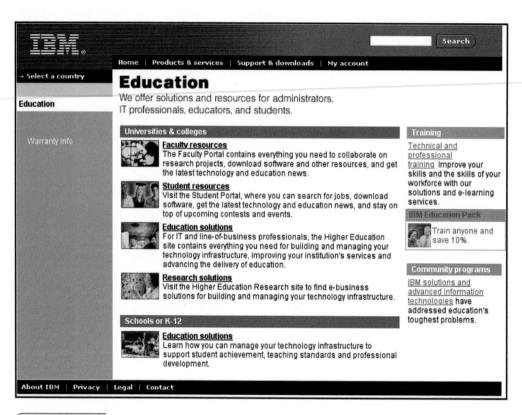

FIGURE 6–6

The IBM site: *www.ibm.com*

FIGURE 6–7

A site for children: ASPCA's Animaland (*www.animaland.org*) Copyright © 2001 The American Society for Prevention of Cruelty to Animals

FIGURE 6–8

A site for environmental issues: Rainforest Action Network (*www.ran.org*)

FIGURE 6–9

High-contrast colors help readability: Creative Freedom UK (*www.creative-freedom.co.uk*)

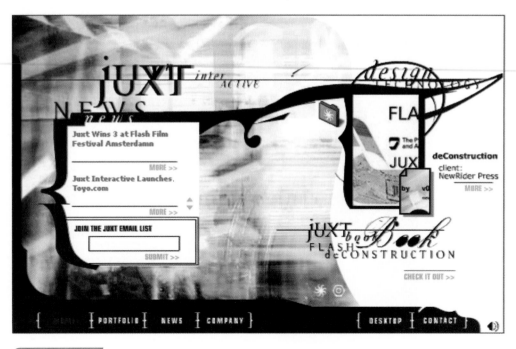

FIGURE 6–10

A unique graphic style: Juxt Interactive (*www.juxtinteractive.com*)

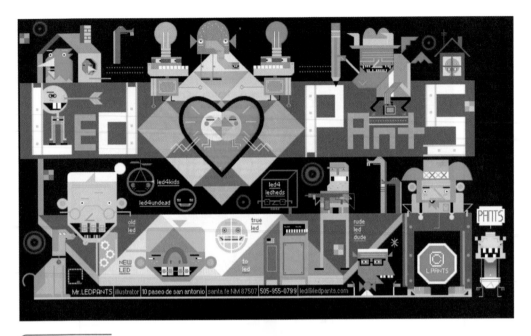

This is Blue text on Black background.

This is Blue text on Red background.

This is Pink text on Yellow background.

This is Yellow text on White background.

FIGURE 6–13

Poor readability: low contrast between foreground and background

HOME | ABOUT CREATIONS | LUNCH | DINNER | RESERVATIONS | DIRECTIONS | RECIPES

Creations is open to the public and a great place for lunch or dinner.

Offering Classical Freanch cuisine and white linen service Creations is the perfect place for a special dinner, lunch, or celebration.

Please see what we have to offer by sampling our lunch or dinner menu on our web site.

Thank you
Chef James W. Paul
Director, Creations

NEW AT CREATIONS
WINE PAIRING EVENING
On November 14 and 16 at 7:00 pm new gourmet dinners offer four spectacular courses accompanied by specially chosen wines. Make the evening an event.

See Wine Pairing Reservations for more details.

The Art Institute of Atlanta

HOME | **ABOUT CREATIONS** | LUNCH | DINNER | RESERVATIONS | DIRECTIONS | RECIPES

menu
ABOUT CREATIONS

ABOUT THE ART INSTITUTE OF ATLANTA

ABOUT THE CULINARY ARTS PROGRAM

ABOUT CULINARY ARTS STUDENTS

The Art Institute of Atlanta

ABOUT CREATIONS

Classical French cuisine and white linen service are the tradition at Creations. Open to the public, the restaurant serves as a dining lab for Culinary students at The Art Institute of Atlanta.

Creations tempting menu offers fine dining courses served in a relaxed, learning environment. Daily tableside preparation and tempting desserts.

Enjoy Fine Art inside Creations

The Art Institute of Atlanta

Home | About Us | Lunch | Dinner | Reservations | Directions | Recipes

New: Wine Pairing Dinners
On November 14 and 16 at 7:00 pm new gourmet dinners offer four spectacular courses accompanied by specially chosen wines. Make the evening an event.

Make the Evening an Event
for more information: Wine Pairing Reservations

Home | About Us | Lunch | Dinner | Reservations | Directions | Recipes   Contact Information

The Art Institute of Atlanta®

online reservations can be made at: **ReservationSource.com**

Home | **About Us** | Dinner | Lunch | Reservations | Directions | Recipes
Creations | The Art Institute of Atlanta | The Culinary Arts Program | Culinary Arts Students

About Creations
Classical French cuisine and white linen service are the tradition at Creations. Open to the public, the restaurant serves as a dining lab for Culinary Arts Students at The Art Institute of Atlanta.

Creations' tempting menu offers fine-dining courses served in a relaxed environment. Daily tableside preparations and tempting desserts are served at Creations.

Enjoy fine-dinning in a relax environment.

Home | **About Us** | Dinner | Lunch | Reservations | Directions | Recipes   Contact Information

The Art Institute of Atlanta®

online reservations can be made at: **ReservationSource.com**

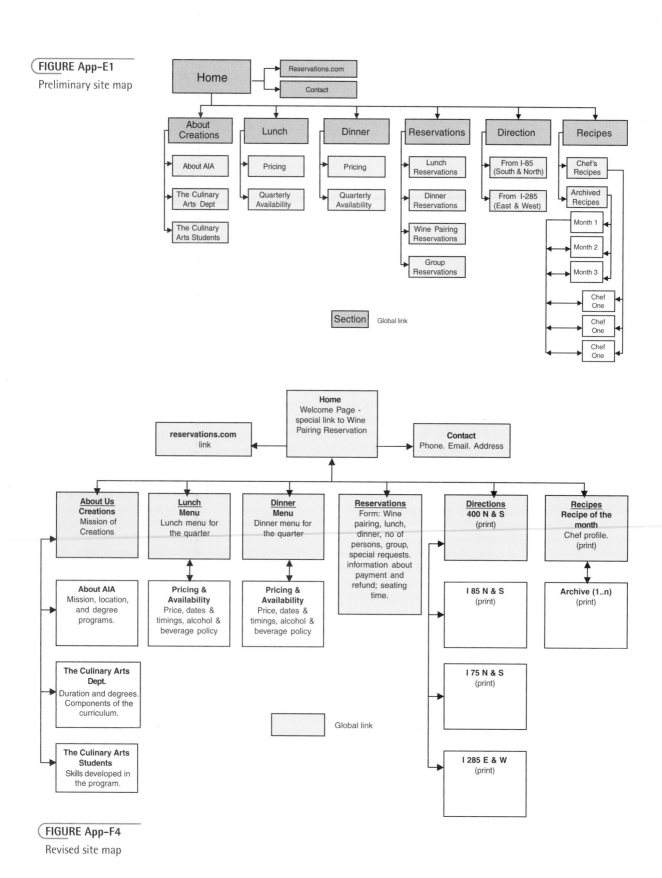

FIGURE 6–4

Image metaphor links without and with text labels

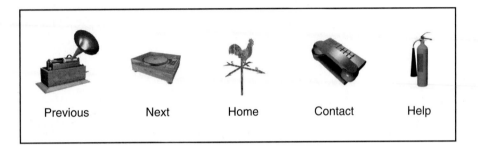

Previous   Next   Home   Contact   Help

FIGURE 6–5

Example of image metaphors: Girlzilla, Inc. (*www.girlzilla.com*)

Project Timeline   Services   Methodology   Contact Us   Jobs   Game Room   H-factor

COLORS

Colors have a powerful significance in communication. They represent emotions, actions, and identities. In this book, we will not explore specific theories of color. Many good books have been written on that topic. However, we will touch on considerations that must go into making decisions about the colors used on a web site.

Colors should depend on who the site represents. For example, certain organizations have strict specifications on what colors could be used to represent them. A web site for IBM with any color other than blue as a prominent color may appear out of character, as the organization is identified as the "big blue" (see Figure 6–6).

Colors also depend on the site's target audience. For example, bright, cheery, bold and fun colors would be a natural consideration for a web site that targets children (see Figure 6–7).

Colors also depend on the topic of the web site. For example, green, earthy colors would be a likely choice for a site dealing with environmental issues (see Figure 6–8).

There are important cultural connotations and preferences for colors. For example, some Asian cultures relate well to earth colors, whereas Western culture tends to

FIGURE 6–6

The IBM site:
www.ibm.com

FIGURE 6–7

A site for children:
ASPCA's Animaland
(*www.animaland.org*)
Copyright © 2001 The
American Society for
Prevention of Cruelty
to Animals

FIGURE 6–8

A site for
environmental issues:
Rainforest Action
Network (*www.ran.org*)

FIGURE 6–9

High-contrast colors
help readability:
Creative Freedom UK
(*www.creative-
freedom.co.uk*)

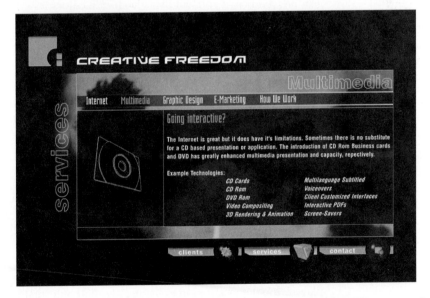

prefer pastels. In some cultures, red is associated with mourning, whereas in others, it is associated with happiness.

Color is the most critical consideration in readability of a web site. Bright, iridescent colors do not do well for backgrounds, especially when there is a large body of text on them. Similarly, low contrast between background and foreground leads to poor readability. Considering that most designers work on large high-end monitors, it is easy to overlook the possibility that lower-end, lower-resolution, and smaller monitors will make the text difficult to read. Effective designers thus seek an ideal combination of contrasting colors and text size to enhance the readability on their sites (see Figure 6–9).

TABLE 6–1   Graphic Styles

Abstract	Art deco	Cartoon
Comic book	Cubist	Cutaways
Impressionist	Line art	Montage
Painterly	Realistic	Stipple
Surrealistic	Three-dimensional (3D)	Typographic

TABLE 6–2   Medium for Rendering Images

Charcoal	Collage	Oil
Pen and ink	Watercolor	Spray paint

Finally, *when selecting colors for a web site, the designers should take into consideration the web-safe color palette.* Two hundred and sixteen web-safe colors appear the same across different browsers and platforms. Items such as text and backgrounds are best displayed using web-safe colors.

GRAPHIC STYLE AND MEDIUM

The graphic style of a web site is just as important as the color. As a designer, you have many styles to choose from. Some of these are listed in Table 6–1.

Though the eventual delivery medium for the images is the computer monitor, you can also consider a variety of media for rendering the graphic style. A few of these considerations are listed in Table 6–2.

As a designer, you may have your own individual style and a favorite medium. If you do, there is danger of getting pulled into using the same style and medium. The style and medium should be a considered decision that could be supported by the overall purpose of the web site. Also keep in mind that you need to sustain the style and medium throughout the web site.

The use of style also extends to the use of photographs. Once the decision to use photographs has been taken, you need to determine how these images will be displayed. Too much variation in the use of different formats (horizontal and vertical), different sizes, and different treatments (sharp edge, feathered edge) needs to be avoided.

Figures 6–10 and 6–11 show two examples of sites that use a unique graphic style that seems to work well with the objective, content, and target audience.

TYPOGRAPHY

The typography on a site is an integral part of the graphic design. The designer needs to consider the cohesiveness and harmony between the graphic style and typography.

FIGURE 6–10

A unique graphic style:
Juxt Interactive (*www.
juxtinteractive.com*)

FIGURE 6–11

A unique graphic style:
Led Pants
(*www.ledpants.com*)

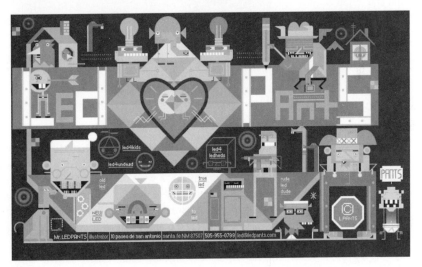

In most cases, type will not be a separate consideration but rather an integral part of the decision on the graphic style. Typography is an important consideration for the following specific components of a web page:

- Headings and subheadings for a body of text
- Pull quotes that summarize the message and draw the reader to further read the copy
- Body copy

In each of these cases, typography can help enhance the communication by ensuring readability and by becoming an integral part of the expression of the site personality.

Effective typography on a site can enhance the mood and the message of the site. At the same time, indifferent selection of typeface can work against the communication objective of the site. Consider the typefaces in Figure 6–12. Which of these best represents "fun"?

FIGURE 6–12
Which of these
typefaces represents
fun?

Which of these fonts represents fun?

Are we having fun yet?   Helvetica

Are we having fun yet? Verdana

Are we having fun yet?   Monotype Corsiva

Are we having fun yet?   Times New Roman

Are we having fun yet?   Tekton

FIGURE 6–13
Poor readability: low
contrast between
foreground and
background

This is Blue text on Black background.

This is Blue text on Red background.

This is Pink text on Yellow background.

This is Yellow text on White background.

Along with making sure that the type represents the message and mood of the site, you need to make sure that the copy is readable. Here are some considerations when using typography on a web page:

Appropriateness of the typography for the resolution of the monitor and the size of the font. Typically, sans serif fonts, such as **Helvetica** and **Arial**, are easier to read, whereas cursive fonts, such as *Script* and Bookman Antiqua, are more difficult (on the computer monitor).

Font color and background color. Some colors may work wonderfully well together in print but be disastrous on a computer monitor. We have already discussed this point in the section on color. Figure 6–13 shows a combination of low-contrast colors that seems to work fine for print but can be quite impossible when it comes to the screen.

Font size. Obviously, the larger the font size is, the easier it is to read it. Unfortunately, as designers, we do not always have control over the font and the size that the visitor will view the site with. One way of ensuring that content is displayed with specific type and size is to display that information as a graphic image. Often, critical headings on a page are displayed as images (with the appropriate *alt* and *name* attributes defined in the *img* tag of HTML, e.g., <img src="home.gif" width="80"height="70" alt="icon linked to the home page" name="homeimage">). This, however, has its own problems in terms of download speed and accessibility by visually impaired visitors. With the growing popularity of Cascading Style Sheets, designers are likely to have better control over how text is displayed in a browser window.

Access by visually impaired visitors. Text that is displayed as a graphic on a web page cannot be accessed easily by a visually impaired visitor. It is thus important to provide redundant text links. Also, as discussed in the earlier paragraph, it is important to use the *alt* and *name* attributes with the image display tag in HTML (*img*). The World Wide Web Consortium (W3C) guide to web accessibility provides the specific production issues that need to be considered when designing web sites.

Use of white space (blank space). We will discuss white space in the context of layout design in the next few pages. In reference to typography, it is important to use white space to distinguish the important messages (e.g., pull quotes) and titles. White space is also important to break the monotony of large paragraphs.

Capitalization. Use of capitalization is good for emphasizing and stylizing a few words. However, a whole paragraph of text in all capitals is very difficult to read. In the web world, the use of all capitals is considered to be equivalent to shouting.

Alignment. Center-aligned headings are good for identification of section content. However, large centered paragraphs can be difficult to read. On the other hand, left-aligned jagged-right paragraphs could aid readability.

LAYOUT

Layout decisions are decisions about the placement of objects on a web page. Many guidelines for the layout of web pages are derived from our past experience with the print media, but research on electronic display of information is becoming increasingly popular. Over the past few years, several guidelines and conventions for web page layout have emerged. For example, it is accepted that all pages of a web site should display common elements in a consistent position. In the next few paragraphs, we discuss some guidelines that you may consider when designing the layout of web pages.

Logo. Logos for the organization or an icon representing the site are used as a link to the home page and are usually placed on the upper-left corner.

Global links. Global links are links that are available from all sections of a web site. They appear in a consistent position on all pages of the site. More often than not, global links are displayed on the left or top of the page. Redundant text links for global navigation are often displayed at the bottom of the page (see Figure 6–14).

FIGURE 6–14 Conventional position for global links

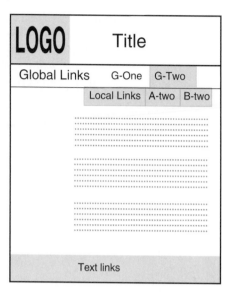

FIGURE 6–15 Conventional position for local links

Local links. Local links are links that are available only on a specific page. Typically, they take the visitor to the subsections of a site. Local links are best displayed such that the association between the currently selected global link and the local links can be clearly established. It is also important that local links for each section be consistently displayed (position, style, color) (see Figure 6–15).

In the example shown in Figure 6–15, the association between global and local links is obvious because of shared background color. The representation of links is also consistent in position, style, and color. These elements help increase the usability of the web site. We will discuss this issue again in the section "Navigation Tools."

White space. White space is blank space on a page or a screen. A screen with a lot of white space appears sparse, whereas one with very little white space may appear crowded.

Although the jury is still out on the importance of white space, the use of white space could result in an aesthetically pleasing layout. At the same time, too much white space could also limit the space available for the content or message.

The context of the message is important in determining the amount of white space on a page. For example, the splash page (that we see first on reaching a site) should typically have a lot of white space so that the visitor's attention is focused on the message. On the other hand, a content-rich news site may use limited white space and display a lot of content in a small space. This is done to prevent excessive clicking or scrolling to get to the information. Such layouts could potentially cause confusion and make it difficult for a visitor to find information. In such cases, it is important to provide an effective labeling mechanism and also design a layout that smartly uses white space, background colors, labels, borders, icons, and pull quotes to increase the accessibility to large amounts of information.

Perceptual organization. Perceptual organization refers to the way in which information is organized on a page. This topic could warrant an entire book on its own. However, you may need to keep the following in mind as guiding principles for information design on a web page:

▶ *Proximity*. Put similar elements and functions near each other. For example, put all links next to each other.

▶ *Similarity*. Elements that perform similar functions or have similar content can be displayed similarly. For example, all headings and links have the same format.

▶ *Continuity*. Create a sense of a "whole" on the site by maintaining the consistency and continuity across different sections. For example, ensure that the link label and the title of the page are consistent across pages.

▶ *Grouping*. Similar elements and functions can be visually organized in a group of items. For example, use color and lines to indicate the association between a section title and the contents of that section.

▶ *Hierarchy*. The hierarchy in visual display should be similar to a clearly established content hierarchy in terms of importance, alphabetical listing, sequence of occurrence, and so on. For example, the main heading should be larger than the subheadings.

▶ *Balance*. Ensure balanced composition of the visual elements on the web page. For example, if you use a heavy illustration on the left side of the page, balance it with a visual element on the opposite side of the page.

▶ *Relationship*. Clearly establish relationship between different elements, such as section and subsection links. For example, visual metaphors, illustrations, or even headings could be used to clearly establish the classification of information on a page.

Scrolling pages. Scrolling on a web page occurs when the page is designed to display a lot of content or when it has a lot of white space and the content is spread out. There is a raging debate in the field about whether typical visitors are inclined to scroll down a web page. While the empirical evidence is being gathered, we must exercise common sense with respect to this question. When a visitor comes to a web page, he or she will immediately see the content that is displayed in the visible area of the page. If there is no indication of what lies buried underneath, it is possible that the visitor will not be inclined to scroll down in search of that content.

Thus, the layout should be designed such that the most important and interesting information is positioned toward the top of the page. Once the curiosity has been piqued, the visitor will not mind scrolling down to access the detailed information about that topic. The layout could also provide visual cues (lines, arrows) indicating that there is more information below the visible screen.

Long pages also need to provide a mechanism for jumping up or down or to specific points within the page for quick access to information in different parts of the page.

Although scrolling cannot always be avoided, you need to make an attempt to minimize it and take steps to ensure that critical content is not missed on account of not being visible.

You must watch out for web pages that require the visitor to scroll not only vertically but also horizontally. Invariably, this happens when the designer has assumed that the visitors will access the site with larger screen resolutions. It also happens when the designer ignores the space that browser borders and scroll bars will occupy. Unfortunately, this space varies across browsers and also across platforms. For

FIGURE 6–16 Heading and subheadings on a web page: Girlzilla, Inc. (*www.girlzilla.com*)

example, when designing for a resolution of 800 × 600 pixels, it is best to plan for a display of 717 × 390 pixels to ensure that the page does not require scrolling (www.hotwired.lycos.com/webmonkey/99/41/index3a_page3.html).

Heading. The heading of a web page serves two purposes. First, it indicates the content on the page, and, second, it informs the visitor of where he or she is on the site. When a visitor comes across a web page without a heading, he or she is likely to experience problems of orientation. The heading is made even more critical because search engines could land a visitor in the middle of the site. Without adequate navigation and orientation cues, the visitor could feel lost on such pages.

We need to keep a few things in mind when designing the heading. First, the heading needs to be consistent in content and form to the icon, graphic, or text link that the visitor clicked on. Second, the heading should be displayed in a consistent position on different pages of the site. Third, the heading should not be so large that it wastes valuable screen estate. It is important that the heading serves as an identifier and navigation aid. But it should not be given so much prominence that it detracts the attention from the content on the page. The heading should ideally indicate the name of the site and also the name of the section (see Figure 6–16).

Subheadings. Subheadings help break up the content and help the visitor during a quick scan of the page. As we know, visitors to a web page rarely read all the text. They are more likely to scan the page and then zero in on the content that is of interest to them. Use of white space and subheadings helps in this (see Figure 6–16). As we have seen earlier, long web pages that require scrolling are usually better off

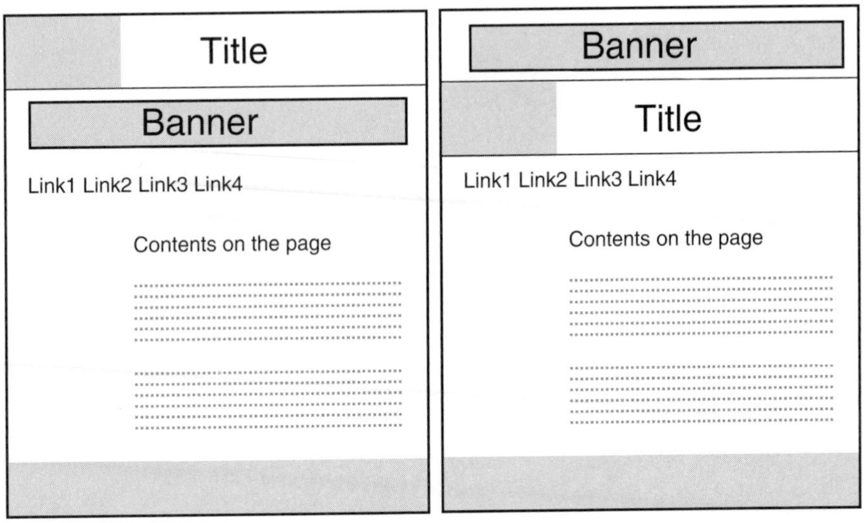

FIGURE 6–17   Banner on a web page

TABLE 6–3   Banner Sizes

Type	Width	Height
Micro button	88	31
Button	120	60
Button	120	90
Square banner	125	125
Half banner	234	60
Full horizontal banner with vertical navigation bar	392	72
Full horizontal banner	460	55
Full horizontal banner	468	60
Vertical banner	120	240

providing not only subheadings but also links within the page that allow the visitors to jump to the different sections on the page.

Banners. More often than not, advertisement banners are a critical revenue source for a web site. Consequently, they are given a prominent position on the web page. Web page designers are not likely to determine what goes on these banners. Thus, the role of the information architect and the interface designer is limited to specifying the number, size, and position of the banners on a web page. When determining the positioning of the banner, it is important to ensure that it does not break the continuity of the content on the page. For example, in the layout on the left of Figure 6–17, the banner breaks the visual and cognitive link between the heading and the content on the web page. This could be avoided by moving the banner to the top of the page (as in the layout on the right).

Standard banner sizes established by the Internet Advertising Bureau (IAB) and the Coalition for Advertising Supported Information and Entertainment (CASIE) are given in Table 6–3. When designing the layout of a page with banners, it is important to specify the size using this chart.

Templates. Templates have a connotation of being uniform, regimented, and maybe even boring. However, templates can be a great boon to web designers and developers. When designing a large web site, it makes no sense to create a different layout for every page on the site. It is usually smart to design a template that can be used across different sections. This is a good approach not only for optimizing the design effort but also for optimizing programming and debugging efforts. Further, templates help in developing a consistent layout and help visitors in developing a cognitive map of the site.

In the last few paragraphs, we discussed some issues critical to the design of the layout of a web page. We will now examine aspects that need to be kept in mind with respect to navigation and interaction on a web site.

NAVIGATION AIDS AND INTERACTION DESIGN

One of the most difficult things about designing a web site is to create an intuitive, easy-to-use navigation design. Often, the problem is compounded by the fact that the web site is a labyrinth of navigation options. The visitor not only needs a clear mental (cognitive) map for the whole site but also needs to be able to navigate to the relevant content in the shortest time and in the most nontraumatic manner.

We discuss this topic by separating the topic into two areas. The first consists of the elements on a page that are used as tools for navigation. This is somewhat like the mechanism for going from room to room or floor to floor in a building (door, foyer, staircase). The other consists of the attributes of these tools that could help or hinder how effectively a visitor is able to use them (a bit like the shape, color, and position of the handles on the doors).

Navigation Tools

Text Links

The concept of hypertext (text links) is older than the web. Text links are words, phrases, or sentences that are linked to a different part of the web site. We can use text links in three ways on a web site.

The first is as a listing of links available on a page. These text links are usually the primary links for the site or redundant links that replicate the links available through images on the page (see Figure 6–18).

The second is through embedded text links within the body of text. This is the simplest and the oldest form of navigation on the web. Even before the web, Apple computers had implemented the concept of hypertext documents where different documents were linked to each other through "hyper" text (original software: Hypercard™). Keep in mind that although hyperlinks can be an excellent method of accessing extra information about a topic, too many text links within the copy can also distract and confuse a visitor.

The third type of text link is popularly known as "breadcrumbs." These are text links that trace the path the visitor takes through the site. Breadcrumbs allow an easy and quick way of randomly navigating through the path taken to reach a particular page.

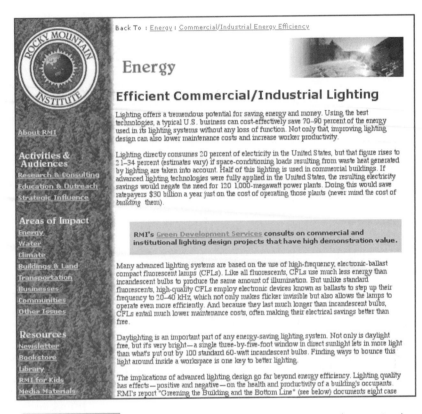

FIGURE 6-18 Text links on a web page: Rocky Mountain Institute (*www.rmi.org*)

As we have seen before, it is important to provide text links on a web page even if they duplicate graphic links. Text links provide several advantages:

▶ Because text loads faster than images, a visitor has the option of clicking on the text link and moving on.

▶ Text links provide a means of navigation for visually impaired visitors who may otherwise not be able to access the graphic links.

▶ The redundancy in access to links can allow for more flexibility in navigating through a web site.

Buttons

As the name suggests, buttons are typically geometric shapes that the visitor clicks on. Buttons provide one of the simpler interface options. Some sophisticated designers actually scoff at their use, probably because they are overused and underdesigned. As with other graphic links, buttons on a web page should be accompanied by redundant text links (usually at the bottom of the page).

Buttons play an important role in form design. Go, Reset, Search, Submit, Send, and Find are some commonly used form buttons. A descriptive text label is important to indicate the action that will take place when a visitor clicks on the

FIGURE 6–19

Form buttons

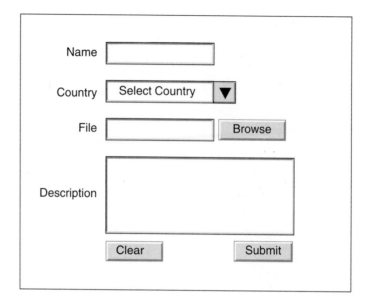

FIGURE 6–20

An icon without and
with a text label

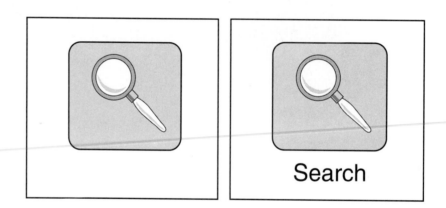

button. It is also important to position the button in such a way that it is easy to associate it with its input field (usually next to or below the input field) (see Figure 6–19).

Icons

Icons are somewhat similar to buttons. Icons are well-recognized visual representations of objects. Unfortunately, there is no guarantee that all visitors will make the right association between an icon and the navigation option it represents. It is thus important to always support an icon with a textual label (see Figure 6–20). This retains the visual interest and yet does not cause confusion in the meaning or representation of the icon. Over time, the visitor will not need to read the label and will relate the icon to what it represents. Figure 6–21 shows some commonly used icons on web pages.

Home

Help

Sound

Previous

Next/Forward

FIGURE 6–21   Commonly used icons

FIGURE 6–22   Image links: © Estate of Keith Haring (*www.haringkids.com*)

Images

Image-based links are a bit like icons, except that we cannot make an assumption of universal association of the image with what it represents. Typically, the image will be associated with the metaphor, the content, or the imagery (graphic style) of the site. The Haring Kids site makes an effective use of images as links. When the cursor moves over an image, the section name appears on it (see Figure 6–22).

Hot Spots

Hot spots are parts of an image that the visitor clicks on. For example, in the map of a country, each state can be a hot spot, and we can click on it to access information about the state.

Hot spots are a popular method of providing navigation that is integrated in the visual presentation on a screen. This eliminates the need for a separate listing of buttons or icons. The disadvantage of hot spots is that they may be difficult to find. A visitor may not know that a specific part of the image is interactive. As with other visual interaction interfaces, it is important to provide redundancy for hot spots through text links.

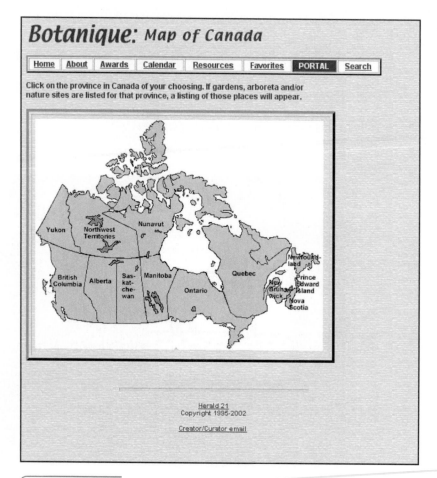

FIGURE 6–23 Hot spots as links: Herald 21 (*www.botanique.com*)

On the Botanique site, the visitor is able to click on each state to access information on gardens, arboreta, and nature sites in that state. Instructions to this effect are provided above the map (see Figure 6–23).

Menus: Drop-Down and Pop-Up

A menu refers to a list of choices. By that token, any list of links displayed on a web page is a menu. However, we will limit our definition to a drop-down or pop-up list that is invoked by clicking or rolling the mouse over a link. A drop-down menu is the list that drops down (see Figure 6–24). On the other hand, a pop-up list appears next to or above the link. The function of both types of menus is the same—the difference is in where they are positioned in terms of the link.

The advantage of the menu is that it does not occupy too much space and can be positioned just about anywhere on the screen. Once the menu pops up (at the click of the mouse or when the mouse moves over the link), the visitor sees a list and can select one of the items by clicking on it. The menu disappears from the screen as soon as the cursor moves out of the menu window or when the visitor clicks outside it.

FIGURE 6–24 The drop-down menu: the Jane Goodall Institute (*www.janegoodall.org*)

Site Map

As the name suggests, the site map is a visual representation of the organization of content on a site. A site map can be presented using many different formats. Indented text and a visual chart are two common formats. The site map presents the complete site structure at a glance. It helps the visitor get a clear mental picture (cognitive map) of the contents of the site. In addition, the site map allows the visitor to quickly jump to any section of the site without wading through the hierarchy in which the content is organized (see Figures 6–25 and 6–26).

Attributes of Navigation Tools

What we have seen so far are the options for designing navigation on a web page. The designer needs to further determine the features of these tools. As you read through these guidelines, you will come across the concept of consistency again and again. One of the easiest ways of avoiding confusion in navigation is to keep the navigation interface consistent. This is also one of the guidelines that is commonly ignored.

Sequence

As a visitor moves from one page to another, if the sequence in which the links are displayed keeps changing, it can cause significant confusion. In the example

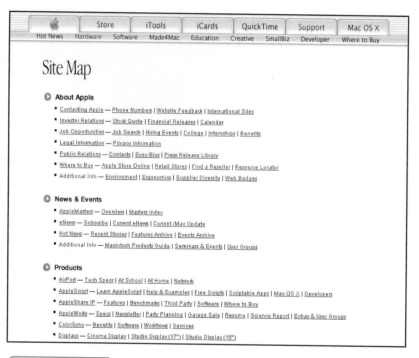

FIGURE 6-25 Text-based site map: Apple Computer Inc. (*www.apple.com*)

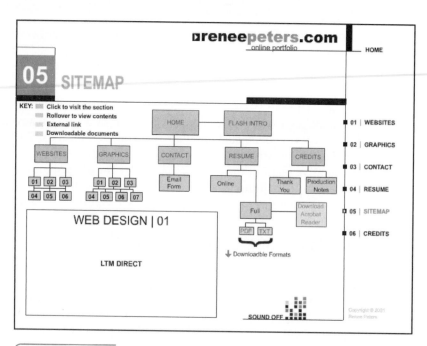

FIGURE 6-26 Visual site map: Renee Peters (*www.reneepeters.com*)

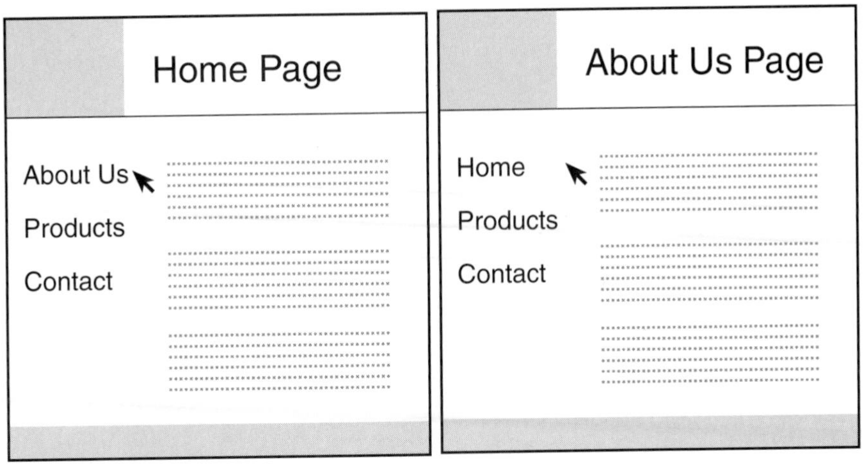

FIGURE 6–27   Inconsistent links

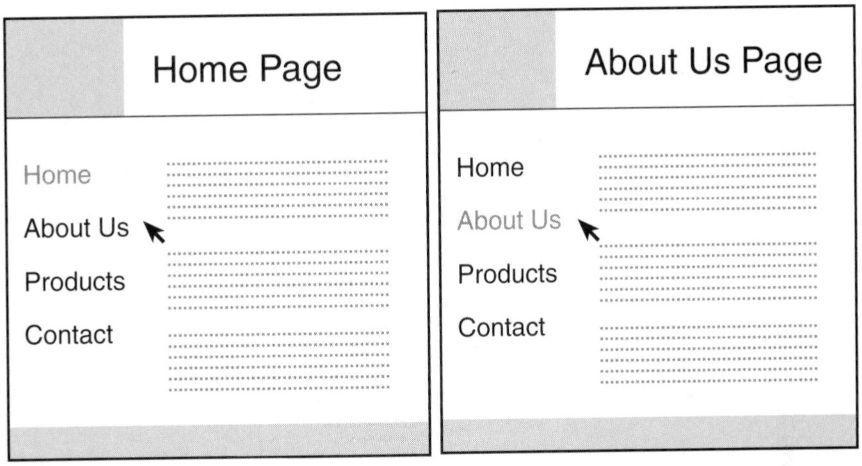

FIGURE 6–28   Consistent links

shown in Figure 6–27, assume that the visitor clicks on the About Us link on the Home page. On the About Us page, the cursor is still in the same position, but it is now over the Home link. This kind of inconsistency in sequence of the links means that on each page the visitor will need to create a new mental map for navigating through the site. Needless to say, that is an unnecessary cognitive overhead. Maintaining consistency in the sequence in which the links are displayed across the whole site is one of the basic tenets of good interface design. See how the consistency issue is addressed in Figure 6–28.

Location and Size

A designer grapples with the positioning of the links. It does not matter what form (text, button, icon, image, menu) they are. There are times when a designer

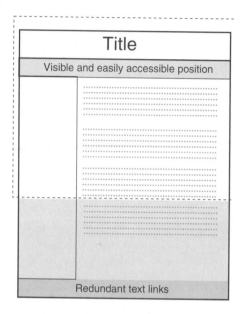

will spend hours trying to figure out the best place to put a link. The ease of finding and using the links on a site is one of the most important factors that affect usability.

The links on a web page need to be visible and apparent as soon as someone visits the page. Designers need to ensure that they follow principles of information design (perceptual organization) when selecting the position for links on a page. Often, designers can get caught up with the aesthetics of the layout and ignore the importance of usability and "stick" the links where they look good rather than where they "work" good.

There are web pages that "hide" the links so that you need to scroll down to click on them. It is possible that the visitor will not be aware of the existence of these links and will leave the site because of the difficulty in finding the links. Some web sites put the links on the right side of the page. If the visitor resizes the browser window and the page is not designed to be scalable (layout gets resized along with the page), it is entirely possible that the links will be hidden from the visitor's view. Still other pages display the links only as images and thereby make the page inaccessible to visually impaired visitors and visitors using text browsers.

Although redundancy can be somewhat boring, it is a good idea to provide the same global text links on a page. Often, these links are displayed at the bottom of the page (see Figure 6–29). In addition to making the page more accessible, this allows the visitor who has scrolled down to the bottom of the page to access the links without having to scroll all the way back to the top of the page.

Although links need to be visible, they should not occupy too much screen estate. The reason is that the links should become an intuitive and noninterfering navigation tool. If they occupy too much space, they will detract the visitor's attention from the content on the page, force the visitor to scroll, and represent unsophisticated design sensibilities (see Figure 6–30).

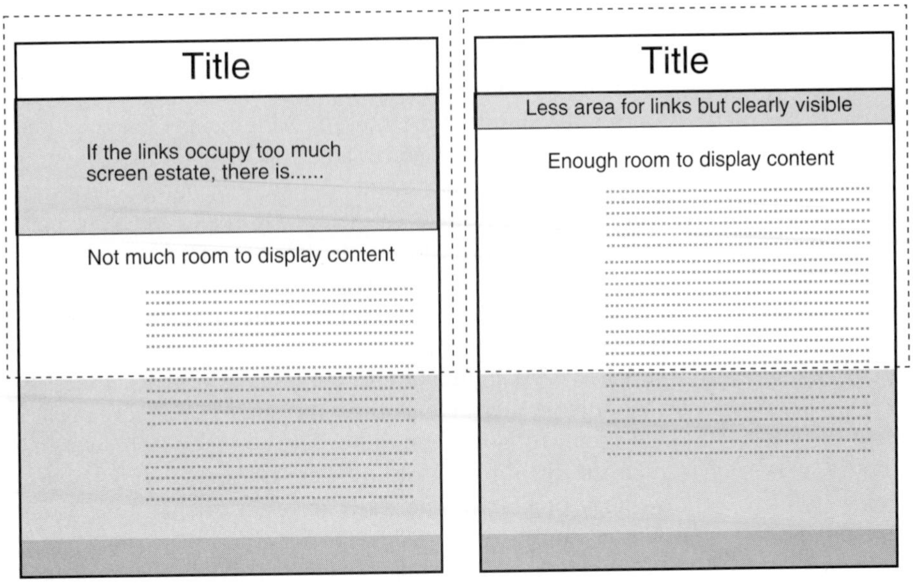

FIGURE 6–30 Space occupied by links

Link Status Indication

Traditional software applications and multimedia titles have used creative strategies for indicating the following states of links (regardless of what format they are presented in):

- Display of available links (links that a user could click on)
- Currently available link (the link on which the cursor is positioned)
- Feedback indicating that a link has been activated (after the mouse click)
- Selected link (for the section that the visitor is currently viewing)
- Not available links (the link is not available on this page)
- Visited links (the links that the visitor has clicked on earlier)

Until recently, technology limited what one could do with interactive interfaces on a web site. However, now, with tools such as DHTML and Macromedia Flash, designers are able to visualize and deploy many creative approaches to interactive interfaces.

The latest tools allow designers to push the envelope and create interesting and effective interfaces. However, certain basic guidelines apply to designing these interfaces regardless of the tools used to develop them.

Let us first consider the selected link. On a web page with text links, the browser automatically changes the link color once it has been selected (see Figure 6–31). This provides an indication of links you have clicked on earlier. The designer's decision is limited to the colors for the link, the active link, and the visited link. However, when the link is represented by an image or is coded using dynamic HTML, the designer could change the color, add an element, modify the texture, and do a hundred other things to indicate that it is currently selected.

As we have seen earlier, consistency in treatment is important. The treatment that indicates "currently selected link" should be uniform across all links.

An indication of availability is another important consideration. The browser provides the standard method of changing the arrow cursor to the hand icon each time it moves over an available text or image link. Conventionally, the browser also underlines the text that is linked. Lately, designers have used newer technologies to create innovative rollover interfaces. "Rollover" refers to a change on the screen when the cursor is positioned on a specific object or area of the screen. A simple rollover results in a change in the image that the cursor is positioned on (see Figure 6–32). However rollovers could also include an audio cue or display of information on a different part of the screen.

A small but significant design issue to bear in mind is that the "rollover image" should *not* be the same as the "currently selected image." If the two are the same, the visitors will not get an immediate cue about which item is currently selected and which they could click on. Although designers often resort to this to optimize the download time, it may be better to select smaller images that are different and avoid potential confusion.

FIGURE 6–31

Currently selected link

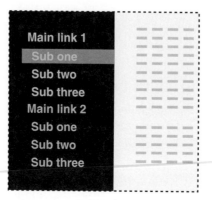

FIGURE 6–32

Cursor rollover with item description

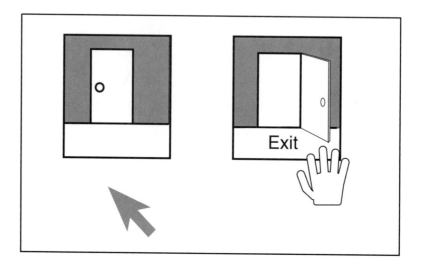

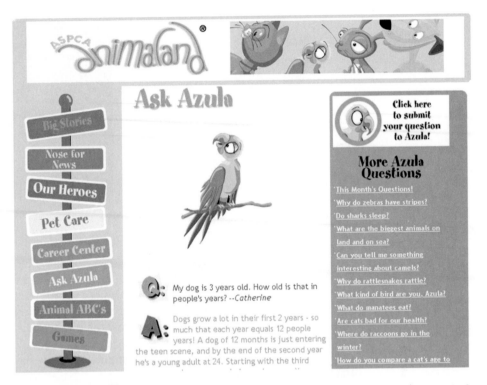

Link Association

An important interface feature is to clearly define the association between the link item (text, icon, image, menu) and its sublinks and also between the link item and its destination page. Color, lines, and text cues are effective methods of achieving this.

Color can be an effective navigation cue. For example, the prominent color of the link image (or icon) could be the color of the title or background of the page to which the image is linked. Such cues create a mental association between links and their destinations without a deliberate effort on the part of the visitors. In the Animaland web site, the color of the link is used prominently on the page it links to (red color of the link is used on the page Ask Azula) (see Figure 6–33).

Another use of color is to show relationship between the main link and the sublinks. This is achieved by using the same background or foreground color for both. Figure 6–34 shows how this can be achieved.

The previous discussion attempts to provide guidelines and considerations when making critical visual design decisions. Considering that the web is still an evolving medium and there is a lot that is still to be discovered about it, evaluation of the interface is just as important as the guidelines that drive the design. We will discuss evaluation in Chapter 8 and examine methods of ensuring that creative design can also be usable design.

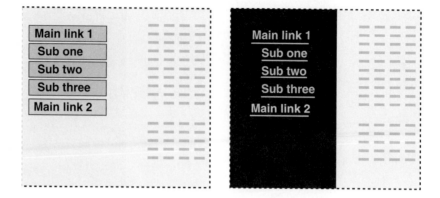

ANIMATION

For a long time, the web was beset with the problem of tacky animations. The early web designers literally stuck animations on a page without heed to their impact or effectiveness. Newer web sites have started to use sophisticated animation for presentation of information, for interactivity, and for grabbing the attention of the visitor.

Animation can help create a rich media experience, but it can also be rather distracting. A constantly moving and changing image in any part of the screen can distract attention and cause strain to the eye.

When using animation on a web page, it is important to determine whether it will help in creating more effective communication. Animation can be used effectively to gain and maintain attention, illustrate a concept or process, and provide an innovative method of interacting with the web page. Technologies such as Macromedia Flash and Adobe LiveMotion provide a powerful means of creating these attractive interfaces. However, the designer often needs to provide alternate web pages, as some installed browsers may still not be capable of displaying the animation without installing a plug-in. The use of such media also creates a challenge of accessibility for visitors who can read only text-based content. Further, the time required to download rich media content is still significantly higher than that for simple text-based pages. With increased bandwidth and better compression technologies, this problem may disappear. Until then, the use of rich media (animation, audio and video) content on a web site needs to be driven by considered assumptions about the type of platforms, technologies, and access abilities that the targeted visitors are likely to have.

AUDIO AND VIDEO

Just as animation can help create a richer, more meaningful and enjoyable experience for the visitor, audio and video content can also enhance and support the communication.

Better bandwidth capability, coupled with smarter plug-in technologies, has made it possible to serve audio and video content on web pages.

Although there is little doubt that audio and video can add significantly to the message and experience of the web visitor, designers do need to be aware of the bandwidth limitations of the target audience. They also need to consider the fact that the visitors will need to install a plug-in. Consequently, a cost-benefit analysis similar to the one described in the earlier section should be used to determine the importance of serving rich media content on a web site.

So far, we have examined the issues and considerations that could form the basis for decisions taken by interface designers. Let us now discuss the documentation of these decisions. The design concept note, storyboards (or comps), and production specifications are generated during the design process, and these documents help communicate the design concepts and aid the production process.

DESIGN CONCEPT NOTE

The concept note captures the thoughts and decisions about design. It serves as a guiding document for future design modifications and decisions. In some ways, this is like the mission and vision statement for an organization. Mission and vision statements guide the strategies, structure, and processes within an organization. Similarly, the design concept note guides decisions about design. Considering this, it is important that the clients contribute to it and most certainly approve it before the design process gets too far. Some topics that could be included in the design concept note are given in the following lists. For each topic, illustration of the approach or examples from similar sites could be provided.

Branding and Identity
- How will branding and identity be achieved on the site?
- What are some critical imperatives for branding (color, logo, icons, metaphors)?

Graphic Style and Typography
- What graphic style and typography will be used on the site?
- Why have these styles been selected?

Layout
- What will be the standard components of the web pages on the site?
- What is the approach to the use of white space in layout? Why?
- How will information on the pages be organized and presented (headings, images, text, columns, footer, links)?
- What identifiers will be used for different sections of the page (icons, text heading, color)?
- What is the approach to scrolling pages? Why?
- Where will the navigation elements be displayed?
- Will the site make use of pop-up windows? For what functions, and why?

Colors
- What colors will be used on the site? Why?
- Provide a color swatch that represents these colors.
- Will certain colors be used for headings, backgrounds, images, and so on?

Interaction and Links
- How will links be represented (text, icons, buttons, image map)
- How will the different states of the interactions (available, active, selected) be represented?

CONCEPT BOARDS (COMPS)

Concept boards visually represent the layout, colors, graphics, images, and input fields on a web page. They are similar to the storyboards that are traditionally used in film, video, and animation work. Film, video, and animation storyboards assume a fixed display area and need to indicate change in scene over time. On the other hand, web concept boards need to consider the possibility of scrolling pages and the integration of animated content within relatively "static" content on each discrete page. Many organizations use the word "comps" to refer to the concept board.

Ideally, all unique page layouts on the web site are designed, and production specifications for these pages are worked out. After this activity is completed, the production of graphic and media assets and programming and integration activities for the web site commence.

Four levels of detail could be associated with this stage: the roughs, the wire frame, the formal visual concept board (comps), and the production specifications.

Rough Storyboard

Roughs could be just scribbles on the back of a paper napkin. Alternately, they could be rough illustrations in the designer's sketchbook. The design team could also work together and brainstorm about the layout and create rough sketches on a white board. These explorations and experimentation in design—the beginning of a creative process—capture random thoughts. Most successful designers generate several concepts at this stage and then further develop a few of them in the next stage (wire frame). By and large, this can be the most enjoyable design stage, as you can conceptualize under minimum constraints and have fun experimenting with ideas (see Figure 6–35).

FIGURE 6–35

Roughs

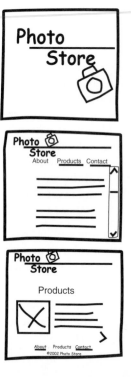

Wire Frames

The wire frame for a web page is a formal outline of the layout for the page. Relative positions of page elements are identified, but without specific details such as color and illustrations. The exercise allows the designer to create a layout structure for the web pages. The wire frames can be evaluated for consistency, space available for display of important elements, relative positioning of items (information design), functionality of interactive elements, and so on (see Figure 6-36). The wire frame serves as a blueprint for development of the final visual concept boards or comps.

FIGURE 6-36

Wire frames

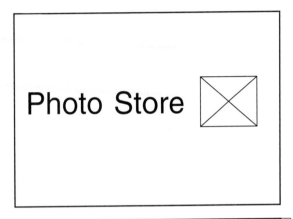

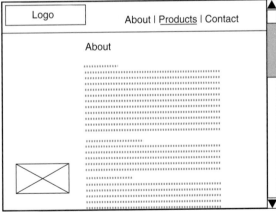

Visual Concept Board (comps)

The visual concept boards (also called comps) capture the design specifications: colors, layout, typography, and interactivity (see Figure 6-37). Many variations of the visual concept board are in use in the industry:

▶ The paper concept boards that are mounted on single matte boards
▶ A series of paper concept boards that are mounted on a large matte board
▶ A flip book of concept boards in a folder
▶ An electronic "slide show" representing different pages of the site

FIGURE 6–37

Visual concept boards (comps)

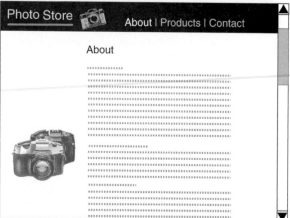

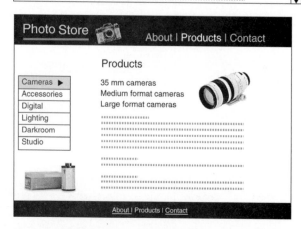

FIGURE 6–38

Design concepts:
PMG.net
(*www.pmg.net*)

FIGURE 6–38

Design concepts:
PMG.net
(*www.pmg.net*)

I personally find the electronic slide show with image-mapped links between different pages to be the most effective method of presenting visual concept boards. However, in some instances, large-size printed concept boards mounted on a matte board have been more effective.

Concept boards are used to share the design concepts with the client and obtain approval for the design before moving on to the next stage. Some designers present more than one design concept to the client and invite the client to select one. Often, the process of getting approval for a design concept can become drawn out and lengthy. The process can become more efficient if the designer presents the pros and cons of each design and talks (walks) the client through the process of identifying the most appropriate design. The evaluative comments from select members of the target audience and heuristic evaluation done by design experts could also help in this process. Figure 6–38 shows two of more than six design concepts that PMG.net developed for its own web site.

Production Specifications

Whereas the visual concept boards present the look, feel, and personality of the pages, the production specifications identify the attributes of individual elements of a web page (image dimensions, color values, table structure, Cascading Style Sheets, HTML structure). The specifications are used by the team in producing the media assets (icons, illustrations, photographs, animations) and integrating them on a web page.

Because the application program and web page scripts are closely tied to the functionality and layout of the web, the systems analyst and programmers are also involved at this stage. The systems analyst works on the technical feasibility and application design document. The process is very extensive and is usually executed by highly skilled information technology professionals.

INTERFACE PROTOTYPE

The interface prototype (also called mock-up) is a functional subset of the complete site. It represents the navigation, interaction, copy style, look and feel, and personality of the site. In addition to providing the designers and the client a means of experiencing the final site, the interface prototype allows the team to establish the technical feasibility for the web site.

When a team develops the interface prototype, they are in effect going through a representative experience of developing the site. All aspects of development (information architecture, software application design, interface design, media production, copy, security of the data, hosting) come together in an experience that is representative of developing the complete site.

The prototype includes pages that are unique and would need to be evaluated (and approved by the client). For example, a prototype for an e-commerce site could have the splash page, the home page, an item selection and features page, the shopping cart and checkout page, and the confirmation-of-order page. As you can see, all the unique experiences on the site are captured in the prototype.

We saw earlier that the copy for the site could be written and presented to the client along with the navigation prototype. Although this would be ideal, it may not always be possible because of the time required for research and information gathering. So, if the copy has not been presented earlier, it should be presented along with the interface prototype. Whereas the industry has paid a lot of attention to the visual experience of a site, writing for the web has not been as hotly discussed. This is somewhat regrettable because most of the information-rich content on web pages is delivered via text. Because of this, the copy of a web site is also a strategic design decision. The style, tone, format, organization, and quantity of text are just as important as the graphic and media elements of a web page. We will discuss this in some detail in Chapter 7.

As with any other production process, the prototype needs to go through quality assurance and testing before it is evaluated and presented to the client.

Ideally, the prototype should be taken through a thorough usability and heuristic evaluation. This is a good time to identify flaws and shortcomings in the interface and fix them. Failure to do so at this stage can result in costly rework after the complete site has been developed. Unfortunately, a number of clients (and many designers) fail to see the value of conducting the evaluation at this stage. One of the most common reasons for this resistance is the extra time and budget that would be required to conduct the evaluation. Fortunately, a number of smart-thinking clients and designers have started to insist on doing the evaluation at this stage. We will discuss various methods of evaluation in Chapter 8.

The evaluation results are presented to the client along with the interface prototype. The client needs to formally approve the interface prototype. In the interest of project efficiency and completion, it is important that neither the client nor the developer change the specifications after the prototype has been approved. Changes in content structure, navigation, copy style, and interface design after this stage can prove to be very expensive in terms of time and effort for both the developer and the client.

PRODUCTION CONSIDERATIONS

An important consideration during the design process is the practicality of design. Sometimes it may be a simple issue, such as understanding how an image is going to be sliced and re-created using a table. At other times, it may be a complex issue, such as understanding how a web page is going to be dynamically generated from a database. A designer cannot be expected to know all the technological intricacies that will form the backbone of the site. However, it is critical that the design be examined for technical and implementation feasibility before it is finalized.

As we saw earlier, in projects that have substantial back-end technology, this task is undertaken by the systems analyst. The technical feasibility and application design establish the technical approach, requirements, and resources that will be essential to implement the site. Sophisticated software design tools could be used to complete the technical feasibility and application design process. In this book, we will not go into any further detail with regard to technical solutions to web site development. However, designers need to recognize that there is a specialized skill set that will go into arriving at this solution, and they need to learn to create designs that work well with the technical solutions for a web site.

The process of web design is certainly a creative one. However, there is a lot of tedium that goes into converting a good creative concept into a workable and usable web site. Effective web project teams develop and adhere to production documents throughout the project cycle. These documents include production specifications, file naming conventions, backup logs, copy style guide, version tracking, and so on.

At the beginning of this chapter, we asked the question about whether web design is an art or a science. I doubt whether we have yet arrived at a definitive conclusion. Designing effective web interfaces is a matter of finding the right balance between creativity, aesthetics, functionality, usability, technology, copy, communication media, and the content (or the message). And it takes both art and science to arrive at this balance.

SUMMARY

In this chapter, we examined various considerations that go into the interface design of a web site. Although creativity is important in designing a web site, the most important consideration is that the design contributes toward achieving the communication objective of the site. We looked at the process of carrying out interface design and established the importance of concept boards, production specifications, and the interface prototype. This chapter focused mainly on visual design, but it is important to note that over the next few years, the web is likely to become capable of delivering rich "multimedia" content. It is thus important to consider the role that animation, audio, and video could play in enhancing and supporting the effectiveness of communication on a web site.

Good design necessitates that design decisions are validated through a formal or informal evaluation with the target audience and design experts. This is even more critical in web design because the field is young, and well-researched, empirically tested design principles for the web have yet to be established.

REFERENCES

Graham, Lisa. (1999). *The principles of interactive design.* New York: Delmar Publishers.

Head, Alison. (1999). *Design wise.* Medford, NJ: CyberAge Books.

Lynch, Patrick, & Horton, Sarah. (1999). *Web style guide.* New Haven, CT: Yale University Press.

GUIDING QUESTIONS

▌ What is the relationship between usability and aesthetic design on a web site?

▌ What is interface design? What is its role in web design?

▌ In your opinion, is interface design an art or a science?

▌ What are some common problems with interface design on a web site?

▌ What can an interface designer do to enhance the ease of navigation on a web site?

▌ What role could animation, audio, and video play on an entertainment site, a training site, and an e-commerce site?

▌ Describe the function and use of the following:
  ▌ Design concept note
  ▌ Roughs
  ▌ Wire frames
  ▌ Visual concept boards (comps)
  ▌ Production specifications
  ▌ Interface prototype

▌ What kind of evaluation should you do before presenting the interface prototype to the client for approval?

EXERCISES

▌ What is a metaphor? Find a web site that uses a metaphor and analyze its effectiveness.

▌ Imagine that you are coaching a novice interface designer. What aspects should he or she consider when starting out on the interface design?

▌ Assume that you have been invited to present a design concept to a client for an on-line magazine. Use the navigation concept you developed in Chapter 5 and design three possible page layouts for the site. For each design, prepare a design concept note outlining your reasons for the specific layout, graphic style, typography, and colors. If you had to convince the client to select one design, which would it be? Why?

Writing for the Web

Writing has long been the domain of journalists, scriptwriters, fiction writers, and technical writers who have traditionally written for print, radio, film, and video. Some of these professionals have now migrated to writing for the web. In doing so, they have had to recast their writing approach to take advantage of the communication opportunities offered by the new medium and also work within the constraints of screen-based communication.

Print refers to media such as newspapers, magazines, and books that communicate primarily through text supported by images. On the other hand, time-based media, such as radio, television, and film, are essentially sensory in nature and communicate through the audio and visual content.

In this chapter, we look at a few unique aspects of writing for the web. But before we do that, let us examine how print, time-based media, and the web compare as modes of communication (see Table 7–1).

Writing for the web is one of the most important and yet one of the most neglected design fields. The number of books and web sites on "visual design of the web" far outnumber the publications on "writing for new media." This is somewhat unfortunate because the primary means of message composition and communication on the web continues to be the "written word."

If we observe someone going through a web site and closely watch his or her reading behavior, what are we likely to see?

- We may notice that visitors rarely read all the text on the screen. They mostly scan the text. They read a paragraph word for word only if something catches their attention or if they are searching for specific information.
- We may find that visitors scroll down only if the initial copy engages their attention and leads them down below the visible page. This means that sometimes they may miss information that is accessible only by scrolling.
- We may see that if the visitors have to make an effort to read text (because of size and color problems), they give up easily and very often exit the site.

You may find that similar behaviors can be observed with any medium that uses writing as a significant means of communication. You may also argue that some of

TABLE 7–1 Print, Time-Based Media, and the Web: A Comparison

Factor	Print	Time-Based Media	Web
Attention	Readers anticipate reading as their primary activity. Patience and a somewhat relaxed absorption of the message can be assumed.	Viewers have a short attention span. The nature of the medium suggests that reading is not a primary mode of communication.	Visitors have a short attention span. In most cases, surfing is purposeful, and finding and carrying out a task in the shortest possible time is important to the user.
Senses	The primary means of communication is the written word. The text is supported by visual imagery. The medium incorporates passive interactivity.	The message is invariably composed through a juxtaposition of visual and auditory communication. The medium incorporates passive interactivity.	While there is potential for communication through the audio/visual mode, the message is conveyed primarily through text (written word). A typical message is a composite of multisensory communication, interactions, and reading.
Continuity	The message has a distinct flow and continuity. Narrative is an important component. Communication is essentially linear.	The message has a distinct flow and continuity. The message is composed through a well-knit narrative. The communication is essentially linear.	The message is invariably broken into bits of information that may be accessed in a nonlinear fashion. Several parts make a whole, though there may be a narrative that ties it all together.
Richness of media	The medium affords a one-way flow of information through words and images.	Rich media could be used but without immersive interactivity.	The possibilities are endless: multimedia and interactivity. There is high potential for active participation of the visitor in communication.
Ability to read	The medium relies on the reader's ability to read.	Ability to read is not always critical.	The medium relies on the visitor's ability to read and interact with the message as well as manage the technology.
Familiarity with the medium	The medium is usually very simple to use.	The medium requires minimal familiarity with equipment (though some high-tech audio/visual devices are rather complicated).	The visitors are expected to be comfortable with the browser interface and be able to use the computer.

the problems identified here are problems not of "writing" but of interface design. A deeper analysis may also indicate that some of these issues are closely linked with the way information is structured on the web site (information design).

In all cases, your observations would be accurate. It is difficult to attribute the effectiveness of the web exclusively to any one design element. The web's effectiveness is governed by how the different components of the site work together in communicating a message. It is thus important that each component is carefully crafted to work with the other components. In the next few paragraphs, we examine the challenges faced by web writers and some tools and guidelines that could aid them in creating an effective and efficient communication design for the web.

THE CHALLENGES TO A WEB WRITER

Web writers have some unique issues to bear in mind, especially if they are trained and experienced in writing for other media.

Roles of Designers

As we have seen earlier, design for the web (information architecture, interface, media, copy, software application design) requires a synergy between the different professionals on the team. A web writer has to work closely with the interface designer, the application programmer, the client, and most of all the information architect.

As we examine aspects of writing for the web, we must keep in mind that the web writer's role is not limited to writing copy. The writer may be involved in researching the content, preparing the proposal for the client, contributing to information architecture, and writing the treatment statement, the design concept document, and the script for the site.

The challenges are in working with the different team members, having a clear understanding of their roles, developing a holistic view of the purpose of the web site, and being able to integrate written communication skills in this melange in a creative and effective manner.

Site Objectives and Communication Strategy

As with any other design activity, the web writer needs to first understand the purpose of the web site. The writer also needs a thorough understanding of the target audience. The communication strategy needs to be built on the basis of this knowledge.

For example, the purpose of an e-learning site could be to foster comprehension, retention, and generalization. The copy style, navigation control, type of interactivity, response–feedback dialogue, and intervention of media will need to focus on achieving these goals for a specific audience.

The tutorials on WebMonkey (*www.hotwired.lycos.com/webmonkey/programming/javascript/index.html*) attempt to do just that. R. Venkatesh and M. Nichani (*www.elearningpost.com/elthemes/monkey2.asp*) identify the following writing features that make these tutorials effective:

- Bite-size bits (breaking the content into smaller bits using bullets, paragraphs, and tables)
- Inverted pyramid (putting the most salient message first and then building the details)
- Writing style (first person, conversational, personal)
- Hyperlinks (allowing visitors to check out further details about specific topics and words)

Similarly, on an e-commerce site, every design element (including copy) focuses on comprehension, persuasion, and action (see Figure 7–1). The writing on the site is succinct and attractive, and most important it addresses the anticipated concerns

FIGURE 7–1 The copy focuses on comprehension, persuasion, and action: Shoebuy.com (*www.shoebuy.com*)

of the visitor (e.g., discount, savings, tracking an order, return policies, shipping, secure credit card transactions, salient features of the products).

Interactivity and Nonlinear Navigation

Interactivity and nonlinear navigation set the web apart from most other modes of communication. As we know well, human beings are prone to free association of thoughts. All of us tend to jump from one thought to another while participating in any communication activity (reading, watching television, or even talking). On one hand, the nonlinear navigation on the web encourages free association. However, it can also hinder comprehensive communication of one composite message. The web writer has to anticipate this possibility and attempt to communicate in the short bursts of attention that the web site is likely to get from its visitors. In some ways, interactivity and nonlinear navigation result in a double-edged sword. On the one hand, they may interfere with continuity of a message; on the other, they allow control to the visitor in accessing the desired information. The challenge to the web writer is to create an effective communication while allowing for the requisite freedom of navigation and also maintaining continuity in the message.

Writing for Many Media

Web writers need to be conversant not only with writing copy for web pages but also with how to integrate multimedia content on web pages. This means that they need to be able to visualize the copy for the web pages as well as the audio and video components of the message. Web writers thus need to be familiar with the guidelines for writing for a variety of media and have the skill to weave a comprehensive message using these different media.

Having examined some of the challenges of writing for the web, let us consider specific activities that could help enhance a web writer's efficiency and effectiveness during the message design process.

DOCUMENTATION

As we saw at the beginning of this chapter, the web writer is likely to be involved not only in writing the copy for the web site but also in information architecture, writing the proposal, writing the concept note, and so on. In fact, some projects involve the web writer in generating all relevant documentation. In this section, we briefly discuss four outputs that the web writer is closely linked with or directly responsible for.

Site Map

We discussed site maps in some detail in Chapter 5. The web writer uses the site map as a starting point in developing the copy for the site. As we saw in Chapter 5, it is a good idea to integrate the copy into the navigation prototype. The client thus gets a clear picture of how the site will be organized and also what message, content, or activity will be incorporated on specific pages.

Design Concept Note

The design concept note captures the approach to designing the web site. It is among the first few documents that are generated during the course of development. It identifies the objectives and target audience for the site, the creative concept, writing style, and approaches to interactivity and navigation. The web writer works with the creative director in collating this information and presents it in a comprehensive document. The design concept note is used to communicate the approach to the client and serves as a guiding document for future design decisions in the project.

Style Guide

As its name suggests, the style guide specifies the way in which words will be spelled, punctuated, and capitalized. For example, there could be many ways of writing time: 1:10 PM, 13:10, 1.10 P, and so on. The style guide specifies how time is to be represented on the web site. Having this specification reduces the chance of similar information being presented in different formats on a site.

The style guide specifies not only the format but also language style. For example, if the primary audience for the site is Australian, it would be important to use Australian spelling and language style (e.g., "Howdy mate" instead of "Hi, how are you"; "organise" instead of "organize"; "centre" instead of "center"; and so on).

TABLE 7–2 A Template for a Web Script

Page/Filename	Script	Production Notes
Home page (*index.html*)	Welcome to the web site of the friends theater . . . <Photograph of a stage performance> On this web site, you will find . . . *Be sure to visit the virtual gallery . . .*	Stage performance file name: stage.jpg On Virtual gallery, go to *virtual.html*

Script

The script is a tool for capturing the time-based flow of events as well as specific words, images, and sounds that will occur along this time line. The script and the storyboard are the guiding documents for video, film, and audio productions. The same is true for the web. However, the challenge is compounded by the fact that a web page needs to be represented in many different dimensions. One is the display of headings, subheadings, graphics, photographs, text, audio, and video. Another is the interactivity that takes place in terms of navigation and user input. Yet another is the linear time-based flow of the audio and video components that are integrated within the page. The web writer visualizes and captures all these details in a web script.

You may want to keep in mind that the content for some web sites that are template driven is served from a database. Such sites may not require a script. These sites are planned in such a way that specific parts of the web page are generated from a database where content is stored. For such sites, instead of a script, the web writer would write and edit the content that is stored in these databases.

Many different formats for the web script are in use in the industry. In many instances, the detailed audio, video, and animation scripts are done separately. The master script will indicate the place where these media assets are to be integrated. Table 7–2 shows an example of a template for a web script.

As you can see, writing for the web is a complex task. The challenge is compounded by the fact that the medium is still evolving. The guidelines and suggestions given in the next section may help a web writer face these challenges.

GUIDELINES FOR THE WEB WRITER

A web writer faces a challenge not only from the nonlinear medium but also from the limitations imposed by technology, the unpredictable behavior of the visitors, and the need to communicate a large amount of information in limited space. In addition, the glamour of the web seems to be reserved for those working on the visual interface. In spite of these challenges, the role of the web writer is one of the most critical in web site design.

Do Thorough Research

As the popularity of the web increases, more people are relying on the web to gather information. Sometimes, critical life decisions are based on information gathered from the web. This puts added responsibility of ensuring accuracy and clarity in the communication. Among the first tasks a web writer should undertake for a site is thorough research of the content, the message, the objectives, and the target audience.

Be Succinct

For the most part, the web is not a place for lengthy narratives and complex exposition. Most visitors want to quickly find the information that is relevant to them without having to wade through a torrent of words. This is probably the biggest challenge to web writers: creating an effective message with few words but without sacrificing the beauty and elegance of language.

Keep It Simple

Not only do web writers need to keep it short, but they need to keep it simple as well. The language needs to match the literary capabilities of the target audience, and it needs to address the largest range of individuals in the audience. Use of jargon is very tempting, but a successful writer avoids it.

Use Pull Quotes or Sidebars

The use of pull quotes or sidebars is an effective way of addressing the fact that most people will not "read" all the text on the web page. Pull quotes stand apart, are brief, and provide an effective method of capturing the essence of the message. Pull quotes are also a good method of capturing attention, appealing to curiosity, and encouraging the visitors to read the copy (see Figure 7–2).

Break It Up

Large chunks of information are best presented by breaking them up. This can be achieved by using paragraphs, headings, subheadings, bulleted lists, and tables. Small chunks of information are easier to manage and also allow the visitors to quickly scan and focus on the information that is relevant to them.

Web writers often need to make a decision about whether the content should be presented on one page (increased scrolling) or on separate pages (greater number of clicks). Engaging the visitor's attention is the most important consideration in this decision. Scrolling down a page is not bad once the visitor has been drawn into reading it. Having attention-grabbing copy at the top of the page can help accomplish this.

Breaking the content up into separate pages can be problematic in maintaining continuity in the narrative. Thus, content is best separated when there is a logical break in the topic and the visitor is likely to get significant new information on the next page (see Figure 7–3).

FIGURE 7-2 Pull quote: The Rainforest Action Network (*www.ran.org*)

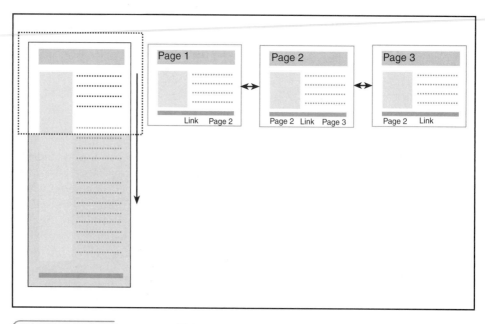

FIGURE 7-3 Scrolling versus multiple pages

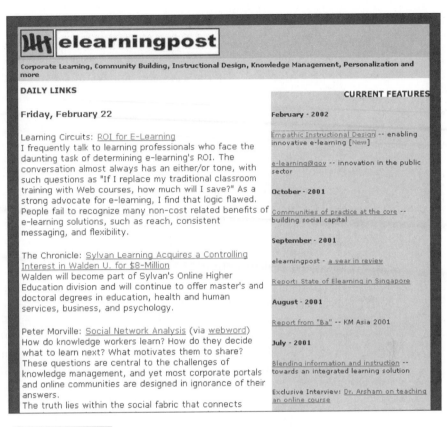

elearningpost

Corporate Learning, Community Building, Instructional Design, Knowledge Management, Personalization and more

DAILY LINKS

CURRENT FEATURES

Friday, February 22

February · 2002

Learning Circuits: ROI for E-Learning
I frequently talk to learning professionals who face the daunting task of determining e-learning's ROI. The conversation almost always has an either/or tone, with such questions as "If I replace my traditional classroom training with Web courses, how much will I save?" As a strong advocate for e-learning, I find that logic flawed. People fail to recognize many non-cost related benefits of e-learning solutions, such as reach, consistent messaging, and flexibility.

Empathic Instructional Design -- enabling innovative e-learning [New]

e-learning@gov -- innovation in the public sector

October · 2001

Communities of practice at the core -- building social capital

September · 2001

The Chronicle: Sylvan Learning Acquires a Controlling Interest in Walden U. for $8-Million
Walden will become part of Sylvan's Online Higher Education division and will continue to offer master's and doctoral degrees in education, health and human services, business, and psychology.

elearningpost - a year in review

Report: State of Elearning in Singapore

August · 2001

Report from "Ba" -- KM Asia 2001

Peter Morville: Social Network Analysis (via webword)
How do knowledge workers learn? How do they decide what to learn next? What motivates them to share? These questions are central to the challenges of knowledge management, and yet most corporate portals and online communities are designed in ignorance of their answers.
The truth lies within the social fabric that connects

July · 2001

Blending information and instruction -- towards an integrated learning solution

Exclusive Interview: Dr. Arsham on teaching an online course

FIGURE 7–4 Text links: ElearningPost (*www.elearningpost.com*)

Use Hyperlinks

One of the advantages of the medium is that you can link just about anything on a web page. Text-based hyperlinks make it possible to provide definitions, explanations, and links to different web pages within and outside the site. Providing these links affords a greater freedom of exploration to the web visitor. Text-based hyperlinks can also enhance brevity in a message because extended information could be provided through the links.

Although text-based hyperlinks can allow freedom of access to the visitors, too many hyperlinks on a page can also distract and confuse them. So we need to design the hyperlinks only for those words or phrases that warrant additional explanation or information (see Figure 7–4).

Start With the Message in a Capsule

We know that most visitors will scan the text before reading it. It thus makes sense to start a section with an encapsulated message. The details can then be elaborated in the following paragraphs. In his book *Designing Web Usability,* Jacob Nielson calls this approach the "inverted pyramid." The intent is to make sure that the visitors get the gist of the message at the very beginning. The message could then engage the visitors and encourage them to read on.

Cater to Varied Entry Points

Keep in mind that visitors may not enter the site on the home page. Search engines or bookmarks may lead a visitor directly to a page deep within the site. The copy on the page needs to provide adequate reference (or navigation) to allow the visitors to quickly get their bearings.

Be Consistent

Along with the visual layout of text, consistency is essential in copy tone (serious, humorous, personal, official, factual, poetic), usage style (use of hyphens, display of specific words and phrases) and spelling (British, American, Australian). The consistency concept is also important in the way titles and subtitles are worded and displayed. Style guides (discussed earlier) can help document some of these elements.

Localize Communication

One of the advantages of the web is that it has a global reach. This in turn can also become a challenge. The challenge is compounded not only because there are many languages and dialects but also because there are many local versions of each language. If the site is to "reach" visitors from various parts of the world, we need to consider the use of the local language and localize the communication to keep it culturally relevant. Alternately, it needs to be generalized (internationalized) to the point that it will appeal to all audiences.

In some cases, localization may mean creating an entirely different site for each geographical location using a completely different language, layout, imagery, and site structure. However, very often we can provide localization of language usage and culturally relevant imagery while retaining uniform structure, language, and treatment. As globalization of businesses through the web becomes more real, localization will become a more critical consideration in web design.

In Figure 7–5, we see that the Apple Computer sites for the United States and Mexico have similar layout and information architecture, but the sites have been "localized" in terms of the languages (English and Spanish).

Personalize Communication

A web site could provide the visitor an opportunity for digital voyeurism wherein he or she experiences the information created for "to whom it may concern." However, in many instances it may be possible to personalize communication (not just by addressing the visitor by his or her name) and address the visitor's needs and expectations. It is also possible to use personal pronouns (I, you, we) when addressing the visitor. For a web writer, this translates into giving a face to the site as well as providing direct communication with the visitor through the use of appropriate language.

Serving content that is most relevant to a specific visitor is another aspect of personalization. For example, the web site can recognize the individual and use preexisting profiling to determine the content to be displayed (e.g., the weather information for his or her city). This feature calls for complex front-end as well as back-end technologies. The feature also raises issues of privacy and the ethics associated with it.

FIGURE 7–5 Multiple-language versions: Apple Computer Inc. (*www.apple.com;* *www.apple.com/mx/*)

Weave the Message With Media

One of the biggest shortcomings of the web as a communication medium is that rarely do we find an integration of the different media in the message. The copy, the images, and the audiovisual media seem to stand on their own rather than work as a composite, integrated communication. Writing for the web cannot be considered in exclusion to the other media that will be used on the site. It is thus important to design a holistic communication that integrates all the media that compose the message for a site.

Run Spelling and Grammar Checks

Typographical and simple grammatical errors are common in the first draft of any professional's work. However, when these errors carry over to the web site, the presentation can easily lose its credibility. The first line of defense is to use a good word-processing program that can do the spelling and grammar checks.

Keep the Search Engines in Mind

The web writer is usually responsible for determining the keywords and description that will be embedded in the metatags (in the HTML code). Thus, the web writer needs to have a clear understanding of how search engines work and how best to include information so that the site receives a high ranking in search results.

Get the Copy Evaluated and Edited

Software applications are limited in their abilities and cannot be a substitute for someone reading the copy. Web writers can benefit significantly from a "manual" human evaluation of the spelling, grammar, style, meaning, and overall effectiveness of communication. A professional editor would be ideal, but having another person read the copy could also provide valuable feedback.

SUMMARY

Text continues to be a significant mode of communication on web sites. Web writers face the challenge of weaving a narrative in the face of the nonlinear and unpredictable navigation behavior of the site visitor. In many ways, web writing is similar to writing for print. Yet there are additional considerations, including the short attention span, the possibility of using more than one medium, the visual limitations of computer displays, and the difficulty of predicting the literary and language expertise of the visitor. The web writer needs to work closely with other members of the development team. Although the challenges are huge, following a few simple guidelines can help the web writer create an effective communication for the site.

REFERENCE

Nielson, Jacob. (2000). *Designing web usability.* New Riders Publishing, Indianapolis, Indiana.

GUIDING QUESTIONS

▶ What is the difference between writing for the web, for time-based media (radio, television, film), and for print?
▶ On a web development team, who will a web writer work closest with?
▶ What are some of the challenges a web writer faces when writing for a nonlinear interactive medium such as the web?
▶ What are some guidelines to bear in mind when writing copy for a web site?
▶ What are some typical deliverables from a web writer?

EXERCISE

Identify a site targeted at children, an e-commerce site, a brand site, and an event site. Compare the copy style on these four sites and analyze the appropriateness of the style for the site objectives and audience.

8

Measuring the Success of a Web Site

So far, we have examined the three main web design activities: information architecture, interface design, and copy writing. These activities, along with technical feasibility and application design, culminate in the development of an interface prototype. The prototype represents the experience of the final site and is evaluated, modified, and presented to the client for approval. Once it has been approved, the project moves into the production phase, where media assets are produced, application programs are developed, media assets are integrated into the front-end and back-end applications, and the integrated application is thoroughly tested. Quality assurance is one of the final activities before the site goes live.

At various stages in the project life cycle, there are opportunities to evaluate the concepts and outputs. As we have seen in the earlier chapters, the client is asked to formally approve the navigation prototype, design concept note, concept boards (comps), technical feasibility document, interface prototype, and the final site. A site that has been in use for a while can also be evaluated to establish its value. In addition to the evaluation done by the client, other methods can be used to systematically collect feedback and improve or establish the effectiveness of the web site.

In this chapter, we look at the following evaluation approaches: heuristic evaluation, focus groups, user feedback, traffic statistics and analysis, task completion on the site, number of inquiries generated by the site, revenue generated through the site, and usability evaluation. We discuss usability evaluation in some detail because formal or informal usability evaluation can make a significant positive difference to the effectiveness of your web site.

HEURISTIC EVALUATION

The phrase "heuristic evaluation" sounds loftier than what it actually represents. Heuristic evaluation refers to the process in which a group of experts uses a set of

141

criteria (heuristics) to evaluate specific features of a site (information design, textual communication, navigation, interaction design). The most commonly quoted set of principles (heuristics) for application software is based on the work of Nielson and Molich (1990). Over the past few years, other experts have identified a set of heuristics that could be used to evaluate specific aspects of web design (see the on-line article van der Geest and Spyridakis 2000).

The process of heuristic evaluation starts with the identification of experts who will carry out the evaluation. These experts may collectively determine a set of heuristics, or they may be given a set of heuristics that they will use to judge a web site. The following guidelines could be a part of such a set of heuristics:

- All elements on the page should be legible.
- Every media element on the page (illustration, photograph, video, audio) should be purposeful.
- The visitor should be able to determine the association between a link and its destination.
- The visitor should be able to access the home page from all sections (and pages) of the site.

The experts evaluate the site from the perspective of these heuristics. It is important to have more than one expert carry out this evaluation, as it increases the possibility of identifying a larger range of problems. The observations of the experts are collated, and a comprehensive heuristic evaluation report is generated.

Heuristic evaluation is especially useful for validating design decisions and identifying potential problem areas during the design stage. The method can also provide valuable inputs about the potential success of a web site after it has been completed.

FOCUS GROUPS

We have already discussed focus groups in Chapter 4. Just as focus groups could be used during requirements analysis to establish the need for a site, they could also be used to gather feedback on the site's design and organization during the design stage. Once the site has been hosted, the focus group could be called on to react to information architecture, interface design, technology requirements, and the general performance of the site.

The focus group could be composed of individuals with varied expertise (design, technology, information architecture, typical visitors, marketing strategists, and so on). The group is presented with the web site and its objectives. The members then express and discuss their opinions about the likelihood of success for the site. The process differs from heuristic evaluation in that the individuals in the focus group do not spend a significant time examining specific features from a particular perspective. Rather, the comments are more generic in nature and primarily opinion based.

Needless to say, the feedback of the focus group is likely to be general in nature. It is possible that the group would indicate potential success and problem areas that then require a follow-up study through the methods described in the next few paragraphs.

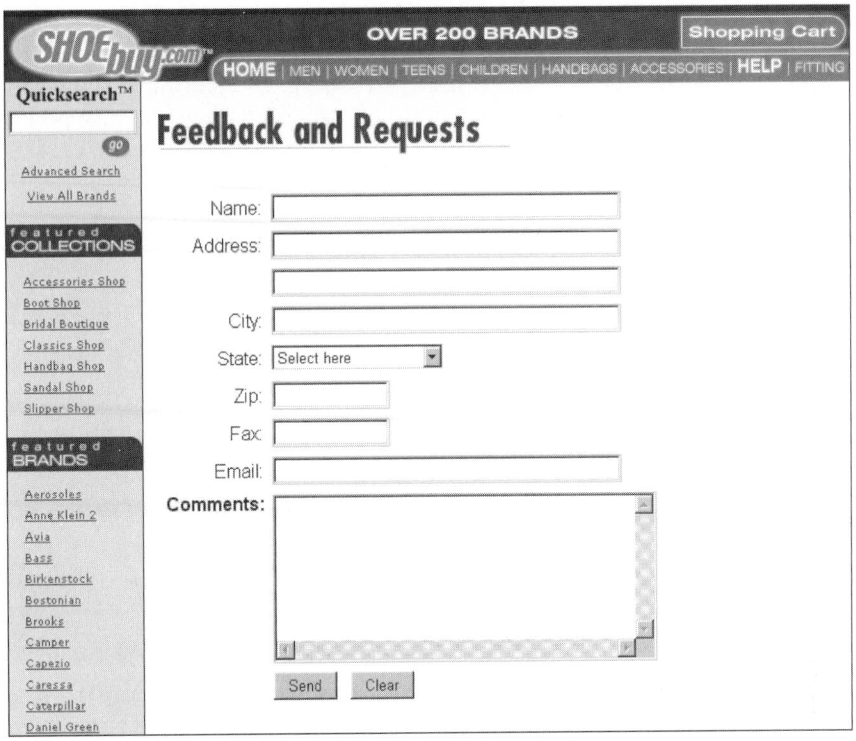

FIGURE 8–1   Feedback page: Shoebuy.com (*www.shoebuy.com*)

VISITOR FEEDBACK

In Chapter 5, we introduced visitor feedback as one of the components of a web page. It usually appears at the bottom of the page and encourages the visitor to send comments about the web site to the web master (see Figure 8–1).

There is no guarantee that visitors will actually click on this link and take the trouble to send their comments (it is kind of like writing a letter to the editor). However, there will always be a few who care enough (or are frustrated enough) to share their experience of using the site. These feedback messages can provide very good design insights. It would be worthwhile to collate these messages over time and examine them for trends and significant issues. Although the feedback messages may not result in a quantifiable and definitive conclusion about the success of the site, they can certainly indicate specific issues that beg attention.

TRAFFIC ANALYSIS

There are several ways of collating data on the traffic to a web site. Large sites may have a built-in engine that allows the web master to track the traffic. Service for tracking traffic is also available from specialized organizations (e.g., *www.hitlist.com*). The statistics can provide an indication of the profile of the

FIGURE 8–2

Traffic report:
Websidestory, Inc.
(*www.hitbox.com*)

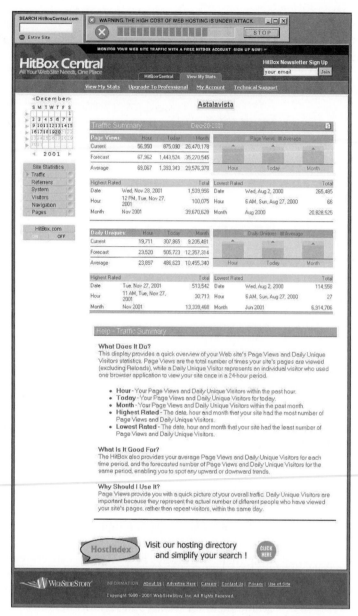

visitors to the site and their behavior on the site. This includes data such as the amount of time visitors spent on each page, the type of browser they use, the browser version, the country, the number of repeat visitors, and so on. A sample traffic report is shown in Figure 8–2.

Each item on the traffic report can potentially indicate a trend that could be further explored. For example, if your site is targeted at an Australian audience and you find that you are getting a lot of traffic from Australia using Flash plug-in, you could safely incorporate Flash content on your web site. On the other hand, if you find that most visitors are using older browsers and do not have the required plug-ins, you may want to reconsider the use of technologies that rely heavily on the presence of a plug-in.

TASK COMPLETION ON THE SITE

Business-to-customer e-commerce sites that have the objective of facilitating transactions could track successful completion of these transactions. For example, we may want to consider the percentage of visitors who successfully tracked the status of their order or placed an order for items selected for purchase.

INQUIRIES GENERATED THROUGH THE SITE

The actual number of inquiries generated from the site (about a product, service, organization, and so on) could be an indication of its success or failure. Analysis of where these inquiries are originating (a city or a country) could help devise a strategy for future enhancements to the site and the overall marketing strategy for the organization.

REVENUE GENERATED THROUGH THE SITE

If revenue generation is an objective of the site, it is possible to determine the actual revenue generated from the site and thereby arrive at a measure of its success. E-commerce sites would need to take this statistic as a critical measure of success.

USABILITY STUDY

Whereas all the previously discussed approaches are important indicators of the success of a site, the usability study is often used as a prediction and a diagnostic tool (see Figure 8–3). The usability study is a method of determining the effectiveness of a web site from the perspective of the user's experience.

The usability study plays an auditor's role in the development process. The study is conceived and conducted like a research study. Objectivity in design, data collection, and analysis is important. Consequently, an external expert is usually called on to conduct the usability study. The role of a usability expert is relatively new to the field of web development. However, in the past few years, several individuals have established themselves as usability consultants. These individuals have backgrounds in human factors engineering, instructional design, cognitive psychology, software application design, and interface design. Invariably, these individuals are trained and experienced in methods of social science research.

The usability study serves as a logical conclusion for two phases in a development cycle: after the interface prototype has been completed and after the site has been hosted. A site that scores highly on usability is likely to be successful in achieving the overall objective for which the client commissioned its development (e.g., increased revenue, brand awareness).

The usability study is valuable for "young" sites, but it often is critical for sites that have been around for a while. A usability study for such sites could serve a

FIGURE 8–3

Usability study and
project stages

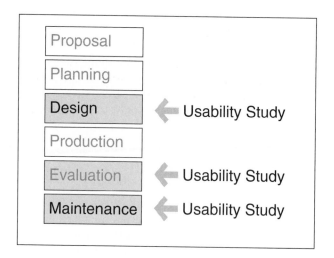

diagnostic purpose, in determining possible obstacles to successful achievement
of the site's objectives. For example, if traffic analysis indicates that visitors do not
access a particular section of the site at all, there may be a reason to conduct a usability study to find out the reasons for this behavior. On the other hand, even if
a site is meeting its target for revenue, it may be worthwhile to conduct a usability study to examine possible ways of incrementing revenue by "capturing" the
visitors who were turned away.

Although the term "usability" inherently indicates a utilitarian predisposition,
it is important that the study examine the totality of the experience. Over time, the
term "usability" may even get replaced by the term "experience." A comprehensive
usability study could examine the following issues:

- How easily visitors are able to learn to navigate through the site?
- How intuitive is the content structure?
- What are the specific trouble spots?
- How successful is the overall experience of visiting the site?

As you can see, the focus of the study is on the experiences of a visitor to the
site. The web development process attempts to *create* the most effective experience
for the visitor, in turn leading to achieving the business and communication objectives of the site. The usability study establishes the likelihood of success of a visitor's experience in the context of the business and communication objectives of
the site.

When we examine usability of a site, we must bear in mind that the visitors
could be broadly classified into two types: expert and novices. Expert visitors are
familiar with the web and experienced with navigating through different sites. These
visitors are likely to figure out the structure and navigation of a web site with relative ease. Expert visitors may expect shortcuts for navigation and transaction interactions on the site. The design objective of the site is to provide the expert visitor
with the features that make their experience on the site comfortable and not tedious.
On the other hand, novice visitors cannot be expected to be familiar or confident
with using the web and may take a while to reach the anticipated level of comfort.
The danger is in their getting frustrated and leaving the site (never to return) before

FIGURE 8–4

Level of comfort:
novice and expert
visitors

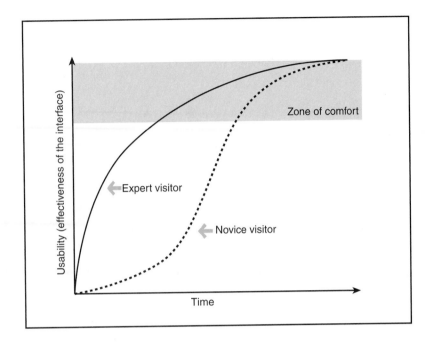

reaching that comfort zone. The design objective of web sites is to minimize the time that novice users require to reach the comfort zone (see Figure 8–4).

At this point, it is important to reiterate a perspective that we have discussed earlier. There are times when we see the professionals in the field aligning themselves in two separate camps: that of usability and that of creative design and cutting-edge technology.

Going back to our analogy, we know that the architects and construction engineers attempt to build buildings that not only look and feel good but that also allow their occupants to carry out their functions and move around with ease. In doing so, they strive to strike a balance between form and function without sacrificing either. They try to use good and dependable building materials, have a resilient structural plan, give the building a pleasing look and ambience, use signage to direct the occupants, and position the utilities (such as light switches) in a way that the occupants can easily use them.

With the growing maturity of the web development field, we can hope to see the evolution of a similar approach. The alignment of the efforts of the client, content expert, information architect, interface designer, application designer, application programmer, media producers, quality assurance expert, usability expert, and project leaders can lead to web sites that are not only usable but also aesthetically pleasing, creative, and technically sophisticated.

The usability expert carries out five main activities during the course of a usability study (see Figure 8–5):

▶ Designing the usability study
▶ Developing instruments
▶ Selecting a sample
▶ Conducting the usability study
▶ Conducting analysis and compiling a usability report

FIGURE 8–5

Steps in a usability study

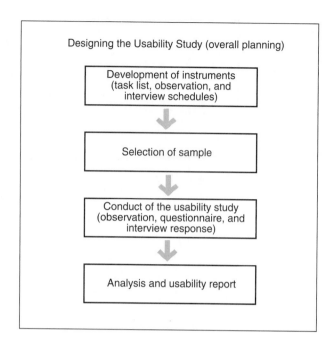

Designing the Usability Study

Let us assume that a site has been live for a few months, and an external consultant has been hired to conduct a usability test. The consultant will most likely start by establishing the parameters of the study. Typically, these parameters will include the purpose of the study, the issues to be examined, and the methods to be used to establish the outcomes. The data from requirements analysis, traffic analysis, visitor feedback, and success in revenue and inquiry generation serve as valuable inputs for this activity.

The *purpose* of the study is determined by the objectives of the web site and specific trends that have been observed in the use of the site. The *issues* examined during a usability study focus on the overall experience of using the web site. These could include the following:

- Learnability (how easy is it to learn to navigate the site)
- Intuitiveness of content structure (how well the content structure maps onto the existing mental map of the visitors)
- Dealing with errors (how well the site handles errors caused by misunderstanding on the part of the visitor or induced by faulty design)
- Memorization (how effectively the visitors are able to internalize and use the interface)
- Affective impact (whether the visitors "like" the site)

The usability study can be carried out using a variety of *methods*. These include observation, interview, and response to a questionnaire.

The study is built around a series of predefined *tasks* (see Table 8–1 for an example) that a visitor to the web site is expected to perform. These tasks are related to the objective of the study. The tasks may be for the whole site or representative sections of the site (see Figure 8–6). The evaluator observes and analyzes the actions and comments of the visitor as he or she attempts to carry out the specified tasks. A questionnaire and an interview follow the observation.

TABLE 8–1   Activity List for a Usability Study of a News Site

Activity

Find the latest world news headline.
Return to the home page.
Find the latest entertainment news.
Find the review of a movie.
Find the list of events for the day in your town.
Send an e-card (birthday) to the following person: John Doe: JohnDoe@anywhere.com
Find the current weather information for Boston, MA.
Send a message to the web master with feedback on the site.
Watch the video clip for the top story of the day.
Go to today's crossword and solve at least one word (Across) and one word (Down) in the crossword. (Don't worry about being right!).
Send a response to the opinion poll.
Send an inquiry for advertising on the site. Type in the following: "Please send the rate for a banner on the 'Weather in Atlanta' page."
Enter the chat area and participate in the chat in any of the rooms.
Return to the home page.
Locate and name any three advertisements on the site.
Spend about 5 minutes just browsing through the site.

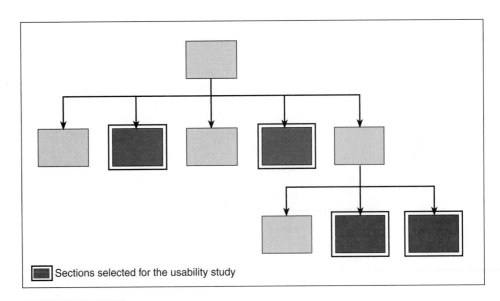

■ Sections selected for the usability study

FIGURE 8–6   Scope of a usability study

Once the overall approach, tools, and method for conducting the evaluation study are determined, the instruments (task list, observation schedule, questionnaire, interview schedule) that will be used in the study are developed, and a sample of individuals who will participate in the study is selected.

Developing Instruments

The instruments that will be used to conduct the study could include the following:

▶ A list of tasks that the participant will carry out (see Table 8–1)
▶ An observation schedule that will guide the observer as the participant is carrying out the tasks (what to look for and how to conduct the observation)
▶ A questionnaire that the participant will be requested to fill out (questions on what worked and did not work for them and on how well they liked the site)
▶ An interview schedule for the observer (what to ask the participant after the tasks are completed)

Task List

The task list asks the participant to carry out specific tasks on the web site. Some examples of these tasks are finding information about a product, placing an order, and removing an item from the shopping cart. As you can see, the tasks are closely linked with the objectives of the study (and the objectives of the site).

As the participants carry out these activities, they are asked to talk aloud and express their thoughts as they go through the activities. This provides a unique usability perspective for the web site, as the participants are likely to share their confusion, frustration, questions, and expectations.

Observation Schedule

The observation schedule guides the observer and indicates specific user behaviors that need to be focused on. It also provides a format for documenting observations and notes. Here is a sample of instructions that may be included in an observation schedule:

▶ Make sure you have put the participant at ease and informed him or her that this is the evaluation of the site and not of his or her skills.
▶ Request that the participant talk out loud about the experiences and emotions that he or she is going through.
▶ Prevent the participant from executing tasks out of order.
▶ If the participant gets very confused and seems to have reached a dead end, help him or her by giving suggestions. Do not volunteer this information until you are asked for help.
▶ Quietly take notes on the following:
  ▶ Options the participant clicks on
  ▶ How much time is spent on each activity
  ▶ Your observations about whether he or she is confused
  ▶ Comments he or she makes when going through the site
▶ Ask the participant to inform you after completion of each activity. Take down your notes and then ask him or her to continue.
▶ Once the participant indicates completion of all activities, request that he or she respond to the questionnaire.
▶ Interview the participant after the questionnaire has been filled out.
▶ Be sure to thank the participant for his or her help and contribution. Give a memento.
▶ Request members of the development team to desist from making comments during observation.

It is important that the observer not interfere with the experiences of the participant. In order to facilitate this, usability studies are often conducted in usability

FIGURE 8–7

A usability lab

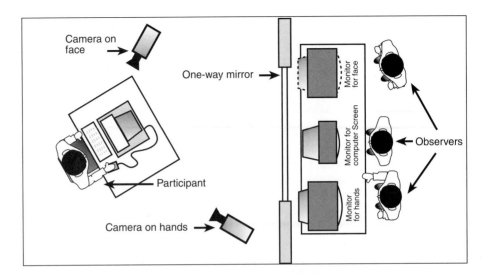

FIGURE 8–7

A usability lab

labs (see Figure 8–7). Such labs have an evaluation room with an attached observer room. A one-way mirror allows observation of the events on the other side. Video cameras track the events in the evaluation room. Depending on the sophistication of the facility, several video cameras could be employed (focusing on hands, face, monitor, and so on). Videotapes that document events can be accessed later for verification or further analysis.

Questionnaire

The questionnaire gathers relatively objective data that can help clarify and validate the information collected through the observation. It could capture the participant's reactions to the experience of working through the activities required in the study. These reactions could be further explored in the interview.

Some questions that could be included in the questionnaire are the following:

▶ Would you recommend this site to a friend? Why?
▶ What was the most enjoyable aspect of the time you spent on this web site?
▶ What was the least enjoyable aspect of the time you spent on this web site?
▶ Did you feel that you could trust the information on this site?
▶ Were you able to find the information you were searching for with ease?
▶ What is your opinion of the visual aesthetics on the site?

The questionnaire should not replace the interview with the participant. Triangulation is an effective method of establishing the validity of the conclusions drawn from a study. Triangulation refers to the process of comparing and validating data collected through different means (observation, questionnaire, interview).

Interview Schedule

The interview schedule lists questions that the participant will be asked on completion of the questionnaire. The interview also provides a means of seeking clarifications for observations during the execution of the tasks and the responses to the questionnaire. For example, if the participant used only the text link to return to the home page, the evaluator may clarify whether this was because it was a preferred method or whether the participant did not know that the logo was linked to the home page. The interview also provides an opportunity to explore affective issues such as the following:

▶ First impression of the site
▶ Impact of colors
▶ Overall aesthetic experience
▶ Likelihood of returning to the site
▶ What they liked best and least and why

A note on the validation of usability instruments might be appropriate here. It may appear that creating a usability instrument (activity list, questionnaire, interview schedule) is an easy and straightforward task. However, you can imagine the havoc that would be caused if these instruments did not measure what they were meant to measure. It is important to evaluate the instrument itself and ensure that it is free of ambiguous instructions, does not list impossible tasks, and addresses all issues that were identified as being critical to the study. Validation of the instrument can be carried out during a **pilot study**. The pilot study is a trial study that is conducted with a small sample. The objective of the study is to establish the practicality of the process and identify any ambiguities in the instruments.

Selecting a Sample

In order to conduct the study, the evaluator needs to identify the participants for the study. The time and budget will determine how many individuals are invited to participate in the study. The larger the sample, the greater the chance that the target audience is accurately represented. Usability studies are conducted with as few as four and as many as hundreds of individuals.

Whatever the size, it is important that the sample represent the target audience. If the profile of individuals who participate in the evaluation does not match that of the target audience, the results of the study become irrelevant. In order to ensure that the sample represents the target audience, the evaluator first compiles the profile of the sample and then selects those individuals who best represent the target audience (see Figure 8–8). Depending on the budget and other resources available to the study, the participants of the study could be compensated for their time.

At this point in the discussion, it is important to discuss ethical considerations in using human participants for such a study. Regardless of the intentions of the

FIGURE 8–8

Selection of a representative sample

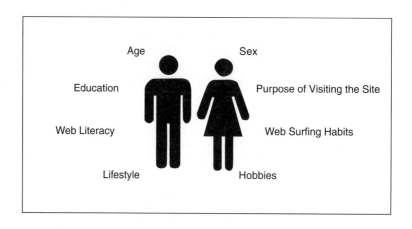

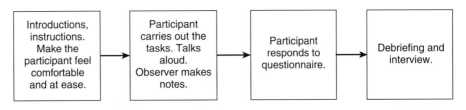

FIGURE 8–9   Conducting the usability study

evaluator, human participants are likely to undergo some degree of anxiety when they participate in the study. It is important to communicate to these participants that the aim of the study is to evaluate the site and not their skills. It is also important to clearly communicate to them the way in which the study will be conducted and how the results will be interpreted and used.

At any time during the conduct of the study, if a participant exhibits anxiety, it is important that the anxiety be addressed and the individual be given the option to withdraw from the study.

The comfort of the participants should be addressed at all points in the study. Provide adequate seating, environmental comfort, and refreshments, if desired.

Even if the participants are receiving payment, it is important that they be treated with dignity and utmost respect. Observers, interviewers, and clients should be asked to desist from making derogatory comments about the performance of the participants, even if the participants are not likely to hear these comments.

Conducting the Usability Study

After the participants for the study have been identified, a schedule for conducting the study is prepared (see Figure 8–9). Typically, one participant goes through the task list at a time. This allows for in-depth observation and interview.

As we have seen earlier, it is important that the participants be made comfortable while they participate in the study. If the participants are comfortable and secure, they are likely to provide unabashed observations and comments about their experiences. Even though the videotape is available for future reference, the observers need to take notes as the participant is carrying out tasks. This will sensitize them to issues that could be valuable for further exploration during the interview.

Very often, the usability expert invites members of the development team to observe the participant as he or she carries out the tasks. First-hand observation allows the development team to "own" the implications of their design decisions (rather than being "told" by an expert).

After the specified tasks are completed, the participant responds to a questionnaire and is interviewed.

Very often, because of budgetary constraints, usability studies are conducted without video recording. This makes it even more important that the observers take detailed notes on the events that occur as the participant is going through the site.

Conducting Analysis and Compiling a Usability Report

After the evaluator has collected the data, it is time for analysis. The analysis could start off with a debriefing and discussion with the development team that was present during the observation. During this complex process, the evaluator looks for trends, commonalties, anomalies, and significant indicators about issues of usability. The evaluator may conduct statistical analysis of the time spent on a particular task or the number of clicks required to accomplish it. This information is invariably supported by data collected through observation, questionnaire, and interview. A problem that recurred with most participants is certainly noteworthy, but it is also important to examine problems faced by specific individuals and determine their causes. For example, if only one participant had difficulty identifying the logo as the link to the home page, the evaluator may decide that it is not a significant issue. However, if one participant repeatedly made the error of clicking on the Company Profile link to navigate to the home page, it may be important to identify the source of the confusion.

The usability report contains a summary of the objectives, the method, and the findings of the study. It may also contain recommendations for modifications. These findings could be categorized by sections of the site or by generalized features of the web site such as the following:

- ▶ Navigation
- ▶ Content structure or hierarchy
- ▶ Labels (naming conventions) used for sections
- ▶ Instructions provided with interfaces
- ▶ Visual layout
- ▶ Language and level of communication
- ▶ Factors that influence the overall performance of the site (use of graphics, text, video)

A usability study report could prompt development of a new version of a product or result in significant enhancements in the current version. Of course, if very few problems are identified, the client and developers will have confidence in their decisions and hope to achieve the objectives for which the site was built.

Formal Versus Informal Usability Studies

So far, we have discussed the design and conduct of a formal usability study. This study is conducted when significant design and development milestones have been achieved. However, effective designers carry out informal evaluation throughout the design and production cycle. This may translate into a simple reflection on an interface by a colleague or a slightly more systematic observation of typical visitors going through a section of the site.

Whatever the method of evaluation and level of formality of the process, it is important that design decisions are validated through the evaluation process. Given the infancy of the discipline and the derivative nature of principles that guide web design, evaluation is one of the most critical means of contributing to an effective process and to the development of an effective and usable web-based communication.

SUMMARY

In this chapter, we examined methods of establishing the success of a web site. We looked at heuristic evaluation in which experts use a set of criteria to evaluate a web site. We briefly discussed focus groups, feedback from the visitors to the site, analysis of traffic statistics, task completion, inquiries generated via the web site, and revenue generated from the site. We also discussed usability evaluation in some detail.

Usability studies can be conducted throughout the development cycle. However, formal studies are best conducted at the end of the design phase (interface prototype), after the site has been hosted and after the site has been live for a while.

We looked at five phases for usability testing: design of the study, development of instruments, selection of a sample, conduct of the study, analysis, and usability report.

The usability study is best conducted by an expert who is not a part of the development team. The study provides an indication of the ease with which a visitor to the site will be able to perform the critical activities that the site was designed for.

REFERENCES

Nielson, J., & Molich, R. (1990). Heuristic evaluation of user interfaces. *Proceedings in ACM Conference on Computer Human Interaction*, SIGCHI, pp. 249–256.

van der Geest, T., & Spyridakis, J. (2000). Developing heuristics for Web communication. *Applied Theory*, 47(3). (*www.techcomm-online.org/issues/v47n3/full/0407.html*)

GUIDING QUESTIONS

▶ What factors will you consider when establishing the effectiveness of a web site?
▶ How is heuristic evaluation of a web site conducted?
▶ What kind of data does a traffic report provide?
▶ What is the purpose of a usability study?
▶ When should the usability study for a web site be conducted?
▶ What are the main stages of a usability study?
▶ What are some tools you could use when conducting a usability study?
▶ Why is selection of the participants so critical in a usability study?
▶ What is the purpose of a usability lab? What are its components?
▶ When conducting a usability study, why it is important that the evaluator not interfere with the activities of the subject?
▶ Why is it important for the development team to be present during the observation of the participants?
▶ What are some implications of the findings of a usability study?

EXERCISE

Identify a news site and prepare a list of activities for usability evaluation. Conduct an informal evaluation with one typical member of the target audience. Prepare a report of your findings and recommendations.

Web Site Development Case Study

This chapter describes the experiences of developing a web site for a specialty teaching restaurant. The web site was developed for the Creations dining lab at The Art Institute of Atlanta. Creations offers an exclusive fine dining experience to its patrons and also serves as a "lab" for the training of students in the Culinary Arts Department at The Art Institute of Atlanta.

This was a pro bono project. As such, it missed the flavor of commercial bottom-line pressures. However, the process and experiences were representative of any small to medium-size web site development project.

THE TEAM

The project started with two team members: Christopher Altman (Chris) and Java Mehta.

Chris started in the role of the project manager and information architect. Eventually, he took on the added responsibilities of interface design, programming, and copy writing. Chris has formal training in concepts of project management, information architecture, usability, HTML, Cascading Style Sheets (CSS), JavaScript, Macromedia Flash, Macromedia Dreamweaver, Adobe Photoshop, and Adobe Illustrator.

Java joined the project as the interface designer and programmer. She was closely involved in project activities during the initial stages of the project: conceptualization, planning, design, and developing the prototype. Unfortunately, Java had to leave the project midway because of conflict with time and work commitments. Java has formal training in fine arts, web design, HTML, CSS, JavaScript, Macromedia Flash, Macromedia Dreamweaver, Adobe Photoshop, and Adobe Illustrator.

Sydney Aron served as a usability expert. She was introduced to the project after it was completed. Sydney also has formal training in concepts of project management, information architecture, usability, and web site development environments.

Kim Resnik and James W. Paul II, CCE, CSC, and FMP, represented The Art Institute of Atlanta.

157

The project team occasionally called on Tim Dempski, faculty member at The Art Institute, for expert design inputs.

I served as an observer and facilitator of all activities that took place during the execution of the project.

Documentation and on-line examples of topics discussed in this chapter can be found at *www.prenhall.com/jadav/*.

PROJECT SUCCESS

The success of any web development project is defined by the following factors:

- Synergy between team members
- The interactions with the client
- The complexity of the content and information architecture
- The team's design and development skills
- "Luck"

The developers adhered to a structured development process. However, they had to contend with several issues throughout the project. Some of these are briefly described here.

Role and Responsibilities of Team Members

The team started with two members (Chris and Java). Chris was to perform the role of a project manager and information architect, whereas Java was to perform the role of the designer and programmer. Unfortunately, about halfway through the project, Java withdrew from the project because of time and work pressures. Consequently, from that point on, Chris became the sole member of the "team." A one-person team is rather unusual in large projects. However, because the project was relatively small and Chris was comfortable with all aspects of development, he was able to complete the project successfully. The change did impact the time to completion of the project.

Interactions With the Client

Chris met the client several times during the course of the project. The client was very clear about the purpose of the site, but it took a while for Chris to get a confident grip on the scope of the content. Chris had to interact with two representatives of the client. The first person was the director of the restaurant (Chef Paul), and the other person was the public relations director of the Art Institute (Kim Resnik). Although there was potential of a conflict (such as contradictory instructions or information) because of a lack of communication between the two client representatives, the team did not notice or experience this conflict. In the initial stages, both the directors were involved in the overall decision making about the project and in giving feedback at each stage. In the later stages, most of the interactions were with Kim Resnik. Timely availability of content and feedback was one of the biggest challenges in the project. Contrary to most commercial projects, the completion pressure from the client was absent. This resulted in some discomfort in the team. Fortunately, very valuable and comprehensive feedback was received before the project was wrapped up. Chris was able to incorporate these suggestions in the web site before it was presented to the clients for the final approval.

Content and Media Resources

After the initial design explorations were approved, the client was requested for a variety of photographs of the restaurant and images associated with it. Although this could have become a bottleneck, the client provided varied photographs that were eventually incorporated in the site. Receiving the photographs from the client addressed the issue of copyright and permissions. Because the client provided the images, the client took on the responsibility for the copyright as well. This issue was clearly specified in the contract. The informal evaluations and the formal usability study conducted toward the conclusion of the project indicated that the quality (primarily brightness) of the images on the site could have been better. This suggestion was forwarded to the clients in anticipation that new photographs would eventually be taken and integrated in the site.

Access to information, such as monthly recipes and quarterly menus, proved to be somewhat difficult. The problem was addressed by putting placeholder (fake) content on the site.

Decisions About Technology

The team had initially decided to use Macromedia Flash for the splash (introduction) page of the site. After many animated discussions, the team determined that although Flash certainly is an impressive tool, the target audience, the content, and the message could be effectively served without using it.

The use of CSS was also discussed at length. Eventually, the team decided that CSS would be used without jeopardizing compatibility of the web site across browser versions 4.0 and above.

The decision about browser version was taken after doing research on browser usage and the assumption that most members of the target audience would be using JavaScript-enabled browsers.

The site was designed to ensure that a web master with knowledge of HTML and JavaScript would be able to update the content. Back-end technologies (such as database) were not used in developing the site.

Deadlines

As we saw earlier, the initial assumption of the project was that there would be two team members. In the beginning of the project, there was some confusion about the process and roles. Adherence to deadlines was rocky at first. However, once the process and role definitions were clarified, the team caught up with deliverables.

As the project was nearing completion, a couple of information design and information architecture issues were observed on the site. Chris and I discussed the cost benefit of making these changes and decided that even though there might be a slight delay in the schedule, we would go ahead with the changes. Had this been a commercial project, we would have discussed this issue with the client, and, depending on how the contract was drawn up, the escalation in cost would have been absorbed by the developers or paid for by the client.

The quality assurance (QA) process turned out to be relatively unpredictable. As changes were made, new issues were identified in the next round of QA. The QA process was somewhat frustrating for Chris because he kept getting a barrage of lists with minor things that needed to be changed. Fortunately, he was able to maintain a focus on quality of the project and also remain detached enough from the process to not take things personally. A few more issues were identified during the final usability evaluation. The team met with the usability expert and prioritized the changes. The most important changes were implemented, whereas the others were forwarded to the client as suggestions for the future. The stretching of the deadline due to these changes was one of the most uncontrolled features of the project.

The team spent approximately 325 hours in completing the project. The original time estimate was 315 hours. Although there was a small difference in the total number of hours, the distribution of hours between the team members changed about halfway. The calendar time spent on the project also increased by about a month and a half. Had this been a commercial project, it would have been essential to find a solution such that the final delivery date did not get affected.

THE PROJECT

The Objective of the Site

The site was designed to meet the following objectives:

- Provide information about Creations' dining lab
- Increase lunchtime reservations
- Increase group reservations
- Support development of a loyal clientele

Requirements Analysis

The team met Chef Paul and Ms. Resnik several times during the first couple of weeks. The initial meetings were exploratory, with the focus on gaining a basic understanding of the purpose and scope of the web site. In subsequent meetings, the discussion was driven by specific questions from the team. The team clarified questions arising from the initial information architecture and interface explorations. The project team also examined web sites of similar restaurants and did a competitive analysis of the features of these sites. The findings of the requirements analysis were incorporated in the project proposal.

Proposal

The proposal was divided into three parts: the requirements analysis, the concept proposal, and the business proposal. The concept proposal was built on the findings of the requirements analysis. The business proposal called for estimation of effort and time. The team was not very confident about their estimates, but they rationally thought through the activities at each stage and used their gut feel about how much time each activity would require. In a commercial project, the effort estimate would have contributed to cost estimation that in turn would have resulted in a pricing exercise.

See Appendix E for the proposal.

Information Architecture and Copy

Chris had some familiarity with the food services business. This background helped in his understanding of the mission and operations of Creations. The team met with the client several times to arrive at the content structure and navigation flow. They went prepared with questions about content, profile of the patrons, objectives of the site, and current communication approaches. After the site map was informally approved, Chris wrote the copy for each page of the site and developed two use cases for typical visitors to the site. The copy was integrated in the navigation prototype and presented to the client for approval.

The site structure did go through changes after the client had given the approval for the navigation prototype. The project team initiated these changes in order to simplify the navigation without making any changes in the overall scope of the content.

See Appendix F for the information architecture documents (user scenarios, original and revised site map, and copy). The navigation prototype can be seen at www.prenhall.com/ jadav/.

Technical Feasibility

As the team was concluding the information architecture exercise, they discussed the use of Macromedia Flash and CSS. Eventually, the team decided in favor of the lowest common denominator. They decided to not use Macromedia Flash and use only CSS that would be compatible across browsers. The decision was driven by the consideration that the site would need to be updated frequently. Because the original proposal had indicated that Flash-based content would be incorporated on the site, the issue was discussed with the client, and on their agreement, the idea was dropped.

In addition to these technologies, the team finalized the decisions about screen resolution, connection speed, and cross-platform and cross-browser considerations. The decisions were documented in a technical feasibility document and presented to the client for approval.

See Appendix G for the technical feasibility document.

Interface Design

Once the client approved the site structure (site map and navigation prototype), Chris and Java conducted several brainstorming sessions. During these sessions, the following issues were discussed: color palette, layout, interaction features, use of images, lines and form, typography, and so on. The team started by designing rough outlines (sketches) on paper. Formal wire frames (specifying relative positioning of elements on the page) came next. Finally, three visual concept boards (comps) were developed using imaging software. The designers carried out informal heuristic evaluation on these designs by seeking the opinions of a design expert. The team made further modifications and then presented these designs to the client. At this time, the team had a recommendation for one design (design 3), and the client concurred with this recommendation. Ms. Resnik was particular about the branding and use of specific colors on the site. The design was revised on the basis of her input, and the final interface prototype was presented to the client for approval.

See Appendix H for the comps that were presented to the client. The interface prototype can be seen at www.prenhall.com/jadav/.

Production Plan

After the client had approved the interface prototype, the team moved into the production phase. At this point, the team identified the media asset requirements (mostly photographs) and content required from the client (recipes, menus, calendar of events). The team then worked out the details of the production in terms of the HTML table structure, color values, styles (CSS), fonts, image sizes, and so on. The file naming conventions, directory structure, testing, and quality assurance plans were also finalized. Several specifications changed during the process of production. The production specifications represented a "living document" that was updated as changes in the production specifications were made.

See Appendix I for a sample of the production specifications (directory structure, production documents).

Production

As the project moved into the production phase, the site structure and copy were finalized first. The basic visual elements (links, images, logo, headings) were incorporated next. The project faced a number of technical challenges. These ranged from simple bugs (forgetting to put the # symbol in front of color values) to complex table structures that enabled a complicated layout.

As the site came together, the team noticed some interface issues. For example, the colors for links and subtitles were too similar, and there was a potential of confusing them with each other. Further, some pages ended up being longer than expected, and there was a need to add the "top of page" link on these pages. The team discussed and decided to add a "print" option to some of the pages at the very end of the project.

After the basic functionality and interface had been integrated in the site, Chris prepared the images that went into the site. This involved cropping and optimizing the images and saving them in the appropriate format. These images were the last items to be incorporated in the site. After this, the testing and QA process started.

Software-based testing was used to detect and fix program bugs. Concurrently, several people evaluated the site. Each person provided evaluative comments on spelling and grammar, usability, headings, and so on.

It was difficult to track a lot of these small changes in design. A system for documenting the changes would have helped track the history for each change.

As we saw earlier, the process of QA and usability study resulted in changes that extended the completion time for the project.

See Appendix J for a sample of quality assurance reports.

Usability Study

Once the site had received a go-ahead from the testing and QA stage, Chris presented it to the clients and also discussed modalities for future site updations. At this time, the clients provided an informal approval of the site. Sydney was then invited to conduct the usability study.

Sydney was given the original proposal that contained the details of the requirements analysis. She first spent some time going through the site and thoroughly examining each page. She identified critical activities that a typical visitor would be expected to perform. In arriving at this, she called upon the use case analysis as well as her own understanding of the site's objectives. This information helped her generate a list of tasks that a visitor would be asked to perform on the site. Sydney then prepared a brief questionnaire and an interview schedule. The process of conducting the study and the three instruments (task list, questionnaire, interview schedule) were evaluated in a pilot study with one participant. This study identified some logistical and consistency issues. The instruments were modified accordingly.

Sydney sought out participants for the study from among her colleagues and acquaintances. She made sure that they matched the profile of the target audience specified in the project proposal.

The evaluation was conducted in a quiet room. Sydney sat unobtrusively behind the participants and made notes on their activities and comments. After the participants had completed the tasks, she requested them to fill out the questionnaire and did a debriefing interview about their experiences.

After all three participants had completed the evaluation, Sydney analyzed the information and wrote the report. Sydney met with Chris and helped him prioritize the changes that needed to be made before the site was formally handed over to the client. The report was presented to the client at the time of making the final presentation of the site.

See Appendix K for the usability study report.

Project Wrap-Up and Client Acceptance

The site was handed over to the client on a CD-ROM. The production document and usability study report were presented at the same time. The Art Institute's web master who was to keep the site current and updated was present at the meeting. The client signed a formal acceptance at the time of handover.

The following comments from the client and team sum up some of the significant experiences of the project.

Comment from Ms. Kim Resnik: *"Chris was very thorough in his preparation and analysis of our goals, the audience, and the design requirements for the web site. This is reflected in the proposal. Although the process of site creation was not "textbook perfect," I felt it went very well. I know that a project like this rarely goes exactly according to plan! Chris was open to suggestions and refinements of content and design from the client side and incorporated them well. We provided information but not a formal script and very few photos; Chris had to learn quickly about the dining room so that he could write the script and have the photos shot. In addition, my work schedule did not allow me to turn around approvals and edits as quickly as we both would have liked; Chris was very patient with me, making sure the project didn't fall too far behind, but always with the utmost courtesy. Finally, Chris provided excellent documentation of the site—the best our web master has ever seen. We were so impressed with his performance that we have asked him for a proposal to do a web site for The Art Institute of Atlanta Library."*

Comment from Chris: *"Working on the Creations web site was a very valuable learning experience for me. While we used a structured development process, I struggled with having to play multiple roles in the project. Working as the project manager, information architect, interface designer, developer, and interfacing with the client taught me one person should not play every project role. A successful project is the fruit of attention to detail; one person cannot focus on every detail and keep a project on schedule. Team-work is absolute to web design. Each person is talented in a specific way, and when these talents work together, first-rate projects are produced. The Creations web site taught me to look at what I do well and surround myself with other talented individuals.*

The experience also taught me that web development requires a lot of patience. I worked with a very pleasant and well informed client. Communication, persistence, and patience were important in making this relationship work. Finally, the project appeared to get drawn out towards the end when I was bombarded with all sorts of quality assurance and usability-related changes to the site. It was important at these times to maintain my focus on quality and not get frustrated with having to rework the same thing over and over. The documentation for the site was tedious, but in hindsight it was one of the most valuable exercises of the project.

All the struggles of the project appeared worthwhile when I received a very positive and appreciative response from the client at the time of the final presentation and handover of the site."

Comment from Sydney: "Working on the Creations project as the usability expert proved to be a positive experience. Performing the usability tests and analyzing the gathered data reinforced my belief that user feedback on site mechanics and their suggestions for improvement are imperative if one is to create a truly useful and intuitive site. Implementing the changes to the site based on this data is equally important. The goal of the web designer is to communicate effectively, and we are in a business where the user and his or her experience is paramount to anything else. Usability testing allows the developers to ensure the delivery of a quality product to the audience."

The Creations site: http://www.prenhall.com/jadav/

Requirements Analysis Outline

Organization Note

▶ Describe the organization for which the site is to be developed.

Goals

▶ What business and communication goals is the site expected to achieve?
  ▶ Foot traffic to retail store
  ▶ Inquiries about products
  ▶ Revenue generated by the site
  ▶ Awareness about the organization
  ▶ Facilitation (transaction) of a business process
  ▶ Access to specific information about the organization and its processes
  ▶ Any other goals
▶ What current method of communication will the site enhance or replace?
  ▶ Print brochures
  ▶ Personal presentations
  ▶ Video presentation
  ▶ Transaction requiring human intervention
  ▶ Classroom training
  ▶ Any other methods
▶ Is the site a part of an overall communication and marketing strategy of the organization? If yes, what role is it expected to play?
▶ What is the unique selling proposition (USP) of the site?

Competition

▶ What other methods of communication will the site compete with?
  ▶ Print
  ▶ Video
  ▶ Television advertising
  ▶ Transaction requiring human intervention
▶ Who are the competitors of this site? How are they successful or unsuccessful?

Target Audience Profiles

▶ Demographics, psychographics, web literacy, language literacy, expectations of the site
▶ Build personas

Target Group and Objectives

Target Group 1	Objective (expected action, change that the site should bring about in the target group)
Target Group 2	Objective (expected action, change that the site should bring about in the target group)

Design Treatment

▶ What are the visual interface imperatives for the site (corporate identity, illustration style, metaphors, colors)?
▶ What are the copy imperatives for the site (level, style, language)?
▶ What are the media imperatives for the site (photographs, illustrations, audio, video, animation)?
▶ What are the other critical considerations for the site design (download speed, ease of navigation, ambience, interactivity, use of technology)?

Benchmark Sites

▶ Which sites should be emulated?
▶ Which sites should not be emulated?

Update Requirements

▶ Which sections will require updating?
▶ How often will the sections require updating?
▶ Who will carry out these updates?
▶ What kind of infrastructure will be used for the updates?
▶ What are the anticipated skill requirements for these updates?
▶ What skill sets are available or will be developed?
▶ What are the logistical considerations for updates?

Advertising Strategy

▶ Who is expected to advertise on the site?
▶ What space needs to be set aside for advertisements on the site?

Traffic Strategy

▶ How will traffic be driven to the site?
▶ What kind of tracking of traffic will be required?
▶ Will the site be registered with search engines? Which ones?
▶ Which pages of the site will need to be prepared for search engine sniffers?

Technical Requirements

▶ Which browsers will the site be expected to work on (browser, version, features)?
  - ▶ Netscape versions_____   ▶ IE versions _____
  - ▶ Mozilla   ▶ Opera
  - ▶ Other _____   ▶ Other _____
▶ Which resolutions is the site to be built for?
  - ▶ Handheld devices   ▶ 640 × 480
  - ▶ 800 × 600   ▶ 1024 × 800
▶ Which hardware platforms is the site to be primarily targeted at?
  - ▶ Apple Macintosh   ▶ Windows
  - ▶ Unix   ▶ Other _____

▶ What are the anticipated media requirements on the site?
- ▶ Voice-over
- ▶ Music and SFX
- ▶ Photographic images
- ▶ Video
- ▶ Virtual reality

▶ What plug-ins should the site support?
- ▶ Flash
- ▶ QuickTime
- ▶ Real Media
- ▶ Other

▶ Describe the features required for
Chat:

Discussion forum:

Search:

▶ What will be the hosting environment for the site?
- ▶ Server and operating system
- ▶ Space
- ▶ Support for CGI, ASP, PHP, streaming media, and so on
- ▶ Will the site need to interface with any existing applications or databases?

Content and Media Sources

▶ Who will be the one-point contact for all content- and media-related information for the site?

▶ In what format is the content for the site currently available?

Content Inventory and Process Flow Representation

List the topics/content that need(s) to be included on the site. This is a complete listing of the content and defines the scope (depth, breadth). Outline the processes and transactions that need to be supported on the site. If possible, draw up a few typical user cases to demonstrate the steps in this process.

(This is an attempt at creating an exhaustive list of all content that needs to go on the site—it is not an attempt to create the navigation structure.)

Project Costing Template

The web organization proceeds to work out an estimate of the time, resources, and effort that would be required to generate the solution suggested in the concept proposal. The method of arriving at the cost estimate varies from organization to organization. However, two methods are popularly used.

The first estimates the number of pages in the web site and categorizes them according to the technology and content. For example, a page may include a form, text, graphic illustrations, scanned images, multimedia, mouse rollover, animation, and so on. The organization works out the cost of developing each page based on a previously established cost metric for these elements on a web page.

Cost Estimate Based on Type and Number of Pages

Type of Page	Number	Cost per Page	Total Cost
		Cost of the Project	

The second method is not page based but effort based. The organization works from a metric of cost estimate for time for different professionals. The project costing involves estimating the effort (time) required to develop the solution. The total cost is the value associated with the time required from different individuals and other resource and production costs. The time involvement from individuals can be associated with different costs. For example, a designer could spend 20 hours on an activity, and this time could be charged at $50 per hour (resulting in a total cost of $1,000). On the other hand, a creative director may spend 10 hours on an activity and this time could be charged at $150 per hour (resulting in a total cost of $1,500).

Effort Estimate

Activity	Person	Time (hrs)

Cost Estimate Derived From Effort Estimate

Person	Time (hrs)	Cost per Hour	Total Cost
Other resource and production costs			
		Cost of the Project	

C

Information Architecture Template

Project Information

Project Name:

Client:

Project Manager:

Information Architect:

Introduction to the Project

> ▶ What is this site about?

Communication and Business Objectives

> ▶ Listing of the communication objectives.
> ▶ Listing of the business objectives.

Target Audience

> ▶ Detailed description of the target audience.

Summary of the Requirements Analysis

> ▶ Briefly describe the outcomes of the requirements analysis.

Method and Outcome of Information Architecture

Method

> ▶ Describe the process of information architecture. What activities did you undertake to arrive at the recommendations in this report?

Competitive Analysis

> ▶ Who are the main competitors for this web site?
> ▶ Describe features that make them successful and unsuccessful.
> ▶ Based on your findings, where are the opportunities and threats to the success of your web site?

Use Case Analysis

> ▶ Provide detailed use case analysis for typical members of the target audience.

Navigation Structure

> ▶ Describe the process that led to the navigation structure (e.g., card sorting).
> ▶ Present a site map.
> ▶ List the global links.
> ▶ Provide a page-by-page definition of links, content and processes.

Information Design

> ▶ What components will be present on each web page?
> ▶ How will titles, subtitles, pull quotes, images, colors, metaphor, shapes be used to present the information?
> ▶ What is the approach to organizing content on the pages (alphabetical, numerical, temporal, perceived importance)?

Process Mapping

▶ Provide a flowchart of the processes that are to be represented on the site.

Traffic Strategy

▶ What steps will be taken to ensure a high ranking with search engines?
▶ What other means of generating traffic to the site do you recommend?

Accessibility

▶ What accessibility standards will the site adhere to? How will these standards be achieved?

Navigation Prototype

▶ Provide the URL of the navigation prototype.

Design Concept Note Template

Project Information

Project Name: *Design Concept #*

Client:

Project Manager:

Creative Director:

Introduction to the Project

▸ What is this site about?

Communication and Business Objectives

▸ Listing of the communication objectives.
▸ Listing of the business objectives.

Target Audience

▸ Description of the target audience.

Site Map

▸ Presentation of the site map approved by the client.

Design

Overall Design Approach

▸ What were the critical considerations behind design decisions?

Branding and Identity

▸ How will branding and identity be achieved on the site?
▸ What are some critical imperatives for branding (color, logo, icons, metaphors)?

Graphic Style and Typography

▸ What graphic style and typography will be used on the site?
▸ Why have these styles been selected?

Layout

▸ What will be the common components of the web pages on the site?
▸ What is the approach to the use of white space in layout? Why?
▸ How will information on the pages be organized and presented (headings, images, text, columns, footer, links)?
▸ What identifiers will be used for different sections of the page (icons, text heading, color)?
▸ What is the approach to scrolling pages? Why?
▸ Where will navigation elements be displayed? What is the reason for displaying them in these positions?
▸ Will the site make use of pop-up windows? For what functions, and why?

Colors

▸ What colors will be used on the site? Why?
▸ Provide a color swatch that represents these colors.
▸ Will certain colors be used for headings, backgrounds, images and so on? Why?

Interaction and links

- How will links be represented (text, icons, buttons, image map)?
- How will the different states of the interactions (available, active, selected) be represented?

Accessibility Standards

- What accessibility standards will the site adhere to? How will these be achieved?

Concept Boards

- Attach concept boards for unique pages of the site. (If you have more than one design concept, prepare the design concept note for each.)

Recommendation

- Salient design features that work and do not work in this design concept.
- Your recommendation for consideration of this design for the web site.

E

Case Study—Creations Web Site Project Proposal

EXECUTIVE SUMMARY

This proposal is based on the developer's understanding of the requirements of the Creations web site. The proposed web site design will focus on achieving the objectives of the site and target the audience specified in the requirements analysis.

REQUIREMENTS ANALYSIS

In order to understand the requirements for the Creations web site, the project team met with the client several times and also looked at web sites for other fine-dining restaurants. The following paragraphs encapsulate the findings.

Organization Note

Creations is an educational dining lab whose mission is to prepare culinary arts students for the pace and complexity of fine dining. Located on the fifth floor of The Art Institute of Atlanta, Creations serves American cuisine in a classical French style.

Approximately 40 students from the Culinary Arts Program operate Creations each academic quarter. These students prepare food, manage business operations, and work as servers in the dining lab.

Creations serves an à la carte lunch menu and a six-course dinner menu with a fixed price. Dinner is served Wednesdays and Fridays. Lunch is served Thursdays and Fridays.

Creations' quick pace is a valuable experience for students. Classroom courses develop fundamental cooking and service management skills, but the dining lab trains students in formal service and guests relations.

The Art Institute of Atlanta is accredited by the Commission on Colleges of the Southern Association of Colleges and Schools to award the associate in arts degree and the bachelor of fine arts degree, authorized to operate and to award the associate in arts degree and the bachelor of fine arts degree by the Georgia Nonpublic Postsecondary Education Commission, approved for the training of veterans and eligible veterans' dependents, and authorized under federal law to enroll nonimmigrant alien students. The associate in arts degree program in culinary arts is additionally accredited by the American Culinary Federation (ACF).

Approximately 400 students are enrolled in the Culinary Arts Program at the Art Institute each quarter.

Site Objectives

The Creations site will have the following objectives:

- Provide information about Creations' dining lab: The dining lab concept is unfamiliar to most guests. Often guests not associated with The Art Institute of Atlanta are uncertain whether Creations is open to the public. The Creations site will invite all interested persons by answering questions about dining times, attire, and directions. After visiting the site, a guest will have enough information and an opportunity to make a lunch or dinner reservation at Creations.

▶ Increase reservations, especially for lunchtime: By increasing lunchtime reservations, culinary students will benefit by the increase in pace and complexity of their training. To attract lunchtime guests, meal times are kept to 1 hour. This time frame is important to the professional during a business luncheon. This demand will allow the students to become more proficient in food preparation and service. The site will provide information about lunch and dinner menus and also allow the visitors to send in reservations for lunch as well as dinner. This feature may appeal especially to professionals working near The Art Institute of Atlanta who are interested in a quick but elegant lunch experience. The site may not have an engine for on-line reservations but will be supported by a 24-hour phone or e-mail response to reservation requests.

▶ Increase group reservations: Group reservations create an excellent opportunity for Creations to partner with other organizations. This network creates professional contacts for students on graduation. The site will provide visitors the facility to make group reservations.

▶ Support development of a loyal community of clientele: Guests who return to the site periodically are more likely to book a repeat reservation to Creations. The site should have features that will encourage repeat visits and thereby build a strong base of loyal clientele.

Current Methods of Communication

The Art Institute of Atlanta promotes the Creations dining lab through the Culinary Arts Program information in the catalogs sent to prospective students. The Art Institute of Atlanta also releases information and photographs about events to the *Atlanta Journal-Constitution* and 450 other media locations each academic quarter. The Art Institute prints a brochure each quarter, and the Culinary Arts Department maintains and updates a list of about 900 people for direct mailing. Recently, it has been possible to make on-line reservations for the dining lab at www.reservationsource.com. The Culinary Arts Department also keeps in touch with its patrons via an e-mail list.

The new web site will help build this ongoing marketing relationship as well as create an important new source of contact for the public.

Target Group

The guest demographic at Creations is composed of 35- to 65-year-old professionals either on lunchtime business engagements or dining as a couple. This audience has a moderate web experience dealing mostly with e-mail and corporate web sites.

The average income level of these individuals is $50,000. This income figure places individuals at a moderate to high economic status. Common places where the target group shops include Macy's, Harry's Farmers Market, and Nordstrom. Restaurants frequently visited by this target group include Houstons, Maggianos, and Ruth Chris' Steak House.

The target group lives approximately 15 miles or less from The Art Institute of Atlanta or works within the Atlanta perimeter area.

Many members of the target group are related to the culinary arts students. These individuals have some familiarity with The Art Institute of Atlanta but may be interested in learning more about the college.

The target group is also familiar with fine-dining etiquette and some culinary terminology. This means that Creations can focus on food preparation and presentation and not focus on educating clientele on what "fonds," "demiglaze," or other unique culinary terms represent.

Treatment

The overall treatment, or feel of the site, must represent the sophistication and elegance of a meal at Creations. Therefore, a site with visual elegance and sophistication will represent the experience of a meal at Creations.

This treatment must comply with *Graphic Standard Manual* developed by The Art Institute of Atlanta. Further, the design must facilitate short download times, ease of use, attractive imagery, and relevant content.

Update Requirements

Some site content will be time based and will require regular updating. Up-to-date information will promote return visits to the site. The web master of The Art Institute of Atlanta will be responsible for updating all content. The web master is proficient in web technologies. Therefore, sections that require updating will be modified through the site's source code. The information that will need to be updated regularly includes menu, service times, and recipe information.

Traffic Strategy

The Creations web site needs to be developed so that search engines can locate and index the site. This strategy will increase traffic from users who search the Internet for fine-dining establishments in Atlanta.

The Art Institute of Atlanta's web site will direct traffic to the Creations site. Visitors to The Art Institute's site interested in Creations will be able to visit the Creations site for in-depth information about the dining lab. The Creations site will also provide a reciprocal link to the Art Institute's web site.

Technical Requirements

The site should be accessible on the Windows and Macintosh operating systems with Netscape Navigator and Internet Explorer version 4.0 or higher. The site will need to be designed for optimum download using 56K modems. Macromedia Flash may be used to enhance the message on the site.

The site needs to be designed for viewing with a resolution of 800 × 600.

Content and Media

The site will display the following media:

- Creations' logo
- The Art Institute of Atlanta's logo
- Photographs of food
- Photographs of chefs
- Photographs of Creations

These media are currently available in digital formats, such as PSD, TIFF, and EPS, with The Art Institute of Atlanta.

Further, the following content items will need to be available on the site:

- Mission of the Creations dining lab
- Current menu
- Service hours
- Directions
- Dress requirements
- Group reservation information
- Recipes
- Chef profiles
- Reservation instructions
- Contact information

Recipe and culinary faculty profiles are currently available in digital text format with the Art Institute of Atlanta.

The Art Institute of Atlanta's catalog, the Culinary Arts Program fact sheet, and the Creations restaurant brochure can be used as content resources for the site.

PROPOSED SOLUTION

The proposed solution is based on the requirements of the Creations site as identified in the previous section. The approach proposed in this section is likely to best accomplish the objectives of the site. The proposal discusses the experience design, site architecture, and technical solution of the project.

Site Personality

The Creations site will impress the visitor by presenting useful information with an intuitive navigation system. Further, a pleasing artistic treatment of photographs, images, color, and type will create a web site that distinguishes Creations as a premier fine-dining establishment.

Experience

The elegance of fine food, wine, and service will be emulated by the Creations site. The site will build a meaningful and enjoyable experience for the visitors and provide them with easy access to the information relevant to them. The site will not use complicated technology that the target audience may not be familiar or comfortable with. The imagery on the site will draw on the elegant lines, typography, and form but will not overwhelm the visitor.

Information Architecture

The content on the site will be organized in intuitive and logical manner. Any information on the site will be a maximum of two clicks away. As such, all content will be organized in two navigation layers.

The main links on the site (Home, About Creations, Lunch, Dinner, Reservations, Directions, Recipes, Contact, and the link to reservations.com) will be global links (they will be available from all pages). Two of these sections (Contact and the link to reservations.com) will be displayed in a new window. This will allow the visitor to access the new information without leaving the main informational pages of the site.

When a visitor selects a section, the first subsection of the section will be displayed by default.

The labels used on the site will be common terms that the visitors are likely to be familiar with.

Sections with lengthy content (e.g., lunch menu) will use subheadings to make it easy for the visitor to identify the information components on the page. The links will be displayed at the top and bottom of the page. The Creations logo will also serve as a redundant home link.

The preliminary site map for the site can be seen in Figure E-1.

The specific content proposed for each section of the site is listed here:

Home
- Creations logo, welcome, information about special events (e.g., wine pairing)

Section: About Creations
- Creations picture, mission of Creations

Subsection: About The Art Institute of Atlanta (AIA)
- AIA's logo, AIA's picture, mission of AIA

Subsection: The Culinary Arts Department
- Pictures of classrooms, labs, mission of the Culinary Arts Department

Subsection: The Culinary Arts Students
- Number of students, students per class, students per lab, students in Creations, chefs in Creations

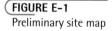

FIGURE E-1
Preliminary site map

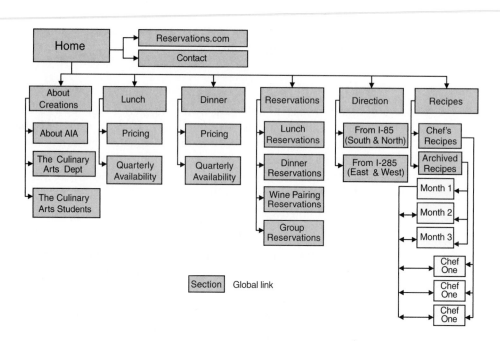

Section: Lunch
- Sample menu

Subsection: Pricing
- Pricing and policy

Subsection: Quarterly Availability
- Timings, dates, link to reservations

Section: Dinner
- Sample menu

Subsection: Pricing
- Timings, dates, link to reservations

Subsection: Quarterly Availability
- Timings, dates, link to reservations

Section: Reservations
- Policy, payment

Subsections: Lunch, Dinner, Wine Pairing, Group
- Timings, making reservations (phone, e-mail, on-line, fax, mail)

Section: Direction
- From GA 400 (map and directions)

Subsection: From I-85
- Map and directions

Subsection: From I-285
- Map and directions

Section: Recipes
- Chef profile, recipe of the month, print option

Subsection: Chefs (Chef 1 . . . Chef n)
- Pictures of recipes, description of recipes, pictures of chefs, chef's biography, print option

Subsection: Recipe Archive (Month 1 . . . Month n)
- Pictures of recipes, description of recipes, pictures of chefs, chef's biography, print option

Section: Contact
- Creations' address, The Art Institute of Atlanta's address, Creation's phone number, contact person's e-mail address, The Art Institute of Atlanta's URL

Link: Reservations.com
- Creations' reservations page

Interface Design

The site will provide an experience of elegance and sophistication. Colors, typography, images, and layout will be selected to work toward creating this experience.

Further, the site's personality will be strengthened by the use of colors that are consistent with the brand (logo). The use of maroon in the Creations logo successfully conveys the fine-dining atmosphere. Therefore, maroon will be the base color of the site's palette. The development team feels that this color creates a sense of refinement that supports the site's personality.

Photographs displayed on the site will be cropped and treated to not only support the content on each page but also help create the ambiance consistent with that of the Creations restaurant. The photographs will support the message but will not compete with it. Photographs used on the site will be from the restaurant, students working in the kitchens and in the restaurant, and images of aesthetic food displays.

The use of clean, crisp fonts for the main copy and links will aid readability. Pull quotes will be used in some sections. The pull quotes will be displayed using elegant, stylish typography. The text will be displayed using high contrast with the background.

A consistent and structured layout will require minimum effort on the part of the visitors to find information and navigate through the site. The integrity of the layout on a page will be maintained on resizing the screen (up to approximately 70%).

To make navigation as easy as possible, the links will be displayed at the top of each page. As mentioned in the section on information architecture, the global links will be displayed at the top and bottom of the page.

The option to jump to the top of the page will be made available on pages that require scrolling beyond one and a half screens.

The links on the site will be clearly distinguished into global and local links. The global links will be available from all sections of the site, whereas the local links will be available in specific sections. Mouse rollover will be used to clearly identify links as currently available. Currently selected links will also be clearly identified using a visual change in the link.

The links for Contact and reservationsource.com will be separated from the other content-oriented links on the site and will open in a new window. Similarly, the link to The Art Institute of Atlanta's web site will be separated from the other links.

Traffic Strategy

The development team recommends that Creations register a unique domain name for the site. This domain name (suggested: www.AIACreations.com) will provide the most direct access to the site.

The site will be submitted to the main search engines on the web. The site will be optimized for indexing by search engines.

In addition, the development team recommends that the URL for the site be printed on all publicity materials associated with The Art Institute of Atlanta and the Culinary Arts Department. Further, the business cards for faculty and the letterhead for the department could also prominently display the URL.

Technical Solution

The Creations site will be developed using HTML, Cascading Style Sheets, JavaScript, and Macromedia Flash.

Supported Browsers
- Netscape Navigator 4.0 and higher
- Internet Explorer 4.0 and higher

Supported Platforms
- Wintel Machines running the Windows operating system
- Macintosh machine with the Macintosh operating system

Target Screen Resolution
- 800 × 600

Other Technical Considerations
- JavaScript-enabled browser
- Image-enabled browser
- Macromedia Flash plug-in

Server Information

The Art Institute of Atlanta will host the site on a Unix server with 30 megabytes of disk space.

Quality Assurance

The development team will perform a quality check of spelling and grammar for the copy, technical solutions, and performance requirements for the site. All issues will be resolved before the site goes live.

Site Completion

The site is expected to be hosted and released on January 25, 2002.

Development Team Information

A core team of two individuals will develop the site. The team has access to and will call on external experts in web design, usability, technology, and project management from time to time.

Contact Information

Development Team Contact Information

Christopher Altman will serve as the project manager for this project and will be the one-point contact for all communication with the client.

Christopher Altman

E-mail: christopheraltman2000@yahoo.com

Creation Contact Information

Chef Paul at The Art Institute of Atlanta will be the content expert. Ms. Kim Resnik will provide branding and design inputs. Approvals for all stages will be given by Chef Paul.

James W. Paul II, CCE, CSC, FMP

Assistant Academic Department Director, Culinary Arts

E-mail: paulj@aii.edu

Ms. Kim Resnik

Director of Public Relations and Marketing

E-mail: resnikk@aii.edu

Schedule

This proposal is being submitted to the client on August 31, 2001. It is assumed that the proposal will be accepted and the contract signed by September 5, 2001. At that time, all brochures and content information will be made available to the development team. The start date for the project is September 10, 2001.

Information Architecture

Site map	September 17, 2001
Copy	September 17, 2001
Navigation prototype (web site)	September 17, 2001
Client acceptance	*September 20, 2001*

Technical Feasibility

Technical feasibility document	September 20, 2001
Client acceptance	*September 25, 2001*

Interface Design

Media assets (photographs and images) from the client	September 25, 2001
Visual concept boards (three comps)	October 5, 2001
Client approval of one design concept	*October 10, 2001*
Production document	October 12, 2001
Design document	October 12, 2001
Interface prototype	October 18, 2001
Heuristics evaluation	October 22, 2001
Client acceptance of interface prototype	*October 25, 2001*

Production

Production planning	October 29, 2001
Production of assets and site integration	November 16, 2001
Testing and quality assurance	November 30, 2001
Usability study	December 15, 2001
Maintenance and update document	December 15, 2001
Site presentation to the client	January 8, 2002
Client acceptance and approval of site	*January 11, 2002*
Project wrap-up, site and documentation handover	January 25, 2002

Assumptions

- The client will provide feedback and approvals within 3 working days after receiving the materials from the development team.
- The client will be available for meeting with the development team at least once every 2 weeks.
- The client will provide photographs and logo in PSD, TIFF, or EPS format.

- The development team will have free and easy access to the Creations restaurant.
- The client will not require changes once approval for specific material has been given.

Copyright

- The client will provide all photographs, and as such the copyright liability for these photographs will be the clients.
- The illustrations used on the site will be original.
- On completion of the site, The Art Institute of Atlanta will have the copyright to all the assets and code used to develop the site.
- The Art Institute of Atlanta will permit Prentice Hall to incorporate the following in the book (*Designing Usable Web Interfaces*) authored by Dr. Ameeta Jadav:
  - The case study of the development of this site
  - All documentation and interim assets produced during development
  - The final site

Total Price of the Project

This project will be developed on a pro bono basis.

PAYMENT SCHEDULE

Considering the nature of the project, there is no payment schedule. However, had it been a commercial project, the payment schedule could be as follows:

On acceptance of the proposal	30%
On acceptance of the information architecture and copy	30%
On approval of the interface prototype	30%
On acceptance of the final site	10%

ARBITRATION AND PENALTY CLAUSES

This section would include legal clauses for the following:

- Delay in delivery schedule on the part of the developers
- Delay in providing feedback and approval on the part of the client
- Delay in providing content and media assets on the part of the client
- Delay and cost escalation resulting from changes required by the client after approval
- Number of times a specific output will be reworked free of cost
- Arbitration in case of dispute

PROPOSAL ACCEPTANCE

The proposed solution for developing a web site for the Creations restaurant is accepted by The Art Institute of Atlanta as per the terms and conditions set forth in the contract.

James W. Paul II, CCE, CSC, FMP	Date
Assistant Director, Department of Culinary Arts	
The Art Institute of Atlanta	

Christopher Altman	Date
Project Manager	

Case Study—Information Architecture and Copy

INTRODUCTION

This document contains the original and revised information that was presented to the client as a part of the information architecture exercise. As such, this was a "living" document. The user scenarios were written after the first draft of the site map was developed. During the process of development, the site map was revised to simplify navigation and create a more intuitive interface. The copy for the site was written after the draft of the site map was approved. The copy was integrated on the site and further revised on the basis of inputs provided by the client.

ORIGINAL SITE MAP

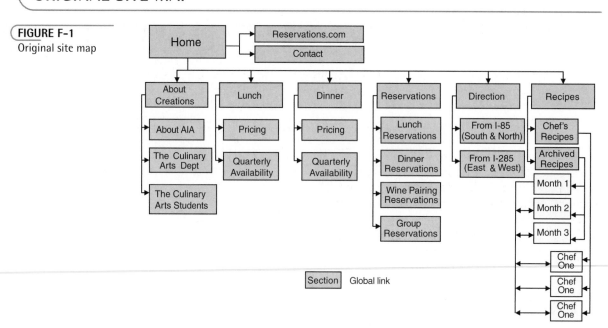

FIGURE F-1
Original site map

USER SCENARIO 1

Blake Jackson is a marketing professional working for a multinational company in the outer perimeter in Atlanta. He sometimes packs his lunch but mostly eats out with either clients or colleagues. As such, Blake is familiar with most fine-dining establishments in the perimeter area. Blake's colleague Sandra Malloney introduced him to the Creations restaurant. Sandra's daughter is a student in the Culinary Arts Program at The Art Institute of Atlanta. Blake's first experience of dining at the restaurant was pleasant, and he had determined that he would take one of his important clients there for lunch.

Blake was expecting a high-profile client from Argentina, Dr. Andrea Perez, to visit in 4 weeks, and he decided to take her to Creations for lunch. Blake is a great fan of the Internet. He does most of his shopping on-line and always has his browser window open on his computer at work. He once commented to his colleagues, "Any business worth its name needs to have a presence on the web to survive."

Event

Blake considered his options and decided that the elegance and educational setting of the Creations restaurant may appeal to Dr. Perez. He considered calling Creations, but given his habit of going first to the web, he searched Google for "Creations, Atlanta, fine dining, and The Art Institute of Atlanta." Creations was easy to identify since it was at the top of the results (see Figure F-2).

When he went to the site, the words "wine pairing" caught his eyes on the home page. Blake is an aspiring wine connoisseur. He clicked on the link for wine pairing and noticed that it took him to the reservations form for the event. He considered taking his mother to the event (as she knows her wines) but then decided to first finish the task at hand. Because he was interested in lunch, he looked for it in the links at the top and quickly found it.

Clicking on Lunch took him to a page that displayed the current menu. Some of the words on that page sounded a bit overwhelming, and he thought for a moment that maybe he should not take Dr. Perez to Creations (in case he had to pronounce some of these words and embarrasses himself). He thought to himself that it would be nice if the web site helped with the pronunciation and explained what some of these "tongue twisters" meant. While he was wondering about these things, he clicked on About Us out of curiosity and was intrigued by the photographs on the page. He clicked on the images and went through the whole list. When he was done, he decided that he was brave and would not get beaten by a few French words. He decided to go ahead and make the reservation. He clicked again on Lunch and looked for a link for reservations. At that point, he noticed that the Reservations link was sitting almost next to the Lunch link at the top.

Blake clicked on the Reservations link and noticed the form on the page. He reached for his wallet and pulled out his credit card. As he was filling in the

FIGURE F-2
User scenario 1

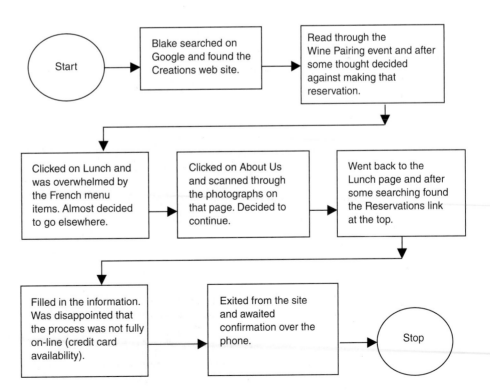

information, he found the calendar on the page very useful. The calendar showed the days on which lunch and dinner were served. Blake knew that the reservations fill up rather quickly and wondered whether the calendar indicated days on which reservations were still open. He found nothing to indicate that on the screen and decided to go ahead with the reservation anyway.

After Blake had filled in all the information, he realized that he had still not entered his credit card number. It was then that he noticed that this was a request for reservations and that confirmation would be done over the phone in 24 hours. He found this a bit odd. He sent in his reservation request and then went back to the stock market ticker that he normally left the browser on.

USER SCENARIO 2

Aretha Solomon is a proud grandmother of a star student, Regina Peters, in the Culinary Arts Department at The Art Institute of Atlanta. Regina tells her grandmother about all the lovely food that she has learned to cook and aesthetically present at the table. Over the 12 months that Regina has been in school, her grandmother has seen her grow in confidence and skill. Aretha wants to show her support to her granddaughter by having dinner at the Creations dining room, where she is getting her practical training in the kitchen. Aretha is planning to surprise Regina by going there on her birthday.

Besides being a doting grandmother, Aretha runs her own business as a florist. She has a regular and loyal body of clientele of offices and private homes in eastern Atlanta. Aretha recently put her business on-line and has started to see a modest growth in her business. Although she does not maintain her web site herself, she does know the basics of web site development and has become quite an avid web surfer of late.

Aretha figured that the Creations dining room would probably have a web site and decided to check out the possibility of making an on-line reservation.

Event

Aretha got the URL for the Creations web site from the school catalog that Regina had left with her. She entered the URL and was intrigued by the photographs on the home page (see Figure F-3). She wondered whether Regina featured in any of the photographs and first went through all the photographs on the home page. She noticed that there was a link labeled About Us and decided to check out that section, just in case there were more photographs in that section. On going to the section, she did see more photographs and some information on Creations. She glanced through the copy and again went through the photographs. As she was doing this, she realized that there was a Students section and decided to check out that section. She read the copy in that section with interest and also went through more photographs. She was slightly disappointed that her granddaughter was not in any of the pictures but was delighted to read about her program and school.

At this point, Aretha got called away to attend to some business needs, so she quickly closed the browser.

Aretha returned to the web site an hour later and clicked directly on the Reservations link. She noticed that she needed to fill out a form in order to make the reservations but that the form did not ask for her credit card number. Aretha was slightly relieved because she had just barely started the credit card transaction on her own site and was very wary about the security of information on the Internet. While she was filling out the form, she wondered whether she could get some details about the

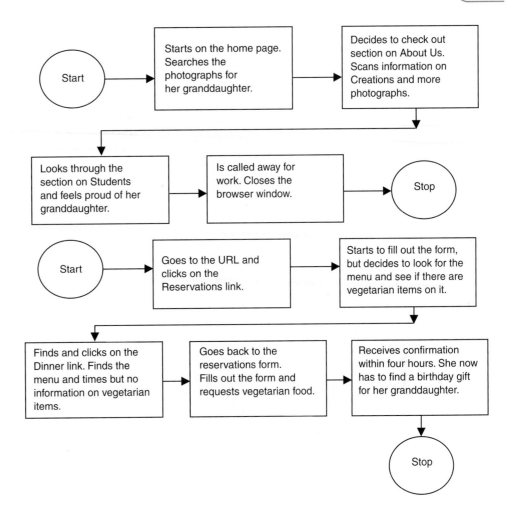

timings for the dinner, the menu, and whether she could make a special meal request (she and her husband were vegetarians). She looked for a link for this information on the Reservations page but could not find it. She then looked for the link in the group of links that she had earlier clicked on and found labels for Lunch and Dinner.

Since her interest was in dinner, Aretha clicked on the Dinner link and found the menu and the calendar with available dates. It was only then that she realized that Creations did not serve dinner every evening, but fortunately it did have a dinner date on Regina's birthday. She looked through the menu and found that most courses appeared to have a vegetarian option. However, there was no specific mention on the page about these meals being truly vegetarian.

As she was searching for the information on the Dinner page, she noticed that there was a link labeled Recipes. She made a mental note of coming back to the site when she had a bit of time on hand and checking out that section.

She decided to go back to the form and send in her reservation and then take it as it came. Back on the Reservations page, she filled in all the information and made use of the calendar to ensure that she got the date/day right. She filled in the special request for a vegetarian meal and clicked on the Send button.

Aretha got a call back within 4 hours confirming her reservation. She gave details of her credit card over the phone and smiled to herself. Her granddaughter was going to have the surprise of her life. Her next job was to pick out a gift for Regina!

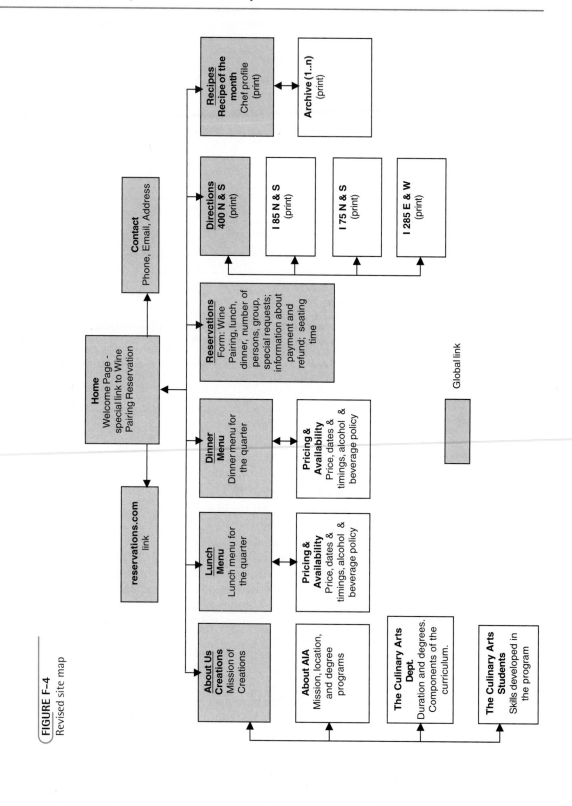

FIGURE F–4
Revised site map

COPY (JANUARY 2002)

Home

New! Wine Pairing Dinners

On November 14 and 16 at 7:00 PM, gourmet dinners offer four spectacular courses accompanied by specially chosen wines. A wine expert will be on hand to educate us all on how the wines were paired and what qualities make good wine pairings. Make the evening an event!

About Us

About Creations (default)

Classical French cuisine and white linen service are the tradition at Creations. Open to the public, the restaurant serves as a dining lab for culinary arts students at The Art Institute of Atlanta.

Creations' tempting menu offers fine-dining courses served in a relaxed environment. Daily tableside preparations and tempting desserts are served at Creations.

The Art Institute of Atlanta

The Art Institute of Atlanta is a diverse, dynamic institution of higher education whose mission is to educate creative professionals. The Art Institute of Atlanta is also the largest provider of culinary arts, web design, and photographic imaging education at the associates degree level in Georgia.

The Art Institute of Atlanta offers bachelor of fine arts degrees in graphic design, multimedia and web design, interior design, and media arts. Also, The Art Institute of Atlanta offers associates-level degrees in graphic design, multimedia and web design, photographic imaging, video production, and culinary arts. Program offerings are designed to prepare graduates for needs of a rapidly changing business environment.

The Culinary Arts Program

The seven-quarter Culinary Arts Program emphasizes hands-on training beginning with basic food preparation skills and continuing through advanced culinary arts techniques. The program includes a foundation in health, safety and nutrition studies, as well as a solid business background in cost control, supervision of food service personnel, and the management of a commercial kitchen.

Culinary Arts Students

Of all 2,000 Culinary Arts Program graduates, 95.5% were working in a related field within 6 months of graduation earning an average starting salary of $27,436. Graduates have joined the staffs of luxury resorts, fine-dining restaurants, and contract food service companies. With experience, graduates can advance to positions such as sous chef, executive chef, or food and beverage director. Others have become personal chefs, opened restaurants, or started catering companies.

Lunch

Lunch Pricing

Lunches are à la carte and range from $9 to $18 per person, plus tax and gratuity. Prices do not include beverages.

Beer and wine are available by the bottle and the glass to compliment your meal. If you wish to bring your own wine, a corkage fee of $7 per bottle applies.

Lunch Availability

Fall quarter service begins October 10 and runs through November 16.

Lunch is served on Thursdays and Fridays with seating starting at 1:30 pm.

Dinner

Dinner Pricing

Dinners include six courses for $30 per person, plus tax and gratuity. Prices do not include beverages.

Beer and wine are available by the bottle and the glass to compliment your meal. If you wish to bring your own wine, a corkage fee of $7 per bottle applies.

Quarterly Dinner Availability

Fall quarter service begins October 10 and runs through November 16.

Dinner is served Wednesdays and Fridays with seating at 7:00 pm.

Reservations

Reservation requests will be filled as long as space is available.

A VISA, MasterCard, Discover, or American Express is required to guarantee dinner reservations. Due to high demand, all dinner reservations (once we have confirmed with you) will be charged to your credit card, even if you do not use your reservation.

Lunch Reservations

Availability

Lunch is served on Thursdays and Fridays with seating starting at 1:30 pm.

This schedule is confirmed for fall quarter 2001 and may vary in future quarters.

Lunch Reservations

On-line reservations at Reservationsource.com

By calling 770.394.4814 ×2111 or 1.800.275.4242 ×2111

By fax 678.579.9124

By Mail: Creations
           c/o The Art Institute of Atlanta
           6600 Peachtree Dunwoody Road
           100 Embassy Row
           Atlanta, GA 30328

E-mail a reservation request: creationsdining@aol.com

Dinner Reservations

Availability

Dinner is served Wednesdays and Fridays with seating at 7:00 pm.
This schedule is confirmed for fall quarter 2001 and may vary in future quarters.

Dinner Reservations

On-line reservations at Reservationsource.com
By calling 770.394.4814 ×2111 or 1.800.275.4242 ×2111
By fax 678.579.9124
By Mail: Creations
c/o The Art Institute of Atlanta
6600 Peachtree Dunwoody Road
100 Embassy Row
Atlanta, GA 30328
E-mail a reservation request: creationsdining@aol.com

Group Reservations

Availability

Group reservations, up to 40 people, are welcomed.
Please call or e-mail for prices and reservations.

Group Reservations

By calling 770.394.4814 ×2111 or 1.800.275.4242 ×2111
E-mail a reservation request: creationsdining@aol.com

Wine Pairing Reservations

Availability

November 14 and 16 at 7:00 pm.
Please call or e-mail for price and reservations. Reservations required.

Wine Pairing Reservations

By calling 770.394.4814 ×2111 or 1.800.275.4242 ×2111
E-mail a reservation request: creationsdining@aol.com

Directions

GA 400
Directions with map
I-85
Directions with map

Creations Chef's Recipes

The chefs of Creations and The Art Institute of Atlanta offer you free, printable recipes to try some of the cuisine we prepare in our dining lab.

To print any recipe:

(1) click on Printer Friendly Version

(2) click on the Print button or select print on
your Internet browser

Case Study—Technical Feasibility Study

INTRODUCTION

The technologies considered for development of the Creations site include HTML 4.0, Cascading Style Sheets, JavaScript, PHP, and Macromedia Flash.

Other considerations discussed within this document include the directory structure and file naming conventions.

TARGET DELIVERY SYSTEM

The decisions about system requirements for the site are based on data from www.browserwatch.com. Browserwatch is a development site that tracks browser type, version, and operating system.

Supported Browsers

As of September 2, 2001, Browserwatch reports that 62.6% of surfers visited its web site with Internet Explorer and 21.7% of surfers with Netscape Navigator. With this data, the development team concludes that Internet Explorer and Netscape Navigator comprise 84.3% of web browsers. The site will be designed to work without errors on Internet Explorer and Netscape Navigator version 4.0 and higher.

Supported Platforms

As of July 2001, The W3School reported the Windows operating system accounting for 94% of web users. The Macintosh operating system accounted for 1% of web users, and other types of operating systems (i.e., Unix and Linux) accounted for 5% (source: www.w3schools.com/browsers/browsers_stats.asp).

The Creations web site will be designed to work on the following operating systems:
- Wintel Machines running the Windows operating system
- Macintosh machine with the Macintosh operating system

Target Screen Resolution

As of July 2001, The W3School reported 38% of web users with screen resolutions of 1024 × 768 or higher, 53% of web users with screen resolutions of 800 × 600, and 4% of web users with screen resolutions of 640 × 480. This data indicates that 91% of web users have screen resolutions of 800 × 600 or higher (source: www.w3schools.com/browsers/browsers_stats.asp).

The Creations web site will be designed for resolutions of 800×600 or higher.

Other Technical Considerations

As of July 2001, The W3School reported that 88% of web users used JavaScript-enabled browsers. The W3School also reported that 11% of web users turn off JavaScript (source: www.w3schools.com/browsers/browsers_stats.asp).

The Creations site will use JavaScript because of the added functionality and large percentage of web users with JavaScript-enabled browsers.

In addition, the site will be designed to work on browsers that support images and Cascading Style Sheets.

Server Information

The Art Institute of Atlanta will host the site on a Unix server with 30 megabytes of disk space. The server will have the capability to run CGI scripts and will support PHP implementation.

HTML 4.0

Hypertext Markup Language, or HTML, will be the primary development and integration tool for the site.

The development team will use HTML 4.0, which has been approved by the World Wide Web Consortium (W3C). More information about HTML 4.0 or WC3 can be located at www.w3.org/MarkUp/.

The *alt* attribute will describe the contents of all relevant images on the site.

In order to facilitate indexing of the site by search engines, metatags (keyword and description) will be used on the home page. The Creations site will use keywords such as "Fine Dining," "The Art Institute of Atlanta," "Atlanta," "French Cuisine," and "Business Lunch" to describe the Creations site.

The use of percent values with the width attribute of the table (<table>) tag as well as the table row and data cell (<tr> and <td>) tags will allow flexibility of resizing the browser window without losing the information on the screen. The Creations site will be designed to be resized to 75% of the maximum screen size.

CASCADING STYLE SHEETS

Cascading Style Sheets (CSS) will be used for specifying display features of text content and layout on the Creations site. CSS have been notoriously incompatible across browsers. At the same time, CSS offer the developers significant control over display features of the web site. In view of this, only CSS that can be supported across browsers will be used on the site.

JAVASCRIPT

JavaScript will add required client-side functionality to the Creations site. Internet Explorer 4.0, Netscape Navigator 4.0, and higher version browsers support JavaScript. It is possible to disable JavaScript from such browsers, but this is rarely done. The development team will assume that most visitors will use JavaScript-enabled browsers.

PHP

Hypertext Preprocessor, or PHP, will be used in the Reservations section. This server-side code is needed to collect data from the reservation form and submit the data via e-mail to the specified address.

IMAGE FORMATS

The JPEG file format will be used for photographic images. Flat art or illustrations will be displayed in the GIF file format.

FILE NAMING CONVENTIONS

Convention 1

The file naming convention will be based on a maximum of eight-character formula that describes the directory/title of the file. For example, The Art Institute of Atlanta page in the About Us section will be named "abot_aia.html."

Convention 2

Convention 2 will be applied to the Recipe section. Recipe files will be arranged by date and placed in an archive directory. The naming convention used for the recipe archive will begin with "rcp" and will be followed by the month and year. An example of a recipe for the month of June 2002 is "rcp_6_2002.html."

Image File Convention

The convention used for image files will describe the section and page of the file. For example, a GIF image on the Lunch page will be named "lun_text.gif."

Some images will be used throughout the entire site, such as spacer images (used to insert blank space). File names for these images will describe the image.

DIRECTORY STRUCTURE

The directory structure for the Creations site will be based on the site's navigation system. The Creations site is divided into six sections labeled About Us, Lunch, Dinner, Reservations, Directions, and Recipes. A directory (folder) will be created for each section.

The directory structure will be based on the navigation system so that the web master can use the navigation bar and flowchart of the site to determine where the files are located on the server.

All images for the site will be placed in an "images" directory. All original image files will be placed in a PSD folder in the root folder.

Case Study—Design Explorations

INTRODUCTION

This document presents three designs that were presented to the client during the design phase of the project. The project team recommended adoption of design 3 and presented their reasoning behind their preference for that design. The client agreed with the team's recommendation. The interface prototype was developed after this approval.

VISUAL CONCEPT BOARDS (COMPS)

FIGURE H–1
Design 1 Home page

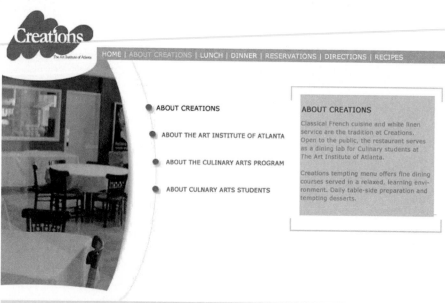

FIGURE H–2
Design 1 About
Creations page

FIGURE H-3
Design 2 Home page

HOME | ABOUT CREATIONS | LUNCH | DINNER | RESERVATIONS | DIRECTIONS | RECIPES

Creations is open to the public
and a great place for lunch or
dinner.

Offering Classical Freanch
cuisine and white linen service
Creations is the perfect place for
a special dinner, lunch, or celebration.

Please see what we have to
offer by sampling our lunch or
dinner menu on our web site.

Thank you
Chef James W. Paul
Director, Creations

NEW AT CREATIONS
WINE PAIRING EVENING
On November 14 and 16 at 7:00 pm
new gourmet dinners offer four spectacular courses accompanied by specially chosen wines. Make the
evening an event.

See Wine Pairing Reservations for
more details.

The Art Institute
of Atlanta*

HOME | ABOUT CREATIONS | LUNCH | DINNER | RESERVATIONS | DIRECTIONS | RECIPES   online reservations can be made at: Reservationsource.com

---

FIGURE H-4
Design 2 About
Creations page

HOME | **ABOUT CREATIONS** | LUNCH | DINNER | RESERVATIONS | DIRECTIONS | RECIPES

menu
ABOUT CREATIONS

ABOUT THE ART INSTITUTE OF ATLANTA

ABOUT THE CULINARY ARTS PROGRAM

ABOUT CULINARY ARTS STUDENTS

ABOUT CREATIONS

Classical French cuisine and white
linen service are the tradition at
Creations. Open to the public, the
restaurant serves as a dining lab for
Culinary students at The Art Institute of Atlanta.

Creations tempting menu offers fine
dining courses served in a relaxed,
learning environment. Daily tableside preparation and tempting desserts.

The Art Institute of Atlanta

Enjoy Fine Art inside Creations

The Art Institute
of Atlanta*

online reservations can be made at: Reservationsource.com

About Creations

Classical French cuisine and white linen service are the tradition at Creations. Open to the public, the restaurant serves as a dining lab for Culinary Arts Students at The Art Institute of Atlanta.

Creations' tempting menu offers fine-dining courses served in a relaxed environment. Daily tableside preparations and tempting desserts are served at Creations.

Enjoy fine-dinning in a relax environment.

online reservations can be made at: **ReservationSource.com**

Case Study—Production Specifications

INTRODUCTION

This is a partial documentation of production specifications for the Creations web site. The complete document was handed to the clients and will be used for future site modifications.

The *Directory Structure* lists the files and folders of the Creations web site.

The *Cascading Style Sheet Reference* lists classes and pseudo classes of the style sheets. The Cascading Style Sheet Reference will be used for changing color, images, or type on the site.

PHP Guidelines explain how to create variables in the PHP code to add and subtract elements of the reservation and contact forms.

HTML Data is a diagram and key to all table data cells for a given file. This section presents the "wireframe" diagram and a key with the table data cell's dimensions and content description.

DIRECTORY STRUCTURE

Folder

File Name	File Description
root	
index.html	Home page
links.html	Text links to every page of the site. links.html is designed to help search engines index every page of the site. links.html will not be viewed by the user.
about	
abot_crea.html	About Creations, information about the dining lab experience
abot_aia.html	About The Art Institute of Atlanta, information about the school
abot_cap.html	About the Culinary Arts Program, information about the program
abot_stu.html	About culinary arts students, information about students
lunch	
lun_menu.html	Lunch menu
lun_pric.html	Service calendar, times, and price information
dinner	
din_menu.html	Dinner menu
din_pric.html	Service calendar, times, and price information

res

res_info.php	Reservation page with reservation request form
res_thanks.php	Page after the reservation request form is submitted with PHP script that submits the form information to creationsdining@aol.com
pop_cal.html	Calendar seen from link on reservation page
contact.html	Contact page with contact information and form
contact_thanks.php	Page after contact form is submitted with PHP script that submits the information to creationsdining@aol.com

dir

dir_75.html	Directions from I-75
dir_85.html	Directions from I-85
dir_285.html	Directions from I-285
dir_400.html	Directions from GA 400
pri_75.html	Printer-friendly version of I-75 directions
pri_85.html	Printer-friendly version of I-85 directions
pri_285.html	Printer-friendly version of I-285 directions
pri_400.html	Printer-friendly version of GA 400 directions

recipe

rcp_info.html	Featured recipe of the month; this is the page that is loaded from the recipe link throughout the site
rcp_temp.html	Template for new recipes
rcp_jan2002.html	Example of archived recipe
rcp_cur_pr.html	Printer-friendly version of the featured recipe of the month
rcp_temp_pr.html	Printer-friendly version template
rcp_jan2002_pr.html	Example of printer-friendly version of archived recipe

images

All optimized images for the site

psd

All original images for the site

style

ie.css	Style sheet for all browsers other than Netscape 4.✕
net.css	Style sheet for Netscape 4.✕

scripts

browser.js	JavaScript file to detect NavApp Version and CSS file
noframes.js	Prevents site from being contained in a frameset

CASCADING STYLE SHEET REFERENCE (PARTIAL) ie.css

```
title {
    font-size : 14px;
    color : #660033;
    font-family : "Verdana", "Arial", "Helvetica", "Sans-serif";
    font-weight : bold;
    font-style : normal;
    text-decoration : none;
}

.title2 {
    font-size : 14px;
    color : 000000;
    font-family : "Verdana", "Arial", "Helvetica", "Sans-serif";
    font-weight : bold;
    font-style : normal;
    text-decoration : none;
}

titlewine {
    font-size : 13px;
    color : #000000;
    font-family : "Verdana", "Arial", "Helvetica", "Sans-serif";
    font-weight : bold;
    font-style : normal;
    text-decoration : none;
}

.titlewine2 {
    font-size : 12px;
    color : #000000;
    font-family : "Verdana", "Arial", "Helvetica", "Sans-serif";
    font-weight : bold;
    font-style : normal;
    text-decoration : none;
}
```

PHP GUIDELINES

```
<?php
if ($BeenSubmitted) {
    if ("creationsdining@aol.com"){
    if (mail("creationsdining@aol.com", "Creations Reservation Request",
            "Creations Web Site","
```

Reservation request from the Creations web site:

name:	$party
reservation date:	$date
number of people:	$persons
email:	$email1
email confirmation:	$email2
phone number:	$phone1 - $phone2 - $phone3 ext. $phone4
special requests:	$request")) {

```
    print ("");
    } else {print ("There is an error. The webmaster has been notified");}}
?>
```

The previous code is an example of the PHP script used in the res_thanks.php file and the contact_thanks.php file. The code collects information from the reservation form and contact form and sends the data to a specified e-mail address.

To change the destination e-mail address, two addresses must be modified. These pieces can be found in the previous example as the bolded **creationsdining@aol.com**.

To add a field to the reservation or contact form (such as an address field), two steps must be taken:

1) Add the field to form and define the *name* attribute of the field.
2) Use the "name" of the field as a PHP variable on the res_thanks.php or contact_thanks.php page. Add a "$" sign to the "name" of the field in the PHP script. The bolded terms in the previous code are examples of "names" from the reservation form.

PHP reference sites:

www.php.net

www.phpbuilder.com

HTML DATA

FIGURE I–1
Table structure for
index.html

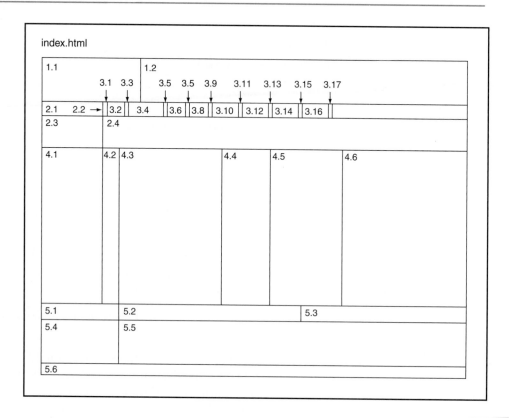

TABLE 1–1 Table Specifications for index.html

Table Ref.	Cell Width & Height	Cell Color	Align	Valign	Table Contents	Image Source	Image Width & Height	Alt Attribute	Link Description
1.10	220×100	#FFFFFF	left	top	Creations Logo	crea_logo.gif	220×100	Creations	
1.20	540×100	#FFFFFF	center	middle	Spacer	spacer_white.gif	540×1	none	
2.10	130×22	#E0E0E0	left	middle	Spacer	spacer_trans.gif	130×1	none	
2.20	100%×22	#E0E0E0	left	middle	Table 3.×				
2.30	130×36	#E0E0E0	left	bottom	Curve Image Top	home_curve1.gif	130×36	none	
2.40	630×36	#FFFFFF	left	top	Spacer	spacer_white.gif	630×1	none	
3.10	9×22	#E0E0E0	center	middle	Navigation Image	home_nav_left.gif	9×22	none	
3.20	46×22	#660033	center	middle	Copy				
3.30	9×22	#E0E0E0	center	middle	Navigation Image Link	home_nav_right.gif	9×22	none	
3.40	70×22	#E0E0E0	center	middle	Navigation Image Link	nav_center.gif	9×22	none	About Us
3.50	9×22	#E0E0E0	center	middle	Navigation Image Link	nav_center.gif	9×22	none	
3.60	50×22	#E0E0E0	center	middle	Navigation Image Link	nav_center.gif	9×22	none	Lunch
3.70	9×22	#E0E0E0	center	middle	Navigation Image Link	nav_center.gif	9×22	none	
3.80	55×22	#E0E0E0	center	middle	Navigation Image Link	nav_center.gif	9×22	none	Dinner
3.90	9×22	#E0E0E0	center	middle	Navigation Image Link	nav_center.gif	9×22	none	
3.10	95×22	#E0E0E0	center	middle	Navigation Image Link	nav_center.gif	9×22	none	Reservations
3.11	9×22	#E0E0E0	center	middle	Navigation Image Link	nav_center.gif	9×22	none	
3.12	75×22	#E0E0E0	center	middle	Navigation Image Link	nav_center.gif	9×22	none	Directions
3.13	9×22	#E0E0E0	center	middle	Navigation Image Link	nav_center.gif	9×22	none	
3.14	60×22	#E0E0E0	center	middle	Navigation Image Link	nav_center.gif	9×22	none	Recipe
3.15	9×22	#E0E0E0	center	middle	Navigation Image Link	nav_center.gif	9×22	none	
3.16	60×22	#E0E0E0	center	middle	Navigation Image Link	nav_center.gif	9×22	none	Contact
3.17	9×22	#E0E0E0	center	middle	Navigation Image Link	nav_center.gif	9×22	none	
4.10	130×374	#660033	left	top	Curve Image	home_curve2.gif	130×374	none	
4.20	37×374	#FFFFFF	right	top	Black Bars	spacer_black_bar.gif		none	
4.30	265×374	#FFFFFF	left	top	Copy				
4.40	6×374	#FFFFFF	left	top	Black Bars	spacer_black_bar.gif		none	
4.50	316×374	#FFFFFF	right	top	Image	pic_home.jpg	267×200	click image	
5.10	167×20	#E0E0E0	left	middle	Image	spacer_trans.gif	130×1	none	
5.20	490×20	#E0E0E0	left	middle	Links				Bottom Nav
5.30	100×20	#E0E0E0	right	middle	Link				Contact
5.40	167×50	#FFFFFF	left	bottom	Image/Link	ai_logo.gif	170×45	The Art Institute of Atlanta	
5.50	100×50	#FFFFFF	right	bottom	Link				Reservation Source.com
5.60	100%	#000000	center	middle	Image	spacer_black.gif	100%	none	

Case Study–Quality Assurance

INTRODUCTION

This document presents some quality assurance exercises undertaken during the process of production. The first report is an example of ongoing QA reports that were generated throughout the production cycle. The second report is a technical quality check provided by an on-line service. The third is a quality assurance report on language that was prepared by a language expert.

ONGOING QUALITY ASSURANCE (PARTIAL REPORT)

Date: November 25, 2001
From: Ameeta Jadav

1. Logo
   In one of my earlier messages I had suggested some ways of optimizing the logo so the AIA text is visible. Let's try it and see if we can improve on the logo.
2. Lines
   You have done a great job of cracking the code for displaying the lines on both sides of the text. My suggestion is that we should keep the same format for both sides (I like the one on the Home page, next to the image). The spoon in About Us is really not working very well.
3. The bottom navigation bar
   The white text is quite lost on the gray background. You may want to consider bolding the text rather than changing its color to white.
4. Contact information
   Needs to be put in.
5. The Dinner link
   The link is displayed in a different size and is underlined in the Recipes and Reservations sections.
6. Spelling of availability
   Needs to be corrected in the Lunch section.
7. Quarter availability
   I am not sure of what you plan to put in this section. It seems like this information may be more appropriate for Reservations. It may also be important to provide a link to Lunch reservations from the Lunch section and similarly for the Dinner section.
8. Redundancy
   The word "reservations" is redundant in the links for the Reservations section. We could remove it without any harm.

WEB SITE GARAGE (PARTIAL REPORT) (websitegarage.netscape.com/)

Date: December 17, 2001

Overall Page Rating	Fair
1. Browser Compatibility Check	Fair
2. !Register-It! Readiness Check	Poor
3. Load Time Check	Good
4. Dead Link Check	Excellent
5. Link Popularity Check	Error
6. Spelling Check	Good
7. Html Design Check	Poor

1. Browser Compatibility Check Fair

This utility checks how well your web page is displayed when viewed with different browsers.
Total Warnings: 21
Compatibility Warnings by Browser:

Browsers	Warnings
Netscape Navigator 4.0	3
Netscape Navigator 3.0	7
Microsoft Internet Explorer 4.0	0
Microsoft Internet Explorer 3.0	3
America Online 3.0	3
America Online 4.0	0
WebTV	5

LANGUAGE REVIEW (PARTIAL REPORT)

Date: December 30, 2001
From: Mrs. Lynn

About Us/Art Institute

Last paragraph has "gradates" (s/b "graduates")

About Us/Cul Art Students

First word "off" (s/b "of"?)

Dinner

In the cursive writing on the right: "dreate" s/b "create" and I think there should be an "e" at the end of "six-course."

Directions

In the directions pages you have used the word "onto," which I don't think is right. It is written in every directional paragraph that way.

Every directional page has "Peachthree," s/b "Peachtree" even on one of the maps (400 N and S).

Case Study–Usability Study

INTRODUCTION

This report was prepared by Sydney Aron after she concluded the study using observation, interview, and questionnaire. Sydney worked with three participants during the study. In a more elaborate setting, the study could have included more diverse and larger number of participants. However, the process is representative of a larger study. The study was approached as a naturalistic, ethnographic examination. As such, it did not rely on statistical data or analysis. A different evaluation model could have included collection and analysis of statistical data, such as time spent in each section, number of errors on each page, degree of confusion with specific interfaces, and so on.

USABILITY STUDY REPORT

Date: 20, February, 2002
From: Sydney Aron

Objective

To determine whether the information in the Creations web site is presented in an intuitive manner by conducting a formal usability study with three subjects belonging to the predefined target audience.

Method

The usability study was designed to test the intuitiveness of the navigation and the functionality of the web site. The study designer began with prioritization of the functions and objectives of the site. Based on these priorities, three instruments—a task list, a questionnaire, and an interview—were developed. Recommendations given in this report were compiled from the analysis of the data from these instruments.

To ensure a degree of validity and reliability of the instruments, a pilot run was performed with one participant. The task list, questionnaire, and interview were modified after this exercise. The instruments were revised on the basis of the fact that some of the questions and tasks were redundant.

The usability study was conducted by inviting three participants in the target audience to execute a list of predefined tasks. The study was conducted with one participant at a time. The participants had moderate to advanced knowledge of the web. Two of the participants had minimal knowledge of web development, and the third had none. None of the participants had any prior knowledge of the Creations dining lab.

The participants were expected to complete the task list while verbalizing their experiences. The participants were directed to talk through their reasoning for selecting one option versus another while the observer recorded the data. To record this data, the observer sat behind each participant while the tasks were completed. Once a participant completed the task list, he or she answered a short questionnaire as well as participated in a short interview. The exercise took approximately one and a half hours each.

Overall Findings

The site seemed to perform well for most participants in the study. Collectively, they thought that the idea of on-line reservations was great. They were especially partial to full menu listings for lunch and dinner. They also said that they would recommend this site to their friends, family, and colleagues who expressed interest in a fine-dining experience in Atlanta, Georgia. Although there was a positive response, some usability issues were identified with the site:

Labels

- Participants found the labels to be very intuitive.
- The Contact section was not located by any of the participants. Participants seem to skip over this section because its location during the time of the tests was in a bar at the bottom of the page. Although contact information was dispersed throughout the site, when asked to complete the task to find information, such as the phone number for Creations, the participant had to hunt to find it. This is categorized not so much a labeling issue as a placement-of-label issue.
- The "Availability and Pricing" label confused multiple participants. The listing of prices of the respective menus was clear, but the label of availability was not. Participants understood the label of "Availability" to mean that Creations would have openings for the dates shown.

Recommendations

- "Contact" should be a part of the primary navigation.
- Rename the "Availability and Pricing" label as "Reservation Dates" and move the pricing information to the Lunch and Dinner sections.

Navigation

- Although the navigation was well organized and easy to use, some issues were identified and suggestions made on how to resize and reorganize the navigation.
- The Contact link at the bottom of the page was not apparent.
- Participants experienced the most issues with the reservation-making process.
- Participants expected the dates in the calendar to be active.
- None of the participants clicked on any of the links located at the bottom of every page on the site.
- Initially, the placement of the secondary navigation was questioned as to whether participants would recognize its presence, as it blends in with the design, but the participants had no problem identifying the location and using the secondary navigation.

Recommendations

- Move the Contact link to the primary navigation at the top of the page.
- Make the dates in the calendar interactive wherein the availability of lunch or dinner could be clearly associated with each date.

Sections

Home

▶ Although the information presented on the Home page is clear, one user requested cross-links be added to the site and especially to the home page to encourage navigation in the site.

Recommendations

▶ Provide cross-links between pages via embedded text links. For example, the reference made to the Culinary Arts Program at the Art Institute of Atlanta should be a link to that section of the site.

About Us

▶ No issues were noted with the information presented in this section.

Lunch and Dinner

▶ The information presented about menu selections was clear.
▶ No information about menu prices was present.
▶ The participants noted that the information on those pages was out of date.

Recommendations

▶ Inform patrons about the prices of menu items.
▶ Ensure that the information on these pages is always up to date.
▶ One participant suggested narrowing the navigation by combining "Lunch" and "Dinner" into a "Menu" tab instead.

Calendar

▶ Although the purpose of the calendar was recognized, there was some confusion concerning how to interpret the information. Participants were baffled by the color coding of available dates. Participants requested that, if a calendar must be used, the dates within the calendar be interactive.

Recommendations

▶ Make the dates in the calendar interactive wherein the availability of lunch or dinner could be clearly associated with each date.
▶ Consider renaming "Calendar" as "Reservation Dates."
▶ Reduce the confusion by finding another avenue to communicate availability of Creations' seating.

Reservations

Specific issues with the functionality of the form were observed in the following areas:

▶ There should be a field where the participant can enter the exact number of their party instead of using the drop-down and selecting "group."
▶ The drop-down to select a date and seating time for a reservation should be reexamined.
▶ The form validation for the e-mail is too case sensitive.
▶ There should be a maximum number of characters entered into the phone number fields.

Recommendations

- Allow visitors to enter the exact number of persons in the party in a text field rather than using the drop-down menu.
- Allow visitors to enter the exact date they wish to dine at Creations in a text field.
- Reprogram the form validation for e-mail.
- Ensure that the phone number field has a limit to the number of characters that could be entered.

Specific issues with the presentation of information of the Reservations page were observed in the following areas:

- The verbiage at the bottom of the page is not displayed prominently enough.
- The link to *creationsdining@aol.com* is not active.
- Arrangements for same-day reservations are not addressed on this page or anywhere on the site.
- Information about the no-show policy of Creations is not addressed on this page.
- Participants did not receive an e-mail response from Creations stating that their reservation request would be processed. Participants also complained about receiving a confirmation phone call instead.
- Information about accommodating large or private parties is not addressed on this page.
- The link at the bottom of the page to reservationsource.com confused the participants and conflicts with the intent of the participants using the form provided on the Creations site.
- Participants suggested that the Reservations form model be something similar to that of www.orbitz.com.

Recommendations

- Move the verbiage above the Submit button. This will help facilitate the patrons' acknowledgment of Creations' reservation process and policy.
- Embed a link to creationsdining@aol.com
- Inform the visitors about making same-day reservations.
- Inform the visitors about no-show policy.
- Consider response via e-mail rather than phone call.
- Remove the link to reservation.com from the site completely. One of the objectives to the site is to encourage the visitor to make reservations for Creations on the site. Also, information about Creations on reservationsource.com conflicts with some of the information presented on the Creations site.

Directions

- The participants found Directions section helpful. The text directions, map, and printable versions create a very participant friendly section of the site. However, they commented that it would be beneficial to add the map to the printable version of the directions.
- Multiple participants also suggested that adding a link to Mapquest.com from this page would be helpful as well.
- Some participants were a little taken aback when the Directions section went straight to the GA-400 section. They had expected an introduction to the section first.
- Participants expected the title of the set of directions to be displayed under the map.

Recommendations

- Add a black-and-white map to the printable version of the directions to Creations.
- Consider adding a link to Mapquest.com from the Directions page.
- Create an index page for Directions with pictures of The Art Institute of Atlanta and information about points of reference.
- Display the title of the map/page under the map on each page.

Recipe

- The participants thought that this section was clever. They commented that they would like a picture of the entrée that correlates to the recipe.

Recommendations

- Provide a matching image of the entrée on this page.

Contact

- None of the participants identified the Contact link at the bottom of the page. Participants located some contact information in different areas of the site.
- No comments form exists on the Contact page.

Recommendations

- Move the Contact link to the top navigation panel.
- Consider adding a comment form to the Contact page.

Aesthetics

- The participants commented that the layout was appealing and simple.
- Participants commented more on the quality of the images than on the content depicted in the images. Participants made multiple remarks during the test-taking process that the images were somewhat muddy, unappetizing, and in need of major improvement.
- Because none of the participants had ever been to Creations, they could not comment on whether the ambience on the site matched the one in the dining lab.

Recommendations

- Improve the quality of images used on the site.
- Communicate the ambiance of Creations through typography, layout, quality of images, and tone of content present.

Technical Performance

- One participant out of three commented that the download was slow.
- The reservation form did work properly, but there were several recommendations on how the functionality could be improved.

Recommendations

- Improve the optimization of images used on the site to ensure a quicker download time.
- Explore more sophisticated features for making on-line reservations.

General

▶ The overall reaction of the participants to the site was positive.
▶ The participants did not require a significant learning curve in getting to know the content organization and interface for the site. Most participants found the needed information in two clicks.

TASK LIST

Dear Participant,

Thank you for agreeing to participate. A usability study is an evaluation exercise that will give the developers valuable insight into the ease of use, functionality, and effectiveness of the site.

The purpose of this exercise is to evaluate the user friendliness of the Creations site. When developing the site, we made a number of assumptions about how it will be used by the end users. We would now like to evaluate our assumptions.

Please remember that this is an evaluation of the site and not of your understanding of how to use it.

In order to carry out this evaluation, we have devised a series of tasks that we would like you to perform.

It is important that you carry them out in the same order in which they are listed.

In order to understand your experiences, we would like to observe your interactions with the site as you use it. A person (Observer) will sit behind you as you go through the site. We encourage you to share your observations and comments on your experiences as you go through the site.

Please inform the Observer when you complete each task. Start the next task after he or she asks you to continue. This is being done so that we do not miss out on any information.

The time taken to complete this exercise may vary from person to person. However, as per our estimates, completion of the whole exercise should take approximately 1 hour. Once the exercise has been completed, we would like you to fill out a questionnaire as well as ask you a few questions about your experience. This should take about 30 minutes.

Thank you once again for your time and interest.

Sincerely,
Sydney Aron

Activities

1.	Access the site by typing the following URL: www.christopheraltman.com/creations/development
2.	Find the mission and the purpose of Creations
3.	Book a wine pairing reservation for February 27 for two people
4.	View the lunch menu
5.	Find out which days lunch will be served for February 2002
6.	View the dinner menu
7.	Go back to the Home page
8.	Find the availability of dinner for February 20, 2002
9.	Find the price of a lunch entrée with two courses.
10.	Inquire about a vegetarian meal
11.	Make reservations for 10 people for dinner on February 20, 2002, and complete the form
12.	Find out which credit cards are accepted at Creations
13.	Get directions to Creations from I-85 South
14.	Print out the directions from I-85 South
15.	Find the telephone number for Creations
16.	Find information about the Culinary Arts Program at The Art Institute of Atlanta
17.	Print out any recipe
18.	Look at the recipe archive for interesting recipes
19.	Spend about 5 minutes just browsing through the site

Questionnaire

1.	Based on the content presented in this web site, would you recommend it to a friend? Explain.
2.	Based on the content presented in the web site, would you make a reservation to eat at Creations? Explain.
3.	Would you return to the site?
4.	What did you like most about the site?
5.	What did you like least about the site?

6.	Do you feel you can trust the information presented on the site?
7.	Were you able to find the information easily?
8.	Was the information clearly labeled?
9.	What is your opinion of the visual aesthetics?

Interview Schedule

1.	What is your level of expertise in using the Internet? How many hours are you on the Internet per week?
2.	What was your first impression of the site?
3.	Could you immediately tell this site was an informational site about a restaurant at the Art Institute of Atlanta?
4.	Is the site easy to use?
5.	Do you feel the information has been labeled clearly?
6.	How do you feel about the aesthetics of the site? In your opinion, are the colors and images used appropriately? Do you like the layout?
7.	Would you recommend this site to your friends who are interested in getting information about restaurants in Atlanta?
8.	How does this site compare as an information source with newspapers and television? (to find out if they perceived anything unique about the medium and the site)
9.	Is there anything you would add to this site?

Participant 1

Observer: Sydney Aron   Date: 6 Feb, 2002   Place: Office Connection: T1

Task List

No	Activity	Target Section	Comments
1.	Access the site by typing the following URL: http://www.christophersaltman.com/creations/development	Home	**How long does the site take to load?** *Site loads quickly. Browses over the page for about 10 seconds and moves on to the next task.*
2.	Find the mission and the purpose of Creations	About	**What options does the participant click before locating About Us?** Goes directly to the About Us section.
3.	Book a wine pairing reservation for February 27 for two people	Reservations	**What options does the participant click first?** Goes directly to Reservations. Experiences no difficulty using the form and selects a date from the drop-down menu. Makes no suggestions on how to improve the reservation process. Does not read verbiage at the bottom of the page. Submits reservations and goes to the Recipes section before completing the next task.
4.	View the lunch menu	Lunch	**What options does the participant click before locating the item?** *Immediately goes to Lunch.*
5.	Find out which days lunch will be served for February 2002	Lunch/ Availability	**What options does the participant click before locating the item?** *From Lunch, participant goes to Availability and Pricing. Participant looks at the calendar and comments that the color coding is useful and intuitive.*
6.	View the dinner menu	Dinner	**Does the participant go directly to Dinner?** *The participant went to the corresponding tab directly.*
7.	Go back to the Home page	Home	**Does the participant click on the Creations logo or on Home in the primary navigation?** Participant clicks on Home in the primary navigation.

No	Activity	Target Section	Comments
8.	Find the availability of dinner for February 27, 2002	Dinner/ Availability	**What steps does the participant take to find this information?** *Participant chooses Dinner and then goes over to Availability and Pricing section. Participant looks at the color-coded calendar and comments that she has no problems using it.*
9.	Find the price of a lunch entrée with two courses	Lunch/ Availability	*Participant has no problem finding this information in the target area and corresponding prices.*
10.	Inquire about a vegetarian meal	Contact	**What options does the participant click before locating the item?** *Participant selects the menu sections first and browses through to see whether Creations offers vegetarian entrées. She also explains that during the reservation process she would inquire about a vegetarian meal by writing special requests in the field provided on the form.*
11.	Make reservations for 10 people for dinner on February 20, 2002, and complete the form	Reservations	**Did the participant experience any problems filling out the form?** *No. Participant uses the special requests box to let Creations know that there are 10 people in her party. Participant experiences difficulty entering her phone number in the fields provided, as she cannot tab over and there is not a maximum amount of characters she can put in the spaces.*
12.	Find out which credit cards are accepted at Creations	Reservations	**What options does the participant click before locating the item?** *Participant goes Home first, then to About Us, then to Directions, and finally to Reservations. Takes her approximately one minute to find the information. She comments that this information about the credit cards needs to be in a more obvious spot on the page.*
13.	Get directions to Creations from I-85 South	Directions	**Does the participant comment on whether the maps are useful and the directions were clear?** *Participant goes to Directions and reads through the directions. She thinks the elements (map and directions) are helpful.*

(continued)

Task List (continued)

No	Activity	Target Section	Comments
14.	Print out the directions from I-85 South	Directions	**Does the participant successfully print the directions? Did they use the close window button, or did they use the "X" at the top right of the window?** Participant does not use the printer-friendly version; instead, she uses the print icon in her browser to print the information.
15.	Find the telephone number for Creations	Contact	**Does the participant locate the contact link at the bottom of the page?** *No. Participant clicks on Home first to see whether the contact information is there. She then tries About Us but has no luck in finding the contact information. Neither section displays the phone number.*
16.	Find information about the Culinary Arts Program at the Art Institute of Atlanta	About Us/ The Culinary Arts Program	**What options does the participant click before locating the item?** Participant goes to About Us but never looks to see whether anything in the secondary navigation leads her to information about the Culinary Arts Program at the Art Institute of Atlanta.
17.	Print out any recipe	Recipe	**Does the participant use the print button on the browser or the "printer-friendly version"?** Participant goes to Recipes and uses the print button at the top of the browser window. She comments that having this section was a good idea. Suggests pictures be added to this section so that the visitor can see what it should look like.
18.	Look at the recipe archive for interesting recipes	Recipe	**Does the participant locate the desired information?** *Yes. Participant sees the recipe archive drop-down with no problem.*
19.	Spend about 5 minutes just browsing through the site		

Questionnaire

No	Question	Response
1.	Based on the content presented in this web site, would you recommend it to a friend? Explain.	*Yes. Clear and straightforward information would be useful to many.*
2.	Based on the content presented in the web site, would you make a reservation to eat at Creations? Explain.	*Yes. I eat out frequently. The menu is tempting, and the prices are reasonable.*
3.	Would you return to the site?	*Yes.*
4.	What did you like most about the site?	*I like the way the directions are presented on the site as well as the way the pricing information is presented.*
5.	What did you like least about the site?	*I had difficulty finding out which credit cards were accepted at Creations.*
6.	Do you feel you can trust the information presented on the site?	*Yes.*
7.	Were you able to find the information easily?	*Yes.*
8.	Was the information clearly labeled?	*Generally, but some information was difficult to find.*
9.	What is your opinion of the visual aesthetics?	*Pleasing and clean.*

Interview

No	Question	Response
1.	What is your level of expertise in using the Internet? How many hours are you on the Internet per week?	*Moderate. Spend about 20 hours per week on the Internet.*
2.	What was your first impression of the site?	*Clean looking.*
3.	Could you immediately tell this site was an informational site about a restaurant at The Art Institute of Atlanta?	*Yes.*
4.	Is the site easy to use?	*Yes. Navigation is designed well.*
5.	Do you feel the information has been labeled clearly?	*Yes.*
6.	How do you feel about the aesthetics of the site? In your opinion, are the colors and images used appropriately? Do you like the layout?	*Yes. The site is clean, and the images are not so overbearing as to take away from the information.*

(continued)

Interview (continued)

No	Question	Response
7.	Would you recommend this site to your friends who are interested in getting information about restaurants in Atlanta?	*Yes. Comments that the menu is tempting.*
8.	How does this site compare as an information source with newspapers and television? (to find out whether they perceived anything unique about the medium and the site)	*Comments that the site is better than a newspaper or television because there is way more information presented on the site. Participant likes that the menu is listed in full.*
9.	Is there anything you would add to this site?	*Wants to add pictures next to the recipes and wants the telephone number for Creations to be obvious on every page.*

Participant 2

Observer: Sydney Aron   Date: 3 Feb, 2002   Place: Home Comp. Connection: 56K

Task List (Partial)

No	Activity	Target Section	Comments
1.	Access the site by typing the following URL: http://www.christophersaltman.com/creations/development	Home	**How long does the site take to load? What did the participant do when the Home page loaded?** (scrolled up and down, read specific items, clicked on an option right away) *Site loads in approximately 1 minute. Participant thinks that by optimizing the images, the download time will decrease considerably. Participant takes time to read information on the Home page before he moves on to the next tab.*
2.	Find the mission and the purpose of Creations	About	**What options does the participant click before locating About Us?** Participant goes directly to About Us to find the mission and purpose of Creations. Participant comments that although he does not see a clearly defined mission in the text, the content he does read will suffice. After reading about Creations, the participant goes back Home to get more information.
3.	Book a wine pairing reservation for February 27 for two people	Reservations	**What options does the participant click first?** *Experiences no difficulty in completing this task and goes directly to Reservations. Clicks the calendar link at the top-right corner of the form. Comments about the calendar being confusing and hard to use. Gets impatient, closes the calendar, and goes back to the provided drop-down menu to select the date to make reservations for the wine pairing. He completes the form and adds that the form could benefit from more functionality. Also comments that he operates on the "don't read policy," which basically means that he ignores verbiage (as seen at the bottom of the form) on web pages. If that information is important, it needs to be at the top. Questions the reservations policy and process of Creations. Participant inquires about the process for same-day reservations.*

Questionnaire

No	Question	Response
1.	Based on the content presented in this web site, would you recommend it to a friend? Explain.	*Yes. I would suggest that they review site for information about Creations and check out the menu.*
2.	Based on the content presented in the web site, would you make a reservation to eat at Creations? Explain.	*Yes. I would like to make a reservation at the restaurant but would not want to book the reservation on-line.*
3.	Would you return to the site?	*Yes.*
4.	What did you like most about the site?	*I like the recipe section of the site where I can view some of the recipes created in the Culinary Arts Department at the Art Institute of Atlanta.*
5.	What did you like least about the site?	*I am not pleased with the reservation-making process. More functionality should be added, and a new system for making reservations should be implemented.*
6.	Do you feel you can trust the information presented on the site?	*Yes.*
7.	Were you able to find the information easily?	*Yes.*
8.	Was the information clearly labeled?	*Yes.*
9.	What is your opinion of the visual aesthetics?	*I would like to see more variations in the layouts on the pages. The site seems stagnant, and the quality of images used is poor.*

Interview

No	Question	Response
1.	What is your level of expertise in using the Internet? How many hours are you on the Internet per week?	*Highly advanced. Spends about 40 hours per week on the Internet.*
2.	What was your first impression of the site?	*Would like to see more details about Creations on the Home page.*
3.	Could you immediately tell this site was an informational site about a restaurant at The Art Institute of Atlanta?	*Yes.*
4.	Is the site easy to use?	*Yes.*
5.	Do you feel the information has been labeled clearly?	*Yes.*

No	Question	Response
6.	How do you feel about the aesthetics of the site? In your opinion, are the colors and images used appropriately? Do you like the layout?	*The site needs some pizzazz. Would like to see pictures of the recipes in the recipe section. Comments that the images were muddy and boring. Also comments that there was not a lot of variation in the layout.*
7.	Would you recommend this site to your friends who are interested in getting information about restaurants in Atlanta?	*Yes. The menu is tempting.*
8.	How does this site compare as an information source with newspapers and television? (to find out whether they perceived anything unique about the medium and the site)	*It is a useful tool for Creations. Comments that he has never been to a restaurant-based web site before.*
9.	Is there anything you would add to this site?	*Would add more functionality to the site, including an interactive calendar and a different method for making on-line reservations.*

Participant 3

Observer: Sydney Aron   Date: 5 Feb, 2002   Place: Home Comp. Connection: 56K

Task List

No	Activity	Target Section	Comments
1.	Access the site by typing the following URL: http://www. christophersaltman.com/ creations/development	Home Page	**How long does the site take to load?** *Site takes approximately 45 seconds to load. Does not comment about a download time.*
2.	Find the mission and the purpose of Creations	About Page	**What options does the participant click on before locating About Us?** Goes directly to About Us to find the mission and purpose of Creations. She follows directions under the image provided and begins clicking. Participant likes the idea of an array of images but suggests the designer add Next and Back arrows so other participants can toggle between the pictures. Participant scans through the About Us subnavigation to view more information about the Creations section.
3.	Book a wine pairing reservation for February 27 for two people	Reservations	**What options does the participant click first?** *Experiences no difficulty in completing this task and goes directly to Reservations. Begins to scroll over the reservations page. She begins to give suggestions on how to improve the form as well as the reservations process. Suggests that the form could be made more functional and that instead of using the calendar to find out availability, there should just be a link that says "lunch" or "dinner." Once the participant had made the decision, then they will be able to fill in the day. Of course, this all has to be databased. Participant also questions what happens if you are a "no-show." What is "reservation source"? Questions case-sensitive e-mail on the form validation.*

Questionnaire

No	Question	Response
1.	Based on the content presented in this web site, would you recommend it to a friend? Explain.	*Yes. The content is solid, clear, and easy to read and understand with the exception of Reservations and Availability and Pricing.*
2.	Based on the content presented in the web site, would you make a reservation to eat at Creations? Explain.	*Yes. I feel that the menu offers a wide range of selections for lunch and dinner. Reservations lacks the desired functionality so instead of booking on-line, I will call Creations instead.*
3.	Would you return to the site?	*Yes. I would return to the site if I enjoyed the dinner from a previous evening or if I had friends interested in the Culinary Arts Program at the Art Institute of Atlanta.*
4.	What did you like most about the site?	*The site is easy to use, and the information is straightforward and easy to find.*
5.	What did you like least about the site?	*The labeling should condense more. The link to ReservationSource.com should be removed to avoid any confusion.*
6.	Do you feel you can trust the information presented on the site?	*Yes.*
7.	Were you able to find the information easily?	*Yes. Clearly labeled*
8.	What is your opinion of the visual aesthetics?	*I feel the images presented in the Lunch and Dinner sections are not appealing. The entrées should be popping off the screen. I like the layout. The use of graphics is appropriate.*

Interview

No	Question	Response
1.	What is your level of expertise in using the Internet? How many hours are you on the Internet per week?	*Highly advanced. Spends about 40 hours per week on the Internet.*
2.	What was your first impression of the site?	*Participant thought the site was clean and was laid out well.*
3.	Could you immediately tell this site was an informational site about a restaurant at The Art Institute of Atlanta?	*Yes.*
4.	Is the site easy to use?	*Yes.*

(continued)

Interview (continued)

No	Question	Response
5.	Do you feel the information has been labeled clearly?	*Yes.*
6.	How do you feel about the aesthetics of the site? In your opinion are the colors and images used appropriately? Do you like the layout?	*Participant would like the pictures to be sharper as well as more appetizing.*
7.	Would you recommend this site to your friends who are interested in getting information about restaurants in Atlanta?	*Yes, especially if I have enjoyed a good meal there.*
8.	How does this site compare as an information source with newspapers and television? (to find out whether they perceived anything unique about the medium and the site)	*Participant thinks the site is useful as a marketing tool. Participant does not know of any other restaurant site out there where you can make reservations.*
9.	Is there anything you would add to this site?	*Participant wants to reorganize the reservation process.*

Credits

ILLUSTRATIONS

G. Raghavendra Reddy

WEB SITES

The inclusion of the web sites in this book has been possible with the kind cooperation of many organizations. In keeping with the nature of the industry, it is possible that these sites will change over time.

Chapter 1

Figure	Credit	URL
3. Site map for www.terraincognita. com © Terra Incognita	© Terra Incognita Printed with permission from Terra Incognita	http://www.terraincognita.com
4. Main page from www.terraincognita. com © Terra Incognita	© Terra Incognita Printed with permission from Terra Incognita	http://www.terraincognita.com
5. Our Studio page from www.terraincognita.com © Terra Incognita	© Terra Incognita Printed with permission from Terra Incognita	http://www.terraincognita.com
6. Behind the Scenes page from www.terraincognita. com © Terra Incognita	© Terra Incognita Printed with permission from Terra Incognita	http://www.terraincognita.com

Chapter 2

Figure	Credit	URL
1. Example of a brand site: Arden's Garden (www.ardensgarden.com)	Printed with permission from Arden's Garden.	http:// www.ardensgarden.com
2. Example of a personal site: Renee Peters (www.reneepeters.com)	Printed with permission from Renee Peters.	http://www.reneepeters.com
3. Example of an Event Invitation by Yuki Kawakita (www.studioyk.com/a.htm)	Printed with permission from StudioYK, Inc., and The Art Institute of Atlanta.	http://www.studioyk.com/a.htm
4. Example of a B2C e-commerce site: Shoebuy.com (www.shoebuy.com)	Printed with permission from Shoebuy.com, Inc.	http://:www.shoebuy.com
5. Example of web-based learning site: On Becoming Human (Learning Activity) (www.becominghuman.org)	Printed with permission from the Institute of Human Origins.	http://www.becominghuman.org
6. Example of web-supported learning: course site designed by Aarron Walter (www.thecreativityengine.com)	Printed with permission from Aarron Walter and The Art Institute of Atlanta.	http://www.thecreativityengine.com/mm120/
7. Example of an on-line synchronous virtual classroom: EpicLearning (www.epiclearning.com) and Placeware; showing one of the delivery vehicles in EpicLearning's patented "Blended Learning" technology	Printed with permission from EpicLearning.	http://www.epiclearning.com
8. Example of a news site: *New Zealand Herald* (www.nzherald.co.nz)	Printed with permission from W&H Interactive Ltd, © The New Zealand Herald 2002.	http://www.nzherald.co.nz
9. Example of an intranet site: Intranets.com (www.intranets.com)	Printed with permission from Intranets.com and The Art Institute of Atlanta.	http://www.intranets.com
10. Example of an on-line game © Estate of Keith Haring (www.haringkids.com)	Keith Haring artwork © Estate of Keith Haring. Web design by Daniel Wiener and Riverbed Media.	http://www.haringkids.com
11. Example of a portal site: Poetry Portal (www.poetry-portal.com)	Printed with permission from (Poetry Portal) Mr. Colin Holcombe.	http://www.poetry-portal.com

Chapter 4

Figure	Credit	URL
1. Project methodology used by Girlzilla, Inc. (www.girlzilla.com)	Printed with permission from Girlzilla, Inc.	http://www.girlzilla.com
2. PMG.net's development process (www.pmg.net)	Printed with permission from PMG.net.	http://www.pmg.net

Chapter 5

Figure	Credit	URL
5. Example of linear navigation: slide show (www.pilarplata.com)	Printed with permission from Pilar Plata.	http://www.pilarplata.com
7. Example of hierarchical navigation: Andy Lim (www.andylim.com)	Printed with permission from Andy Lim.	http://www.andylim.com/play_dreamscape.htm
9. Example of grid-based navigation: Shoebuy.com (www.shoebuy.com)	Printed with permission from Shoebuy.com, Inc.	http://www.shoebuy.com/shoebuy/FC_Sandals_W.jsp
11. Example of hyperlinked navigation: Jane Goodall Institute (www.janegoodall.org)	Printed with permission from the Jane Goodall Institute (www.janegoodall.org).	http://www.janegoodall.org/jane/essay.html
14. Components of a web page: Jane Goodall Institute (www.janegoodall.org)	Printed with permission from the Jane Goodall Institute (www.janegoodall.org).	http://www.janegoodall.org/chimps/social.html
15. Title of a web page: The Art Institute of Atlanta (www.aiawebraising.net)	Printed with permission from The Art Institute of Atlanta.	http://www.aiawebraising.net
20. Example of a subscription form: The Nature Conservancy (www.tnc.org)	Printed with permission from The Nature Conservancy.	http://www.tnc.org
23. Example of a process flowchart: Jennifer English, Kim Garrett and Sacha Pearson (www.sims.berkeley.edu/courses/final-projects/travelite/)	Printed with permission from Jennifer English, Kim Garrett, and Sacha Pearson (School of Information Management and Systems, UC Berkeley).	http://www.sims.berkeley.edu/courses/final-projects/travelite/
26. Splash page © Terra Incognita (www.terraincognita.com)	Printed with permission from © Terra Incognita.	http://www.terraincognita.com

Chapter 6

Figure	Credit	URL
1. Example of a metaphor: The Volkswagen Beetle	Printed with permission from Volkswagen of America.	
5. Effective image metaphors: Girlzilla, Inc. (www.girlzilla.com)	Printed with permission from Girlzilla, Inc.	http://www.girlzilla.com
6. The IBM site: (www.ibm.com)	Reproduced by permission from IBM. Copyright 1994–2002 by International Business Machines Corporation.	http://www-4.ibm.com/software/info/education/
7. A site for children: ASPCA's Animaland (www.animaland.org)	Copyright © 2001 The American Society for Prevention of Cruelty to Animals. Reprinted with permission of ASPCA. All rights reserved.	http://www.animaland.org
8. A site for environmental issues: Rainforest Action Network (www.ran.org)	Printed with permission from The Rainforest Action Network.	http://www.ran.org/info_center/factsheets/01c.html
9. High-contrast colors help readability: Creative Freedom UK (www.creative-freedom.co.uk)	Printed with permission from Creative Freedom, UK.	http://www.creative-freedom.co.uk/
10. A unique graphic style: Juxt Interactive (www.juxtinteractive.com)	Printed with permission from Juxt Interactive.	http://www.juxtinteractive.com)
11. A unique graphic style: Led Pants (www.ledpants.com)	Printed with permission from Mr. Led Pants.	http://www.ledpants.com
16. Effective use of heading and subheadings: Girlzilla, Inc. (www.girlzilla.com)	Printed with permission from Girlzilla, Inc.	http://www.girlzilla.com/services_proto_dev.asp
18. Text links on a web page: Rocky Mountain Institute (www.rmi.org)	Printed with permission from the Rocky Mountain Institute.	http://www.rmi.org/sitepages/pid297.pH
22. Image links © Estate of Keith Haring (www.haringkids.com)	Keith Haring artwork © Estate of Keith Haring. Web design by Daniel Wiener and Riverbed Media.	http://www/haringkids.com
23. Hot spots as links: Herald 21 (www.botanique.com)	Printed with permission from Herald 21.	http://www.botanique.com/tours/canmap.htm

Figure	Credit	URL
24. The drop-down menu: Jane Goodall Institute (www.janegoodall.org)	Printed with permission from the Jane Goodall Institute (www.janegoodall.org).	http://www.janegoodall.org
25. Text-based site map: Apple Computer Inc. (www.apple.com)	Screen shot reprinted by permission from Apple Computer, Inc.	http://www.apple.com/find/sitemap.html
26. Visual site map: Renee Peters (www.reneepeters.com)	Printed with permission from Renee Peters.	http://www.reneepeters.com/site.html
33. Color as a navigation cue: ASPCA's Animaland (www.animaland.org)	Copyright © 2001 The American Society for Prevention of Cruelty to Animals. Reprinted with permission of ASPCA. All rights reserved.	http://www.animaland.org/azula
37. Design comps: PMG.net (www.pmg.net)	Printed with permission from PMG.net.	http://www.pmg.net

Chapter 7

Figure	Credit	URL
1. The copy focuses on comprehension, persuasion, and action: Shoebuy.com (www.shoebuy.com)	Printed with permission from Shoebuy.com, Inc.	http://www.shoebuy.com/shoebuy/dept.jsp?Dept=Child
2. Pull quote: The Rainforest Action Network (www.ran.org)	Printed with permission from The Rainforest Action Network.	http://www.ran.org/info_center/about_rainforests.html
4. Text links: ElearningPost (www.elearningpost.com)	Printed with permission from ElearningPost.	http://elearningpost.com
5. Multiple-language versions: Apple Computer Inc. (www.apple.com www.apple.com/mx/)	Screen shots reprinted by permission from Apple Computer, Inc.	http://www.apple.com/mx/ http://www.apple.com

Chapter 8

Figure	Credit	URL
1. Feedback page: Shoebuy.com (www.shoebuy.com)	Printed with permission from Shoebuy.com, Inc.	http://www.shoebuy.com/contact/feedback_products.shtml
2. Traffic report: Websidestory, Inc. (www.hitbox.com)	Printed with permission from WebSideStory, Inc.	http://www.hitbox.com

Chapter 9

Site design, development, project management: Christopher Altman
Site design: Java Mehta
Usability study: Sydney Aron
Clients: Kim Resnik and, Chef Paul (The Art Institute of Atlanta)
Case study included with permission from The Art Institute of Atlanta

Index